Best wishes
to a wonderful &
generous person Pat
fondly Victoria Parian
4/20/17
Duarte

The Girl from Jerusalem

Memoirs of

Victoria Parian

Edited by
Levon Parian

Published by
Parian Photographic Design
9175 Tujunga Canyon Blvd.
Tujunga, California 91042

TABLE OF CONTENTS

PROLOGUE

My life has been a journey filled with adventure. Like most people, I harbored the desire, even at an early age, to build the vessel of my life with sturdy lumber so that I could sail it not only in calm seas, but also through storms and turbulent waters.

Thus, I prepared for my life's voyage with a bachelors degree in education.

After college I married, had children, taught grade school and traveled with my family.

My parents Sarkis and Haigouhi fled historic Armenia in 1915 during the Ottoman Empire's genocide of Armenians, and settled in Jerusalem, Palestine.

I was born in Jerusalem, the fourth of five children.

In 1947, because of the Arab and Jewish fighting, our family was forced to flee. Thus, as a twelve year old child, I too became dispossessed and had to bid farewell to Jerusalem, Palestine, my birth place.

My family then settled in Amman, Trans-Jordan, and later in Beirut, Lebanon, where I spent my teenage years.

In 1953 I married Benjamin Yotnakhparian, a professor of electrical engineering at the American University of Beirut. In 1957 we migrated to the United States with Levon, our two and a half year old son.

Through Ben's electrical power planning consulting to overseas governments, we were given the opportunity to experience different cultures. Living and teaching overseas gave me the opportunity to advance my degree in Education (MA), but at the same time exposed the family to numerous political upheavals. We lived through three wars and several forced evacuations.

When Ben and I became grandparents in 1998, I was inspired to write these memoirs. I wanted to share my life with my grandchildren, and relate to them how each of us must pursue our dreams, develop our individuality, and work to make the world better.

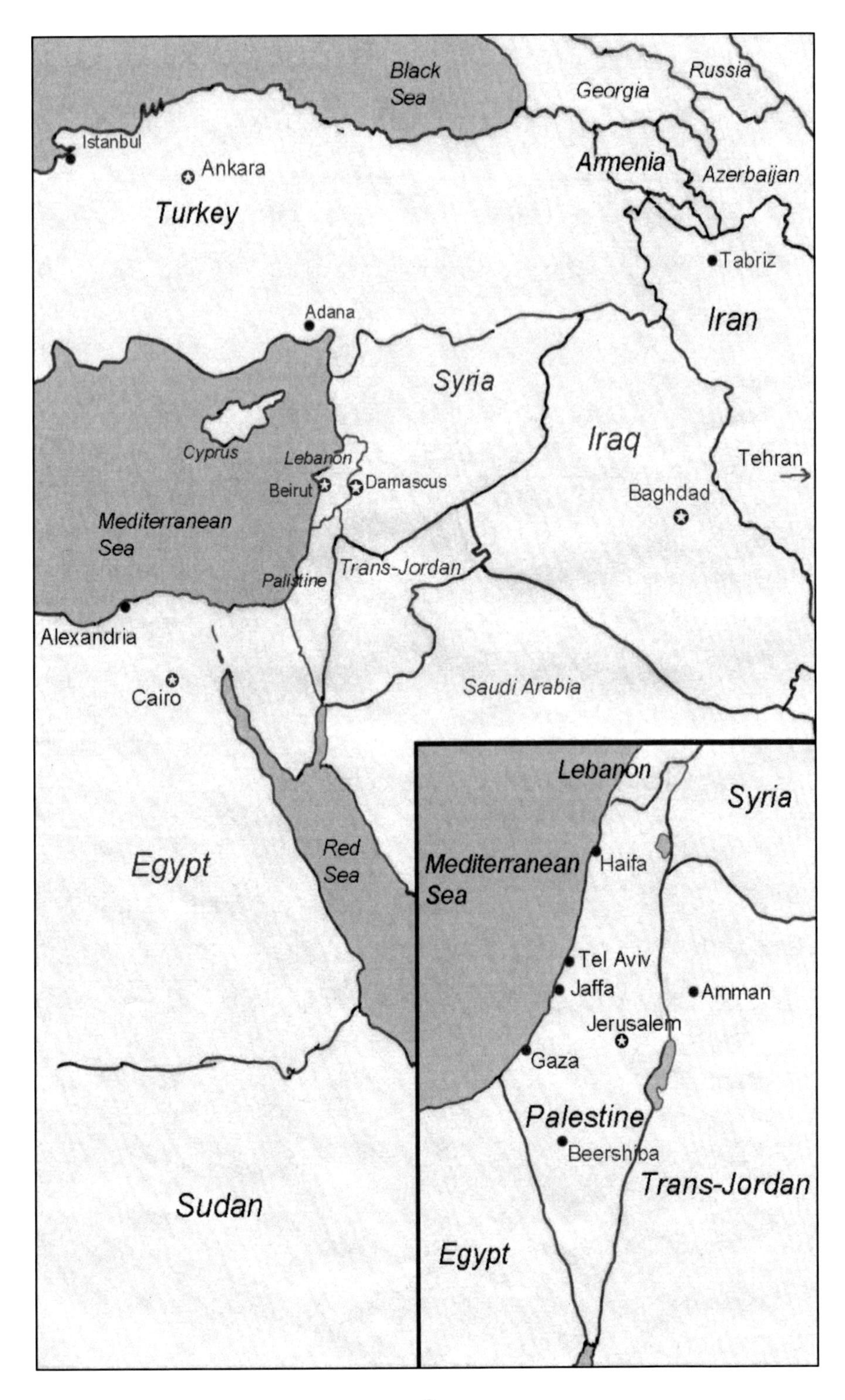
Black Sea
Russia
Georgia
Istanbul
Ankara
Armenia
Azerbaijan
Turkey
Tabriz
Adana
Iran
Syria
Iraq
Cyprus
Lebanon
Tehran
Beirut
Damascus
Baghdad
Mediterranean Sea
Trans-Jordan
Palistine
Alexandria
Cairo
Saudi Arabia
Lebanon
Syria
Red Sea
Egypt
Mediterranean Sea
Haifa
Tel Aviv
Jaffa
Amman
Jerusalem
Gaza
Palestine
Beershiba
Trans-Jordan
Sudan
Egypt

MEMORIES

Mother! Mother! Mother!

This was 1947, I was barely twelve years old and had just stepped off bus number thirty seven, which brought me home from school. As I walked down the hill playing around the boulders and singing, I passed the British Royal Air Force (RAF) military camp. I saw uniformed men hurrying from barrack to barrack. Men in groups talking fast and others gesturing and giving orders.

Every day on my way home, I passed by this camp which consisted of six two-story buildings for the British RAF officers, but I had never seen this much activity, which surprised me. I wondered what they did in their barracks. Sometimes soldiers played cricket across from our house. Mother always warned me not to go out for fear I would get hit by the ball. I would climb a tree to watch them play. I always wondered about the rules of this game.

On this particular day, in the spring of 1947, the sun shone brightly and there was a slight breeze. I intended to go home, drop my books, my lunch box, and run over to the boulders to play. Red wild poppies scattered among other wild flowers with their dazzling colors elated my spirits. As I approached my home I realized there was something different today.

Suddenly, I saw a circular barbed-wire fence surrounding our house and property. As I walked down the field I remember thinking, *maybe there is an opening,* but there was nothing like that, so I started calling my mother.

"Mo-ther! Mo-ther!"

My mother, knowing that I was coming at that hour, was waiting inside and listening, but she did not hear the initial call. I panicked and I started screaming at the top of my lungs, this, she heard, and she came out.

Mother was angry at the British and worried. I was trying to understand what she was telling me from the other side of the barbed wire fence.

"I don't know where the gate is, walk around and follow the fence until you come to an opening."

"Yes mother, don't worry"

The British had divided the city of Jerusalem into sections; each section was divided into zones to protect the people. Each zone covered about ten city blocks and each was surrounded with barbed wire and only one entry way.

I threw the lunch box and my satchel of schoolbooks over the fence to my mother, and started walking down the hill following the barbed wire. My worried mother was shouting instructions; "Don't talk to strangers! Don't go anywhere else; only follow the barbed wire until you come to the gate. Remember our house is in zone number four..."

By creating zones with barbed wire, the British hoped to have more control over the warring groups: the Arabs and the Jews. The Haganah, a strong Jewish terrorist group, was putting bombs in buildings, killing many people. At the time, the British proposed to divide the city into two sections, the small Arab section and a larger Jewish section, but the Arabs did not accept this proposal.

I was scared and didn't know what to expect. Fortunately, I knew the area very well. And I knew the neighbors. I followed the barbed wire fence for about an hour and, finally, I saw lots of people standing in line. There were many military cars, and soldiers, standing around with machine guns; I realized I had come to the opening of the fence. It had a long bar with black and white diagonal lines painted on it. A narrow opening was at the end of the bar, where people could walk through. A guard with a machine-gun stood alert by the gate, and everyone who came had a paper or booklet in their hands to show; otherwise they were not allowed to go through the gate. I had nothing to show.

Every so often, a military car came by, and that same bar was lifted, allowing the car to pass. My whole body shook with fear, I walked passed the gate and came back to it. I saw that other people were going in after a lot of questioning; I stood a few feet away for a while, then, I started walking at a very slow pace toward the narrow opening. Closer and closer I came, trying to find a way to cross. Suddenly I saw an officer signaling and pointing at me. I jumped! My heart was pumping so hard that I thought it would jump out of my chest!

"Come here little girl,"

I was so scared I was shivering! I thought of going back, but where? Then I decided to approach the officer. I had no choice I was caught.

"What's your name?"

"Vicky"

"Where do you live?'

"I live up the hill beyond the field."

"Here take this paper, show it to the officer standing by the small gate and go home."

I felt an enormous relief! I hopped over to the gate and showed my paper. Within seconds I was running at high speed toward home.

I was so absorbed with the barbed wire fence and the gate, that I did not realize that I had walked all the way to the German colony, which was normally more than half an hour's walk from our house. The gate was the entryway to the largest football field in Jerusalem. I rejoiced at my freedom, and ran with joyful jumps across the field.

I saw many military vehicles but I did not care, I was **free! Free**! I knew my way around. I started to shout and sing with delight. I also knew that my worried mother was waiting for me.

Next, I passed my favorite stops. There was a dog barking at the British Council's house, which was a few blocks away from mine. There was a huge field separating our properties. I waved at the dog from the high fence and started running faster. As I passed the field where we used to play, it reminded me of the time when we noticed a man sitting at the top of the hill of our field, reading a paper. He was there for many days, and my friends and I thought this person was enjoying the beautiful sunny weather.

One day, our neighbor Garo Oshagan, the youngest son of the famous Armenian writer, Hagop Oshagan, found a round object close to the road while playing in the fields with his friends. As he picked it up he found there was a long wire attached to it. By following the wire, he ended up where the man was sitting. Garo was scared and told his parents. When they saw the round object, immediately they knew that it was a bomb. The police came, and picked it up. They found some other evidence that this person sitting and reading a newspaper was actually stalking the British consul and waiting to kill him, he was a Jewish Haganah member.

Everyone was upset. They said that the bomb was big and very powerful and if it had exploded it would have destroyed half the buildings on the block. After that incident, we always were on the lookout.

I continued my walk home and passed the Oshagan's house, no one was in the yard. The large white stone house looked deserted. Finally, I came to our neighbor's house, a three story stone building belonging to Dr. Wahid. The Wahids lived in Gaza; but in the summer they came to live on the third floor of this building. No one was playing in the large sandbox, but the swings, were moving slightly from the gentle wind. The breeze passing through the leaves of the large trees that surrounded the yard were making a swishing sound, creating an eerie tranquility.

Fortunately, the gate between our two properties was open, so from the yard, I crossed over and hopped toward home. This was my territory. I was free, running and jumping over the rocky steps, smelling the rosemary bushes, and the beautiful wild flowers of our huge property. I passed the one and only palm tree, the scent of the rose garden next to it gently came to me. After the bomb incident, I was more aware of my surroundings. I loved my home and the wild land.

My mother was waiting for me. She was standing tall by the front door in her blue flowery dress. Her dark brown eyes searching, her curly dark brown hair pulled back with the help of a blue ribbon. As soon as she saw me, she started to cry and hugged me.

With neighbor's house in the background, Mary, Berjouhi play with the family dog -circa 1930

Our home in Jerusalem, Palestine, was a large house, built of stone, with three huge bedrooms. It was double walled, with six inches of space between the outer and the inner walls for natural insulation. In the summer, all the rooms were comfortable and cool, and in winter the house stayed warm.

The structure was built in 1925. During this period, there were no roads to this area, and my father went there on a donkey from the Armenian convent of the old city of Jerusalem.

My parents always related, and laughed about the adventures they had, traveling back and forth, during the construction of the house. They recalled how my mother felt; it was a remote and lonely place to live. How she was terrified as she sat on the stubborn donkey that would not move and how my father had to pull and coax the donkey to continue walking.

Palestine was a British Mandate, before building a house; the landowner had to sign a paper that any excavations or anything found on the land will belong to the British government. The property was part of an upward sloping hill. My father decided to build the house in the center of the hill. As they started digging, they realized there was solid rock underneath, and unexpectedly they found a tomb of an ancient Hebrew leader. The archeologist estimated that this was a tomb built 200 years before Christ.

The tomb was carved out of a rock, and had two levels. The door was about four and a half feet high, and four and a half feet wide, almost like a square. When entering, you had to sidestep onto a ledge, which was the first level of the tomb. If you missed it, you ended up falling into the lower section, which was over five feet deep.

On the first level there were little cubicles. These cubicles must have contained artifacts and jewelry that belonged to the deceased family.

The tomb itself had a rectangular shape. Across from the door, there were stairs leading to the lower level of the tomb, which was flat and led to another entryway. Through this door you saw a circular area covered with dirt. This is where five marble sarcophagi, or burial containers were found, each was about three feet long, one-and-a-half feet deep, and one-and-a-half feet wide. All were plain without ornamentation. The names of the people were carved in Hebrew letters on each sarcophagus.

"According to legend, the Greeks believed that sarcophagi literally ate the bodies stored inside, dissolving the bones within a very short period of time, especially when they were carved from limestone. In Greek *Sarx*, or "flesh", and *phagein* meaning eat."

Granite or marble is used for prominent dead, like royalty and civic leaders, and were often elaborately carved. For example, King Tutankhamen's famous sarcophagus was made of granite."

The British government took the sarcophagi away, and gave my father two replicas made of marble. The originals were taken to the London museum. Many years later, we were able to view them.

As they continued excavating, they found the gate of the tomb. It was a large rock chiseled and shaped exactly the shape of the entryway of the tomb. Obviously robbers had opened the tomb and taken the artifacts and jewelry from the upper level. My father had no choice but to comply with the government order. The excavation left a big pit. He built stairs to go down the excavation and fenced the whole area. Consequently, he ended up building the house at the upper crest of the hill.

My father planted pine trees on the level where the tomb was found. As I grew up, I used these trees for climbing and hiding from my parents. This was the area where we had long picnic tables and benches. In summer, visiting friends and family gathered there for barbecue and shish kebab.

Above the tomb, my father had planted grape vines and fenced them in a large gazebo. I remember how beautiful the arbor looked with red grapes hanging inside this fenced area. There was something unusual about our grapes; they ripened at a later season than the rest of the regular grapes. To protect them my father covered them with paper bags. On the name day of my brother, St Garabed, he prepared a basket filled with these grapes. My brother took the basket to the Armenian Patriarch and in turn received his blessing.

As children, we opened the gate of the gazebo quietly and with joyful anticipation snuck in to eat some of those delicious fruits.

To go down the hill of our land, you had to descend a set of rough cut stone stairs. Here my father planted special pine trees that produced edible pine nuts; he also, planted pistachio nut trees. I used to climb the pine trees and collect the pine cones just before they matured, and opened. My father always made a big fire, and set the cones upright around it so they would spread open from the heat, revealing the nuts with their hard shells. We turned the cones upside down to get the shelled nuts out.

It was fun to crack the shells between two rocks. I used a large flat stone and a smaller smasher to expose the soft delicious nuts. Some we ate, and some my mother used in her cooking.

My father built a small water fountain next to a huge eucalyptus tree. I loved climbing this tree. I used to challenge my friends as to how high and how fast they could climb.

In the house, I loved the unusual living room. It was enormous, with large windows, draped with velvet material with little pompoms hanging on the edges. I played with the pompons, and was fascinated by the twisted ropes with tassels that held the curtains attached to the walls. The sofas were covered in dark brown velvet with geometric designs, and matching soft pillows. Large portraits of my grandparents framed in gold hung on the walls. An antique carpet adorned another wall.

One of the walls was covered with ceramic ornate tiles.

"Father, where did these tiles come from?"

"*Kutahia*, an ancient Armenian city presently part of Turkey"

"Why do we have them here?"

"These tiles were given to me by two men, Balian and Karakashian, in appreciation for my financing the opening of their ceramic factory. They also painted the ostrich egg and presented it to me, which you see hanging on the tiled wall."

My father explained to me that Ohannessian, a ceramist around 1925 brought Mgerditch Karakashian and Nshan Balian from Kutahia, Turkey (Ancient Armenia) to work on the renovation of the Mosque of Omar in Jerusalem. Mgrditch, being the artist, did the drawing, Nshan was specialized in shaping clay tiles, vases and plates, and baking them in the kiln. After they finished their work on the mosque, both Nshan and Mgrdich did not want to go back to Kutahia. They did not have enough money to stay and start a business in Jerusalem. So my father, and grandfather, financed a fac-

Tiles on the wall of the Jerusalem house

tory for them under the name 'Palestine Pottery', thus starting the first Armenian pottery art and design in Jerusalem, which exists to this day. Presently the company is known as 'Jerusalem Pottery'. Their work is so highly prized, that it inspired others, to imitate them.

They hardly had started building the factory, when my grandfather passed away; my father continued helping them financially, until the factory was ready and started to operate.

Aside from the ceramic tiles, the most precious thing in the living room, for me, was the upright, hand carved piano. I loved to caress the beautiful ornate carvings and enjoyed examining them. Listening to my mother and sisters playing, I fell in love with Chopin and Beethoven.

I took lessons from my mother, she was a strict teacher. She insisted that I count my measures while playing. As a child I always wondered how she knew, from another room, that I was not counting. I loved playing but hated practicing.

The bedrooms of the house were large. My parents' bedroom was bright and cheerful, with two large windows, overlooking the front garden, and two small ones on the side. From one of the large windows I could see the road beyond the bottom of the hill. There was a sofa under the window.

Early one morning, I walked into the bedroom and surprised my parents. The sofa was pulled away and both my parents were bending over a safe built in the wall, it contained money and jewelry. They told me that this was our secret and not to tell anyone. My parents had their morning coffee everyday on that sofa, while I sat and played on the wide ledge of the window.

The room had two armoires; one of them was modern styled, with three divisions. One division had fur and winter coats. The second division had evening dresses, and the third division had shelves filled with all kinds of sweaters.

My favorite was the second armoire, a large mirror covered its door and it was hand carved with lovely designs. All my dresses were hanging in this armoire together with my mother's and sisters'. I, like a typical little girl, loved to look at myself in this mirror.

The second bedroom had plenty of room for four beds, an armoire and a chest, where my grandmother kept all kinds of memorabilia and enough space for playing and running around. The room had two large windows overlooking the side courtyard.

The third bedroom, where Uncle Stephan-my mother's youngest brother - slept, was also used as a guest-room as well as a library. It had a basic armoire where the bedding was kept. When relatives and cousins visited, those beddings were brought out and spread all over the house.

My cousins were well known for their tricks, especially Haroutyun and Simon. In the middle of the night, they wore this long white garb that my father used as a nightgown, put all the lights out and with their arms stretched out they walked with a flashlight on their faces as though they were ghosts. The younger children screamed both from fear and excitement.

One wall of this bedroom was covered with shelves of books from floor to ceiling. There was a small ladder that one climbed to pick books at a higher shelf. I loved this room, I spent hours there looking for books and reading them. I was fascinated with the collection that my father had. Ancient books in Arabic script, but the language was Turkish. There were books published by the Armenian Patriarch of Jerusalem, and magazines and periodicals in Armenian, English, and Arabic.

This also was the room where my great grandmother slept when visiting. She read the Bible and told stories from the Holy Book. She taught me how to pray.

This was the only bedroom that had a door leading out to the side courtyard. The door was made of iron with a large iron key. This room had a window on one side, and because the house was built on a hill, The north windows were only about a foot or so above ground.

The dining room was large with a table long and wide enough to play table tennis on. This room also had two sofas that converted into beds. This was the coolest room in the whole house. It was built

Iron back door of the house facing the side courtyard (detail). My Neice Arda with my cousin Meline and family visiting the house- 1980

on the north side of the building, where the slope of the hill was level with the window.

On the east side of the room was the water well for the house. At that time our house was the only one for many miles around. There were no roads or infrastructures, and we depended on well water. There were special containers that collected the rainwater, and, through pipes, the water was directed into the well. There was a big tank on the roof. Every so often, we pumped the water up from the well, and filled the huge tank. It was covered, but unprotected from the sun, therefore on warm days we had lukewarm water.

The dining room was where most of us congregated. It had two doors. One led to the third bedroom, and the second led into the hall/den. This door had a translucent glass, etched with flower designs. It had two sections that folded. One side of the room was covered with closets that contained dishes, hand made cutlery and a variety of fancy serving plates. My favorite was the filigree ornate dessert cutlery made of silver. The handles of the forks and spoons were all made of unique and intricate designs. There were matching filigree tea and lemonade glass holders, where the blue colored glass enhanced the elaborate design.

On the other side of the dining room was another closet. Here, my mother kept the winter food supply for the whole family. Such things like; white goat cheese in large cans, butter for the winter, oils of all kinds, large bottles of olives, and *labni*, made of yogurt, and even lemonade.

LABNI

Place yogurt into a cheese cloth bag and hang in a cool place allowing all the liquid to strain out. After two or three days make small balls with the drained and hardened yogurt. Fill a medium size jar half way with olive oil, and drop each ball into it, making sure that each is submerged in oil. To eat gently remove one of the balls from the jar and spread on toast with a layer of thinly sliced cucumbers.

My favorite was the home made cherry liquor. This was served to special guests in silver containers, with a single cherry in it. Mmmmm! I loved tasting those cherries. My mother did not allow me to have any, but I always stole one while serving the guests.

The top part of this closet also served as a medicine cabinet for my Uncle Stephan, who was a bacteriologist. He brought all kinds of medication and stored them there. When someone was sick, all they had to do was look for the right medication. I used to watch my uncle with fascination, especially when he ground iodine crystals to make medications. In the cabinet there were spatulas, small pumps, eye droppers and many other items that I loved to know more about.

"Stephan *Daee*,(uncle) when I grow up, I want to be a bacteriologist just like you,"

"You can be if you work hard and bring good grades."

I dreaded when he cleaned my infected throat with rolled cotton on a long stick dipped in iodine.

The dining room opened into the den which was a large hall with sofas set in clusters, giving a cozy atmosphere. The front door was an iron gate with a large skeleton key. It had two little glass windows, that allowed you to see who was on the other side. The entryway had a floor to ceiling maroon velvet drapes. The ceramic tiled floor was covered with an enormous Persian carpet which I enjoyed walking on; I always made a game of it by not stepping on certain designs in the weave of this beautiful rug. On the left-hand side of the entryway next to the large window, there were corner shelves with rows of potted greenery. The windows, on each side of the entryway, were almost floor to ceiling, with lovely plants perched on wide ledges.

The radio was the focal point in this happy room. As there were no televisions at that time, the family always gathered round the radio to listen to the news or to popular music. Next to the radio was a wind-up gramophone.

My parents loved dancing, and were excellent dancers. Their favorite was the tango. I was surrounded with music.

My father, tall with dark eyes and dark hair, prematurely graying, was very handsome. He played the violin and the *oud*; which is an eleven stringed old Armenian instrument.

My mother played the piano and the mandolin. I loved the mandolin; I wished I could play like her.

Every Sunday the den was filled with relatives and friends. Music was everywhere. My father, Sarkis, played the violin accompanied by my mother Haigouhi on the piano. Mesmerized I watched and listened. There was pride in my father's eyes as he looked around to the small gathering of friends and relatives who listened with intense concentration. My father decided to change instruments, picked up the *oud*, and my mother rushed to get the mandolin. Together they moved to the balcony and started playing songs familiar to all. Everyone gathered around and began singing and swaying with the beat of the music. My father's clear voice rang above the others and led them into a joyous crescendo of past memories.

Family picture on the front porch of the house, 1943 (top). Arda at the front door revisiting the Jerusalem property in 1980 (above).

The Escape

My parents were very young when their families ran away from historical Armenia during the Genocide of 1915. Western Armenia was under Ottoman rule and is now part of Turkey. The Turkish mayor of the city of Adana had advised my grandfather saying, "The political situation is dangerous and intolerable for the Armenians, you should gather your family and get out of the city."

Armenians represented a quarter of the population of the city of Adana, they were especially recognized as making up a majority of the merchants, artisans, and intellectuals of the area.

Grandfather, Ohannes Kavoukian was married to my maternal great-grandmother's sister Mayrenie. After discussing about escaping the city with my grandfather, Ohannes thought *he should use his artistic skills.* From a small photo, he sketched a black and white portrait of Jemal Pasha, the commanding officer of the Turkish Army. He wanted to present the drawing to Jemal Pasha hoping that he and his family would not be deported to Der-Zor. He was afraid and excited at the same time; he wondered *how Jemal Pasha will react when he sees his drawing.*

He showed the portrait to some friends in the military, they admired it and somehow the news went to Jemal Pasha, who immediately summoned the artist with the portrait. After mustering some courage, grandfather took the portrait to Jemal Pash. The guard seeing him come with the drawing in hand told him.

"Get in! The Pasha is expecting you."

He took a step, and then stopped, his heart was pounding so hard that he held his hand to his heart in order to slow it down; He started sweating, his hands became wet, he asked himself, *what if he dislikes the picture and sends me to jail for drawing it.* He jumped when he heard again the booming voice of the guard,

"What are you waiting for! Get in!" He finally took a few more steps and suddenly found himself in front of the desk of Jemal Pasha.

He turned the picture and showed it to him. Jemal Pasha looked at it and pondered, there was no expression on his face, he played with his mustache and gradually brought his left hand down to his jaw. Grandfather started to sweat more and shiver, he wondered, *what he is thinking.*

To his great surprise, Jemal Pasha started talking in a pleasant tone. He asked uncommitted "Who made this portrait?"

"I did, sir," Jemal Pasha stopped and started thinking again. Then he started talking in an authoritative voice.

"We need a drawing instructor in our schools in Jerusalem, now take your family and go there and start teaching." he ordered.

Grandfather Kavoukian again mustered his courage and asked for papers that would give him, and his family, permission to leave Turkey. Jemal Pasha granted his wish, gave him the necessary papers for himself and his family to travel. What a great relief!

Within one night grandfather Kavoukian and my grandfather gathered their families, including aunts and uncles- about 25 to 30 people.

The group consisted of grandfather Kavoukian with his children and grandchildren. My maternal great-grandmother Matossian and grandparents Markarians with their children and grandchildren.

My father, a cousin to the Markarians was visiting them from the city of Marash. He was hardly eleven years old. He was sent to Adana from Marash to learn the art of goldsmith. He was unhappy in Marash and he had an argument with a Turkish boy. The Turks might have killed him if he stayed in Marash. In Adana he stayed with my mother's parents and was learning the art of being a goldsmith. Thus he was included in the group of travelers that started their departure from Adana.

Fearing the group will attract attention, they walked at night and slept in barns during the day. After many days of travel and hardship, they crossed the border of Turkey into Syria.

Those papers that Grandfather Kavoukian received from Jemal Pasha were vital in allowing them to cross cities. Many times soldiers stopped and questioned them, always looking lustily at the women. At one station a guard while checking the papers pushed one of the ladies and almost cornered her, when one of the men realized what was happening, he rushed to her rescue. All along, the soldiers gave them a hard time, but because of those papers, they let them go.

In Syria, which was still occupied by the Ottoman Turks, the Arab population greeted them with open arms. They rejoiced but continued their way to Jerusalem, where there was an Armenian convent.

"Look the walls of Jerusalem!" everyone kept on shouting with excitement,

"I can't believe we're here", echoed grandmother Matossian

"Thank you God for bringing us safely to Jerusalem," said grandmother

Markarian in an emotional voice, they all chimed in "Amen." All knelt down and prayed and thanked God for their safe arrival. As they walked toward the gates, they all had tears in their eyes.

Old Jerusalem has seven gates. The streets are cobblestones and the walls have ramparts. The Armenian convent is surrounded by high double walls. The thick iron gate of the convent, is inset with a smaller gate, and the small gate is used for late comers. The gates are locked at 8:00 p.m., latecomers knocked on the smaller gate; the night guard opens it, making sure that the late comers are residents or guests of the convent.

The convent is within the old city, built around the fourth century. Almost one thousand years later it became a haven for many who were lucky enough to survive the Ottoman Empire's genocide of the Armenians. Inside the convent, a cobblestone passageway leads to a gateway opening into a courtyard housing one of the most inspiring churches in all of the Middle East, *St. Hagop* (St.James), where the head of St James is buried, built around the twelfth century. There is an ornate iron fence surrounding the front of the church, protecting the entrance to the Sanctuary. In the seventeenth Century the Cathedral was designated to be the seat of the Armenian Patriarchate.

Jaffa Gate of Jerusalem

The only sources of light for the huge sanctuary are the elaborate *ganteghs*, (oil lamps) hung strategically everywhere. Its three alters decorated with more *ganteghs* and candles, and the floor covered with attractive hand made Armenian carpets. People worshiped standing up or kneeling on the floor, there were no chairs.

Outside, continuing along the passageway around a corner was a large courtyard with cobblestone floors. People living in the convent congregated here.

The convent is enormous, and is divided into sections called *'tagh'* (quarter). Each quarter has its common oriental series of bathrooms. There are many *taghs* and many families live there. One can easily get lost in this labyrinthine environment.

My parents and relatives were given a unit per family in the section that was called *Choratagh* (Dry Quarter). This was on the right side of the main courtyard. After climbing a steep set of stairs, you reached smaller courtyards with apartment like units surrounding them.

Gate of Saint Hagop (James) Church in the convent (left). Gate of Armenian Convent in Jerusalem with night entrance (right).

The large courtyard of the convent.

Some of the units had one room with a kitchen; others had two or three bedrooms. My grandparents, the Markarians, felt lucky that they were able to get a unit, and so did the rest of our group, the Kavoukians, and the Matossians, (my great grandmother and her family.)

Grandfather Kavoukian was persuaded by a French artist to go to Cairo and work with him. So he and his family moved and settled in Cairo, Egypt. They wanted my grandparents to join them. During this time there was a political upheaval in Egypt and my grandparents were not able to go. They decided to stay in Jerusalem.

Kavoukian was an artist and photographer. His son, Haroutyun, became a famous portrait photographer of such dignitaries as King Farouk of Egypt, photos of politicians and also that of the Pope. He signed his name as "Cavouk". After his death, his son Onnig took over the business and became equally famous. Onnig's younger brother, a troubadour of children's songs became the internationally famous "Raffi." His music has nurtured children for decades including such hits as; Baby Beluga Willoughby Wallaby Woo, and the Bananaphone.

My father bought a jewelry shop in the old city of Jerusalem. The family objected "Why are you buying this shop? His reply was:

"We need to work and make a living,"

"But soon we will be going back to Adana," the family tried to discourage him:

He bought it anyway and opened a jewelry store and eventually my grandfather joined him.

A street in the old city of Jerusalem.

The Family

Five generations- my sister, Mary and her daughter, Arda, my mother, Haigouhi my grandmother, Parantsem and my great-grandmother, Aigul.

I loved my great-grandmother, Aigul Matossian, who was called Aigul *Khanum* (Lady Aigul), (I called her *Medzmama*). She was blue-eyed and fair-haired, a very intelligent and fascinating woman. She knew many languages; she could read the Bible both in Armenian and in Greek. She also spoke the literary Greek language.

"*Medzmama,* where did you learn the Greek language?"

"I went to a special school, they taught me how to read and write in classic Greek,"

I loved visiting her. She was the one who taught me the Lord's Prayer when I was young.

"Come Victorig kneel by me and let's pray together."

"But *Medzmama* I don't know it well."

"Just repeat after me. I want you to learn the *Havadamk* (the covenant of Christianity)."

"After we say the *Havadamk* will you tell me a story?"

"Yes of course" She was an excellent storyteller; I was mesmerized with her stories. Her daughter, my grandmother, did not speak Armenian.

I was always curious why not, since her mother knew so many languages; her daughter, Paramtzem (my grandmother), (I called her *medzmayrig*) could speak only Turkish.

"Medzmama, why *medzmayrig* can only speak Turkish, you speak, read and write Armenian, Greek and Turkish?"

"When Paramtzem was young, she was very pretty, many Turkish men looked for pretty Armenian girls to snatch and make them their concubines. I was worried that I might lose her; so I insisted that she cover her face with a veil when she went out. I allowed her to speak only Turkish, so the Turks will not know that she was Armenian."

Medzmama was very fond of me. Whenever she saw me she hugged and kissed and wanted me to sit next to her. She knew I loved to listen to her, so she always had a story to tell.

"Come Victorig sit next to me cover yourself with this blanket and I'll tell you a story"

"*Medzmama*, will you tell me the story of the king's daughter?"

"Yes *anoushiges* (my sweet) I will."

"*Once upon a time, there was a very rich king, who had three daughters. He wanted to find out how much they loved him. He called the eldest daughter and asked, "How much do you love me?"*

"Why father! As big as the sky!"

The king was happy; he sent her back to the house. He called the second daughter and asked her "How much do you love me?"

"O father! I love you as big as the oceans!"

Again the king was happy and sent his second daughter back to the house. He called his youngest daughter whom he loved dearly, and asked "How much do you love me?"

"Dearest father! I love you very much, hugged him and kissed him saying, "As much as salt" The king was furious.

"How dare you say that? Guards! Guards! Take this ungrateful daughter of mine and give her to the wolves!"

"Please father don't do that, I really love you," pleaded the lovely princess.

The father did not listen to her and the guards by force took her away. In the forest they did not have the heart to kill her, she was so young, innocent and beautiful that they told her "We will not kill you on condition that you will not come back to the city."

"I promise I will stay as far away as possible."

The guards took a piece of her dress covered it with the blood of a lamb and brought it to the king saying "Sir, here is the cloth that your daughter wore covered with blood." The king was very sad for he loved his youngest daughter more than the others.

The poor girl walked in the darkness, she was terrified, she could hear the noise of the wild animals of the forest, she started shivering from fear and from the cold of the night, she found a tree with a wide opening and curled in it hoping that animals will not come by and kill her, eventually she fell asleep.

On the edge of the forest a woodcutter lived with his wife in a small hut, everyday at dawn he went into the forest, cut and collected wood, carried them on his back to the market and sold them. On that day at dawn he took his ax and went into the forest to cut some wood.

As he was walking he noticed a little girl curled into a ball and in deep sleep. He was puzzled. "Little girl! Little girl! Wake up! Wake up!" woodcutter with long hair and long beard with torn pants and old wrinkled shirt, stood in front of the girl with an ax in his hand and a bag hanging on his back. At first she thought she was dreaming, suddenly the old man started to speak, "Dear girl where did you come from and why are you here alone?"

"I got lost."

"Where are your parents?"

"I don't know."

"Will you come with me, I will take you to my wife she will know what to do."

"Yes, thank you,"

The woodcutter took her to his house.

"Here wife, God sent us a little girl, now you won't be alone, she will help you with your housework and keep us company."

When the wife saw the little girl she was pleased, she always wanted a little girl but never was able to have one.

Hearing this, the little girl was delighted. She helped around the house. Few days later she went with the old man and helped him carry wood to the city. She started calling them father and mother.

One day when the woodcutter was cutting wood, a piece of the tree trunk broke revealing large amount of gold pieces hidden in the trunk. He was delighted, started jumping with joy, he decided to take it and show it to his daughter, he knew that she is intelligent and will find a way to take care of that much gold.

"Father, where did you get all this gold?"

"Down at the forest, as I was cutting I found it in the tree."

"Let's go and see and make sure it doesn't belong to anyone."

They both went and realized that indeed it was a miracle and it did not belong to anyone.

"Dear father from now on you will not work, we have enough money to live a comfortable life."

"I knew you will know what to do with this money!"

"The first thing we will do is buy a house and nice clothes."

So she bought a big house in the center of the city and some nice cloths for her old adopted parents. They started having a happy and comfortable life.

One day they heard that the king had gone hunting into the woods and will be passing by this small city. The daughter asked the old father to go to the kings camp and invite the king to dinner for the next day.

"But daughter, he is the king he will not want to come to an old man's house for dinner."

"Tell him that my daughter invites you to a special feast and please come."

The old man did what he was told reluctantly, but was surprised when the king accepted the old man's invitation. He came happily home and told his daughter that the king and his helpers will be there the next day.

The girl prepared all kinds of food with the help of cooks that she hired from the city.

The next day the king came to the house with his helpers, he sees the beautiful and tastefully decorated house. The tables were set, the king sat at the head of the long table, chef after chef brought all kinds of food, but everything was tasteless, he refused to eat, after the long table was filled with tasteless food the daughter opened the wide door and walked in saying, "My king, why are you not eating?"

"None of the food has any taste."

"Yes, because there is no salt in any of the food." replied the daughter.

The king was puzzled,

"Father this is why I loved you as much as salt."

Suddenly the king recognized his daughter, who had grown tall and more beautiful. She rushed toward his father, and they hugged each other.

"Chefs! Take all the food back, add salt and bring them back!"

Oh! What a feast they had!

The king rejoiced for finding his daughter, and wanted to take her back to the palace.

"No father, I will not go without my adopted parents, they found and took care of me all these years. I will not leave them behind."

The king agreed and they all went to the palace and lived happily ever after."

"*Medzmama*, I will always love you!"

I always thought about her and often my mother would prepare care packages for *Medzmama* that I would happily deliver on my way to school, it gave me an excuse to visit her and talk with her.

Her second daughter, Victoria, a vivacious and talented 21 years old, was engaged to be married. While making all the wedding preparations, she was cleaning the front of the house in the rain; she caught pneumonia and died two weeks before the wedding. The family was devastated, *Medzmama* almost lost her senses. She never forgot Victoria and always talked adoringly of her. She had a huge portrait of Victoria hanging on the living room wall in her house.

When I was born, I was named in her honor, but with a slight variation- VictorAni. The interesting thing was that I looked exactly like her, the same color eyes, and hair. Unfortunately, after Victoria's untimely death, her fiancé never married.

Medzmama also had a son, a jeweler. I felt him to be very odd in that he did not mingle or like to be with children. He scolded them constantly and when we visited he would leave. He never married, but he loved his mother and stayed with her until she passed away.

My father, Sarkis Behesnilian, grew up with my maternal grandparents, Garabed and Paramtzem Markarian. As he grew up, he became very fond of their daughter, Haigouhi. Garabed taught my father how to be a good jeweler and treated him as his own son.

Grandfather Garabed had two sons, Pierre and Stephan. Pierre was blue eyed and blond like his grandmother; he was tall and handsome, and attracted attention everywhere he went. He loved to party and also was the friend of all the Armenian priests. He studied dentistry in Paris. He looked very distinguished and was loved by everyone, especially by my mother, his sister. He, in turn worshipped his sister. Every time he traveled, he brought clothes,perfume and all kinds of presents to her. She became known as one of the best dressed people in Jerusalem.

My maternal grandfather, Garabed (left). My mother Haigouhi with her bothers Pierre and Stephan (right).

Pierre

My uncle Pierre met Hela, a German lady, who had a son named Hantz. They fell in love and got married. She was beautiful-tall and very attractive.

"Son, why did you marry a non- Armenian and with a son?"

"Father, I love her,"

"How will she converse with your mother, who knows only Turkish?"

"Don't worry father, she is able to communicate with her, you'll see."

His parents were very upset about the marriage but could do nothing about it. He opened a dental clinic in Jerusalem, and raised her son like his own. They never had a child of their own.

"Paramtzem, my love, we will have to accept this marriage, otherwise we will loose our son." The father tried to persuade the mother, who was in tears and could not stop crying.

Hela, Pierre's wife, was aware of Pierre's family feelings; she made every effort to gain their confidence and respect. She became a good friend of my mother, Pierre's sister, and always visited his mother and conversed with her in sign language.

Uncle Pierre used to give me, his favorite niece, a ride in his yellow car. The trunk like back opened and became a convertible. I loved it. I sat there and pretended I was a queen with the wind blowing my hair and feeling important. He spoiled me by giving chocolate every time I went to their house.

Stephan

Stephan, like his brother, Pierre, also was attached to his sister. Being the youngest in the family, Stephan was pampered and loved by everyone. His mother always cooked his favorite foods, and took care of him; he in turn took good care of his mother. He was of average height with dark eyes, light skin, attractive and very active. At a young age he was loosing his hair.

Stephan loved to travel. One day he was angry about something and he surprised his parents by leaving the country and going to Bulgaria, where he stayed with his cousin Hagop Atamian. Stephan was a bacteriologist and worked in a Laboratory.

He and his mother, my grandmother, lived with us. One day a friend invited Stephan to a party where he introduced him to a young lady. Stephan was attracted to her, she was light skinned, green eyed with blond curly hair. She had a beautiful voice, and was visiting from Gaza.

Stephan wanted to know more about her; he visited Gaza and spent some time with her family, the Yotnakhparians. A few months later my parents with Stephan went to Gaza to ask her hand in marriage. Not knowing many years later I too would connect with the Yotnakhparians.

The wedding took place in Bethlehem, at the holy Sepulcher. Reception followed the wedding ceremony at one of the halls next to the sanctuary.

After the wedding, Stephan and Aznive settled in Jerusalem not too far from where we lived. Eventually they had four children, three girls and one boy, Paramtzem, Salpi, Seta, and Garabed. Stephan's hobby was collecting stamps. He collected stamps from all over the world, and hoped that one day his collection will be worth thousands of dollars and that his children will benefit from the collection.

Aznive's family lived in a house next to a cemetery. Before entering their courtyard, there was a dark tunnel. I remember how afraid I was and how my grandmother refused to go through the tunnel.

'I can't see anything! It's dark!"

"Don't worry I am next to you." My father said.

"I refuse to go." Replied my grandmother.

"Here give me your hand, walk with me."

We walked together with me tagging along by holding my father's jacket. Once we crossed the tunnel we came to a green garden filled with trees and high brush. It was pleasant and cool.

The house was part of an old convent. The bedroom was connected to the other rooms by a covered patio. The front of the patio was a large courtyard full of plants, some high enough to get lost in. There were pigeons flying around. The bathroom did not have a toilet, but a hole in the ground with space for your feet. I always was afraid that I would fall in the hole.

Haigouhi

With the blessing of Garabed and Paramtzem Markarian,(my mother's parents), Sarkis and Haigouhi were married in 1922. Their first child Mary was born in 1923, a beautiful girl. Two years later, Berjouhi was born, another lovely girl. That year, Sarkis decided to build a house on the large estate that he had bought a few years back on the spacious hills of suburban Jerusalem. His father-in-law, Garabed, had bought the adjacent lot, which was slightly smaller. There were no roads to this area of the country, so the only way to go to their home was by donkey.

Grandmother Paramtzem lived with her daughter Haigouhi and Sarkis (my parents). She was fond of baby boys. At the time families always wanted to have boy children, for they were the bread earners, the head of households, and carried the name of the family for future generations. When my brother Garabed was born in 1927, she was thrilled; she did everything to help my mother, and took good care of the baby. But, during my birth seven years later she became very angry at her daughter for bringing a girl into the world and not the boy she was hoping for. She decided to leave the birthing room and not help. She was heard screaming at her daughter, "You brought her, you take care of her!".

My mother, Haigouhi, had five children. Eventually, my grand

Engagement & wedding of my parents; Sarkis and Haigouhi Behesnilian, 1922.

mother loved all the children and took care of them. She was the best *munti* and *soo borak* maker, these are very tasty Armenian dishes made with dough. All the children got together to help her make it.

MUNTI

After grandmother kneaded the dough, she opened it into a thin layer and cut the thin dough into small squares, we helped by putting cooked ground meat in the center of the square and squeezing both sides together. She arranged the pieces in a large pan and cooked it on two gas burners.

SOO BORAK

For soo borak my grandmother again kneaded the dough and with a thin long stick-like rolling pin rolled the dough and opened it into a large round thin layer. Then she put each layer gently into boiling water for a short time, removed it and placed them one on top of the other into a round pan. She then covered each layer with butter and cheese. The last layer she covered with butter and egg yolk and baked it. The process of preparation took a long time and was exhausting, but it was a labor of love for special occasions.

My mother did not ever allow us to speak Turkish except with my grandmother, who did not speak any other language.

Six years later, when my sister Artemis was born, I don't remember being jealous of her, but rather protective.

I was in the habit of writing the names of the family. When my baby sister came I made a list of the family as; Mary, Berjouhi, Garabed, Victoria, all with the last name of Behesnilian, but Artemis I wrote as *Hivantanosian* (hospital-ian).

One day a few of my mother's friends came to see the new baby and congratulate her. I excitedly introduced my baby sister to the guests; "She is my sister, Artemis Hivantanotsian," I explained to them.

From the left standing, Mary (my sister), Penyamin, Aunt Nazenik, Haigouhi (my mother) Sarkis (my father), Hela (Pierre's wife), Paramzem (my grandmother), Hantz, Stephan, Hela's mother, sitting- Uncle Pierre, Vicky (me), Luther, Garabed, Berjouhi, and Simon

"What a beautiful name! but why Hivantanotsian?" asked one of the guests.

"Because she came from the hospital," I announced proudly.

I was puzzled why they thought this was so funny.

My father, after getting married and settling down, started looking for his two brothers and sister. During the Armenian Genocide, he lost his parents and did not know what happened to his younger sister and brothers. He started looking in different orphanages. After a few years he found his sister and later the youngest brother. He brought them over and took care of them, but kept on looking for the middle brother. He almost gave up looking when by sheer luck he heard of an orphanage; sure enough his brother was there. He became the happiest person, he united the family. Eventually they all married and had their own families.

His sister married an Armenian who spent his childhood in the German military orphanage. They had three sons, Haroutyun, Simon and Luther Deyirmenjian.

The middle brother married a beautiful girl with a lovely sense of humor he had met at the orphanage. They had three children a boy Haroutyun, and two girls, Anahis and Arpine.

The youngest brother married a beautiful blue eyed girl. They also had three children, a girl Meline, a boy Aram and a girl Alice. I was fond of my cousins, most weekends the cousins who lived in Jerusalem were at our house. They were older than I, except for Alice and Arpine. My youngest uncle lived in Haifa, so I did not have the chance to see them as often as the cousins who lived in Jerusalem.

My parents in Jerusalem, circa, 1923

Childhood

Author in front of house in Jerusalem

At four years old, my mother took me to the Armenian convent school, I was excited. For many children, the first day of school is a frightening experience-- but for me, it was an adventure! When I sat down in one of the small chairs which filled the room, I felt like Goldilocks, because those chairs were not too high not too low, but "just right." While my mother and my teacher held an impromptu conference, I watched older boys and girls cutting paper in different forms and pasting them. Oh! How I wanted to cut and paste paper like them. I watched and played with blocks. My mother reached for my hand and we went to the principle's office to register. Ninety percent of the Armenian children living in Jerusalem attended this school.

The Author in Jerusalem, 1936

When I visited in 2011 the school was the same and I felt like I had returned to the ghost of my childhood.

The four story school was built on an incline. A large foyer with advertisements and messages greeted visitors. Two of the kindergarten classes were

Armenian Convent School, 1945 Vicky is in the center top row.

Saint Translators School at the Armenian Convent

held on the right, next to a large hall, where every morning, all the students congregated to pray and sing the good morning songs. Our principal, who was a priest, also gave us a morning message.

The school supply store, and the principle's office occupied the mezzanine or the second floor. The third floor housed seven classrooms and a teacher's lounge. This floor was the center of activity,

Vicky in grade school and the girls in her class (vicky fourth from the right standing)

rooms on one side of the hallway stretched from one end of the building to the other.

The fourth floor had two classrooms across from each other; these were for the final two grades of the school.

The basement level had two classrooms and the huge dinning room with rows and rows of tables. All children coming from a distance brought their lunch boxes and ate in this dinning hall. The supervisor of the lunchroom was a very nice lady; we used to call her *mairig*, (mother). If food needed warming, she warmed it for you and made sure you ate and did not fool around. She also made sure that after school we picked up our lunchbox from our place. One

Fortress along the walk to school.

advantage for me was that she was a friend of my mother and took good care of me.

The school had four kindergarten levels. *Mangabardez*, Children's garden. *Pokhpoch*, flower sprouting. *Gogon,* the flower is a bud, and *Dzaghig,* flower in full bloom. Within these four years, students learned to read and write Armenian, and perform all the basic arithmetic skills. We also learned singing and dancing, specially Armenian folk dancing.

One day, when I was in *pokhpoch,* two boys in the lunchroom began to push and shove each other near the stairs of the classroom. By accident they pushed me, I fell on the sharp edge of the stairs, and hit my nose. I bled profusely. *Mairig* carried me and took me directly to Dr. Yaghlian, a very good doctor and a family friend. When he saw me he looked upset and immediately applied medication. My parents came and took me home. Within a week, infection set in and my face was swollen like a balloon. For about a month I was unable to attend school.

Once a child graduated from *Dzaghig*, he or she entered *Nakhagertaran* (grade school) which lasted six years. I was very glad to graduate from *Kindergarten.* For one thing, I wore a black uniform with a white collar. Although I liked the red uniform worn by Kindergarden students, the black uniform was a sign of growing up.

I had a teacher in *Gogon*, who was very strict, she carried a stick, if you were bad you got a beating with that stick. Sometimes the whole class misbehaved so everyone got a one strike on their hand. To this day I remember how frightened this teacher, Miss Terengouhi, made me. Whenever I saw her I turned around and went in the other direction. I was extremely happy when I got out of her class.

When I graduated from kindergarten, I had learned how to dance in a group and I played the piano. I took lessons from my mother who was a very devoted piano teacher.

Nahkagertaran (grade school) was fun and hard work. I was ready for the challenge.

In convent school in Palestine we had to learn three languages, English for the British mandate, Arabic for the language of the country and Armenian for being an Armenian convent school. Church attendance every Sunday was a holy obligation.

On Sunday mornings each class lined up in the school playground in a single file. Our teacher walked with us to Saint Hagop Church near by. She took us to the second level of the church where we stood in rows and followed the mass. Because traditionally there was no seating in Armenian churches, we sat on the floor. We also followed the mass via our little books called *Jhamakirk*.

By now, my sister Berjouhi had graduated from the Armenian school and was attending the British college. My brother Garabed was going to a French school, so I commuted alone.

My parents worried, "Vicky be careful and go straight to the bus and straight to school, don't talk to strangers."

The bus stop was about a ten minute walk from our house, I had to walk down the hill to the main thoroughfare, past the Egyptian consulate, and wait for the bus.

The Egyptian Consulate was a beautiful circular building with high walls and a green iron gate, the Egyptian flag was always on the top of the building.

As I waited at the bus stop, I got acquainted with the people around me. Sometimes the bus was full and did not stop. For that reason, I had to give myself some extra time. I made friends with bus drivers and some of the neighborhood people who helped me board the bus first. Once I arrived at my destination, I still had to walk for another ten minutes to reach the convent.

The convent stood in the old city of Jerusalem. I walked through Jaffa Gate (*bab-el-khalil)*, and a fortress. Those huge gated walls always fascinated me. At first, they looked menacing, I felt the gate would close on me and trap me, I imagined that there was a man hiding behind each parapet and any moment would jump at me. But as I grew older I got used to them.

The fortress housed British soldiers. Military activity never stopped. Soldiers marched up and down at all hours.

I traveled past small shops that lined the streets of the old city. Being a tourist center, shops sold expensive items, unusual cloths and souvenirs that caught my attention. They sold fruit wrapped in fine paper and displayed in enticing ways. I always had to repress a temptation to pick up an apple and bite into it.

Reaching my daily destination on my own terrified me for the first few weeks. For a long time I imagined someone coming after me, chasing me. I ran with all my might until I was breathless, and reached an area where there were people.

As time went by, I got used to commuting on my own, and stayed out of trouble. I started to feel and know the changes and the little nuances of a market. I learned to recognize the shop owners, the native shoppers and the tourists.

One day, when I was about seven years old my mother decided that we will go to the *hamam* - public baths; a left over from the Ottoman empire. I had never been in one but I had heard all kinds of stories and did not want to go, but she insisted. As we approached the *hamam* the building looked like a pink castle with rounded domes. It was surrounded with archways and cobble stone walkways. I was scarred. My mother realized my hesitation and took my hand leading me to the women's entrance.

As we entered the first thing that I felt was the warm humid suffocating atmosphere. My mother paid at the counter and led me into the inner section of the building. This place was a huge circular hall with water fountains everywhere and steam rising from hot water fountains. Huge women wrapped in towels were lounging everywhere. In one corner someone was lying on the floor and another woman was rubbing her back with *kasa*- a black rough cloth for exfoliating your skin. I was terrified thinking that one of them will capture me and rub my body. We took all our clothes off and wrapped ourselves with large towels. Privacy went out the window. There was no way for me to run away, so I joined my mother in one corner and started soaping myself. My mother came and rubbed my back with the *kasa*. Surprisingly it felt good. My body became soft and tingling. I felt relaxed. My face felt warm and mother said I looked pretty with red cheeks. There were no showers so you filled a large kettle with warm water from the fountain and poured it over your body. At the end I wrapped myself with a huge towel and joined the other women sitting in one corner and listened to gossip.

School was hard but fun at the same time. I made good and lasting friends. The students of my class were friendly; we decided and planned activities together. Many times we went to picnics and field trips, without our parent's knowledge. By living far, I was unable to join the after school social life that my girlfriends who lived in the convent or inside the walled city had. I enjoyed living at our house, but at the same time I missed the camaraderie of my classmates.

I loved visiting *medzmama* (great grandmother) at lunch hour at the convent. The love was mutual, she always offered all kinds of sweets, and talked with me until it was time to go back to school. Even though I had my uncle's family living in the convent, I felt more at ease visiting with *medzmama*. Her house was one large room with a kitchenette, located at the end of the row of houses in the

Vicky and her sister Artemis with their pet lambs

Choratagh (quarter). The same area, where my parents and grandparents came to live when they escaped from the Ottoman Empire's Genocide of the Armenians in 1915.

The last time I went there for lunch, it was six months after her only daughter (my grandmother) had died of cancer. I saw the sadness in her 82 year old face, her voice quivered as she spoke about her daughter, she repeatedly said, "I should have died and not her."

Her anguish made me very sad; I tried to cheer her up but to no avail. Once, when she was preparing eggs for lunch, the oil from the pan spilled a little, the flame was too high, and the pan started burning. I rushed and helped put out the fire. I told my parents about that incident. They were alarmed. They visited her and asked the neighbors to keep an eye on her. As the days went by, she became worse, as if she willed herself to die; she kept saying that she wanted to be with her daughters.

Joined by their brother Garabed

A month or two after this incident she passed away. I lost a loved one, the only person who sat with me and told me stories about life, about people, about the old times. She taught me the Lord's Prayer. No one but her read the Bible to me and narrated stories from the Holy Book. Thanks to her I memorized verses from it.

I grew up in a happy environment. I remember my pet dog, 'Bijou', who followed me everywhere. We also had a cat that looked like a tiger, she had kittens every year. She was a loving member of our family. One day we found her dead in the hallway, we were devastated, my parents told us that she died of old age.

We were all sad but when my father came home that night, he had a beautiful kitten in his lap, who had green eyes and light brown fur with white spots. She became attached to my father and followed him everywhere. She waited at the bottom of the hill for his return from work, and walked up the hill with him. After a year she disappeared. We looked all over for her. A short time later my father found her crushed under a large rock. We were very upset especially my father, he tried to find out who had done such a brutal deed.

Vicky and Artemis in front of their house

We also had pet lambs and turkeys at different times.

One day I came home from school and found one of the lambs missing, I looked everywhere but could not find him. Suddenly in one of the enclosed gardens I saw a man skinning my lamb, I was horrified and started crying. The person who was cleaning immediately covered it up and my mother rushed to whisk me out of there. I was crushed and never got over loosing my pet. I found out later that my lamb was being raised as a religious sacrifice. The meat was cooked and given to poor people living around our church.

My parents both musicians always were involved with music. Our house was always filled with company. Amongst them were composers, conductors, and famous singers. Many times I visited with them and listened to their singing and playing their instruments. My sisters were in choirs and the whole choir came and rehearsed at our house.

Shahan Berberian, the famous composer and conductor, came to the house with his wife and son Barrett for choir practice. Barrett and I played hide and seek amongst the trees, while the choir practiced and later the parents visited with each other.

I started taking piano lessons from my mother at the age of five. My eldest sister, Mary, took over from my mother and eventually I started taking lessons from Ohan Khatchadurian (Durian). He was my first teacher outside the family. Many times, he made me sit and wait until he finished a measure or two writing his composition, after which he played it for me and asked "Did you like it?"

My reply was always "Yes."

He became a famous international conductor. He conducted symphony orchestras in Switzerland, and Israel, He settled in Yerevan, Armenia, and became the conductor of the Yerevan Symphony Orchestra.

Aside from being musicians, my parents were prominent in the community. My father was one of the founders of the *Marashzi* (Armenians from the city of Marash) club. He was respected by the community and was one of the well known leaders. He also was a philanthropist, a friend of the Armenian Patriarch, and good friend of the priests. People called him Sarkis *Agha*, the title *Agha* is used when a person is respected by the community. My father was tall and handsome with dark brown eyes and black hair which was graying prematurely.

My mother was equally known amongst the community for her involvement in volunteer work. She was a major founder of the Armenian Red Cross in Jerusalem. She organized musical groups and helped many musicians. She was one of the best dressed women in Jerusalem. She was tall; light skinned with beautiful dark brown eyes, dark hair, and soft features.

I cherished the times when my mother read in French as five of us snuggled in bed around her, and listened with fascination to the adventures of the Three Musketeers.

I looked like my father, with dark brown hair with slight reddish highlights, and dark brown eyes. I was the shortest in my family. My father's favorite word for me was "*geojal*"- beautiful. Every evening, when he came in from work and held his head between the velvet drapes that divided the door and the living room, he called

"Where is my *geojal?*"

I always screamed with delight and ran to hug him.

As I grew up, my father and I created a routine where we moved our heads in unison, front, back, and sideways. Every time we had company we performed.

I can never forget the time, when my father had a heart attack, a few minutes after we had a demonstration of our routine to my uncles, who were there to celebrate the message that came from a lost cousin.

Earlier, my brother had come back from Beirut after passing an admittance exam for the French University. I offered a cup of coffee to my father and at that moment he collapsed.

They said it was thrombosis: hardening of the arteries. My world was turned upside down. I already had lost a grandmother and a beloved great grandmother. But this was different. Many times I stood by the porch and prayed and waited thinking he would come back.

Since my father was very well known and liked by everyone, people came from all over for his funeral. The church was full; people were standing in the courtyard. After the service, his casket was carried on the pall-bearers' shoulders all the way to the cemetery, a distance of about half an hours walk, the hearse followed the procession without the casket. He was buried in *St Pergitch* church. He was only 52 years old and his death was so sudden and unexpected that it was hard on everyone.

My mother took it very hard. In fits of uncontrollable sorrow, she kept on banging her lap and legs. Her thighs started getting red and swollen. We placed pillows on her lap. She was in shock for many days and could not cry. The whole family was in a state of despair.

In the middle of all this mourning, a truck came to the house filled with iron shutters for all the windows of the house. We had forgotten that my father had ordered them a month before his death. Later during the many upheavals, those shutters became shields that stopped bullets from harming anyone inside the house.

According to Armenian tradition, the family mourns for forty days. During this time relatives and friends bring food. We had a constant flow of visitors coming to the house. My uncles, aunts and cousins stayed with us more than a month. At the end of forty days, the family goes to church and to the cemetery; the priest prays for the soul of the departed and performs a ceremonial blessing.

It was during this time in 1946 when Arab and Jewish clashes started. Unfortunately my family was unable to go to the cemetery. My mother and brother, with great caution, hiding behind walls and trees did go and do the blessing with the local priest. They had some terrifying moments, with guns and bombs going off at every corner. My sister Mary and her three year old daughter Arda, had come for our father's funeral. When my brother–in-law came to take them back to Amman, he was very disturbed at the situation we were in. He advised my mother to take a vacation and stay with them in Amman until the conflict settled down and she and the family could return.

The political situation continued to deteriorate, with more fighting betweenArabs and Jews. The *Haganah* (Jewish terrorists) put a bomb in the King David Hotel and killed 91 and injured 46 people including passengers in a public bus that was passing by. By sheer luck my sister Berjouhi was saved, she ran to catch that same bus, but missed it, she waited five minutes and took the next bus.

Our house stood on a hill, where the Jews controlled the northern section and the Arabs the southern. As the fighting became intense we could hear the bullets flying overhead.

The ricocheting bullets banged and hit the house and the iron window shutters frightening everyone. We decided to sleep in one room. We moved all the beds into the central bedroom and slept there. Many nights we woke-up from the gun shot noise.

One night, an unfamiliar noise awoke me. I could hear clip clop at every few intervals. I thought everyone was asleep; I was so petrified that I could not utter a word for fear that I also will scare the rest of the family, little did I know that others were awake, and were as afraid as I was! No one in the room dared say a word thinking that all were asleep. They all thought that there was someone outside, we were afraid to make any noise for fear that this person would open fire on us. The noise was clip-clop as though someone took a step then stopped and listened, then took another step and stopped. It was strange. No one dared to move until there was enough light outside to see. Right about that time, there was a huge explosion! The whole place shook and lit up! Everyone jumped up, terrified! "What was that?" we all screamed in unison.

The window shutters were closed so we could not see outside. That clip-clop still continued, it was terrifying!

"There must be someone out there." my mother said in a shaky voice.

My sister Berjouhi said, "Let's open the shutters about an inch and see who's out there."

"What if this person has a gun?." I said in a scared voice.

Finally my brother Garabed decided, "I'll go and investigate."

He cautiously went to the back room, the rest of us followed him, and he carefully opened the window shutter, "Oh! What a relief!" exclaimed my mother.

What we saw was a donkey with his hind legs tied. The donkey took a step with the front legs, than hopped with his hind legs; this created the unusual clip-clop noise on the concrete of the backyard. We could not imagine how it had come there. Later we found out that the owner had tied the donkey's hind legs so the donkey would not run away. But the donkey kept on grazing and found its way into our backyard.

We all breathed a long sigh of relief, but still, we were troubled because of that blast we had felt and heard.

"Victorig, go to your uncle's house and see if they're ok."

My Mother prepared a large bag of food and fruits for my Uncle Stephan and family, who lived about half an hour's walk in the direction where the blast came from. Mother was worried and wanted to know if they were doing well.

As I walked towards that part of the city, I could hear ambulances and a lot of traffic and activity. I was nervous and at the same time curious to know what was happening. I went closer and closer, and as I turned the street corner, I had the shock of my life. The hotel Samiramis, which was half a block away from my uncle's house, was almost slashed in half, bodies were hanging from the gaping rooms, ambulances were taking the injured away, while others were being put into plastic bags. I started to get nauseous, I began running toward my uncle's house screaming his name and crying.

"Stephan *Da-e-e*! (uncle) Stephan *Da-e-e*!"

As I came to the door I realized there was no door! No window! Shattered glass everywhere! I was terrified! Especially when I saw that the one year old baby's crib was covered with glass and no one around! "Aunty Az-ni-ve!"

I thought may be they were hiding, or gone to the hospital. After about five minutes of panic, which felt like hours, I heard my uncle coming, I had a sigh of relief.

"Where were you? Where's the baby? Is she alright?"

"Don't worry, we all are well."

"The crib is all filled with glass! I was worried when I saw that!"

"In the middle of the night, baby Paramtzem cried, so we removed her from the crib and she was sleeping with us in our bed when the bomb went off. We did get some pieces of glass but we were covered so everyone is ok. We were petrified! We went and stayed with one of the neighbors." My uncle continued "When the blast occurred, Aznive and I ran out. Soon I asked her, where's the baby? She said, **you** have her! I screamed, No! I don't! Then we both ran back in and found her sleeping peacefully in our bed... Aznive was crying and we both were shivering. We had thought to go and stay at the hotel, as many of our neighbors did." He became emotional.

"They were afraid of the *Haganah* coming, raping the women and killing everyone to make room for the refugees coming from Cyprus." He continued shaking his head. "Poor things, look what happened, they ran from rain and were caught in hale!"

"Thank God you're safe" I replied

"The Arab league was having a meeting the night before at the hotel. After the meeting all the delegates stayed there." He continued, "The Jewish *Haganah* group had planted a bomb in the hotel and killed all of them, including many visitors and tourists. Aside from that we also knew the *Haganah* was going from house to house killing everyone and taking over the houses and buildings. At night many of the residents of our area fearing this attack went to stay in the hotel. A-h-h! They thought they would be safe."

My uncle was shook up and sad; many of his neighbors were killed. He felt lucky. He decided to take his wife and child and walk back with me to our house. My mother was relieved when she saw us coming.

"Stephan, I insist that you, Aznive and the baby stay with us until things quiet down."

"Fine sister, I'll go and salvage whatever I can from the house and bring everything here."

A Few days later friends of the family, the Ojenie Keshishians, her husband and three children, Ankine, Onig, and Oshin who also lived in that area, ran away from the threat of the *Haganah*. They came and stayed at our house. All felt relatively safe in our house because it was built almost like a fort. Later on the Bedros Balian family, whose daughter Nanig was about my age, joined us.

Life at the house was happy and sad. I enjoyed the many people in the house, and the children playing together. Each family occupied a bedroom. But at the same time every night was filled with fear as we heard the sound of guns with bullets hissing by and occasionally hitting the shutters.

One day a neighbor, Anahid Oshagan, who worked at Barclays Bank, came rushing to our house. Anxiously she said, "The British are starting to collect and pack their belongings, they're getting ready to evacuate."

That meant more trouble, more fighting and who knows what else. The Keshishian family decided to go to the Armenian convent where it was relatively safe. A few days later the Balian family left for the Armenian convent. Later my Uncle Stephan decided to do the same. My mother decided that it was not safe to stay in the huge house alone since we were all young and the only male in the family was my eighteen year old brother. Winter was approaching and she was afraid of the rampage that the *Haganah* was committing to open living space for the Jewish refugees that were coming from Europe and Cyprus. She decided to take her son-in-law, Hovig's advice and leave for a short vacation.

So my mother, fearing for our lives, decided to go to Amman, Trans-Jordan, for a few weeks, where her eldest daughter Mary lived. We all thought that within two to three weeks, the political situation will settle down, and we would be able to go back to our home.

Alas! Little did my mother know that she will never see her own house and properties again.

Around 1949, my cousins Harry and Simon Deyirmenjian took a trip with a jewish tour group from the United States to visit Jerusalem. They went to all the religious sites and on one of their free days, they managed to go and see our house. They were surprised to see a jewish family in each of the rooms, the den being large was divided with a curtain, accommodating two families in it.

They were told that the *Haganah* had used torches to open the iron door of the house. We were terribly upset, when we heard this news. Especially since we wanted to go back but were not allowed to cross the borders.

For many years my brother tried to recover our properties but there were always obstacles put in his path.

Leaving Jerusalem

It was decided that my brother Garabed will leave before us with a small truck, so a few days later he left home with a small truckload of household items. On his way, he stayed in Jericho for one night. As he arrived in Amman, my brother-in-law sent Babek, a taxi driver, and a friend, to pick us up from Jerusalem.

In my minds eye, I still see the unforgettable day we left Jerusalem with every movement we made. The taxi driver, who knew my family very well, came to the house and insisted that we hurry because the roads were dangerous. Everyone pitched in and filled the trunk, a section of the back seat, and the roof of the taxi.

We locked the doors, closed all the shutters, and left hoping to return within two weeks, when the political situation calmed down. My mother sat by the driver, and the three children squeezed in the back, we were holding tight the miniature grandfather clock which we had on our laps.

My brother Garabed already in Amman waited for us.

As we neared downtown Jerusalem, we saw barrels blocking the road, forcing us to zig-zag through the barricades. Every few feet soldiers stood with their machine guns pointing toward anything moving. We were terrified; I was shivering. At every barrel or blockade, we stopped and the soldiers examined us, asked questions, and then allowed us to cross to the next blockade. The driver instructed us not to say a word. After a long tiring and tense journey we reached Jericho.

Fortunately we found a room at a hotel. We all had a restless night. In the morning we looked forward to crossing the Jordan River over the bridge to Trans-Jordan, Amman was not too far from there.

As we got ready to go, word came that the river had swollen, and that the car will not be able to cross the Allenby Bridge. The Bridge was completely closed.

"This is a bad omen!" said my mother .

The weather was clear and beautiful, but my mother was frustrated and unhappy. We knew we had to stay in Jericho until the waters subsided. We still were afraid for our lives. My mother made sure that we, the children stayed indoors at all times. This made us very unhappy but we tried to behave and not aggravate the situation. Everyday, the driver went to check on the bridge to see if the waters receded.

The waters became low enough where riders were allowed to cross the bridge on horseback. In order to check on us, my brother Garabed crossed the Allenby Bridge by horse from the Trans Jordan side. He returned back the next day.

For me everyday that passed felt like a month. Being cooped up in a hotel in one room was not fun. After a few miserable days, the bridge was cleared for departure. What joy!

On the other side we met my brother. All that night we sat in a circle and listened to his story.

"You can't imagine how high that water was! I felt the water rushing between the horse's legs below me. It was so treacherous! In the middle of the bridge, the horse stopped! I could feel the horse hesitate. I started shivering thinking that we won't make it to the other side; fortunately the horse took a majestic pose, collected his strength, with his head high and straight, resisted the rush of the water. With painstakingly slow strides we finally made it to the other side."

"Thank God you made it safe and sound" said my mother.

We all chimed in "Thank God!"

My sister Mary and brother-in-law Hovig were worried and were relieved to see us arrive safely.

Elated, I felt free again. My sister Mary lived in a villa on top of a hill in an exclusive area. I went out and twirled around, looking up and absorbing the rays of the sun, which cast an amber glow over the city. It was a joy to be in Amman.

The city was built on seven hills. The hills surrounded the main shopping center in the valley. Each hill had its own name and unique character. My sister lived on *Jabal* (hill)Amman, which was one of the most well known hills and where the effluent lived. Her house had a large living room, three bedrooms and a den. Her mother-in-law and brother-in-law lived with her.

Although it was crowded at my sister Mary's house, we were happy and wishfully thinking that after a week or two we will go back home. At night I slept at the house of Dr. Etyemezian. (He was the uncle of my brother-in-law Hovig). I enjoyed that very much, because they had six children. I was welcomed there and became good friends with Anahid. Her older sister, Mary, ordered everyone around, but I was on good terms with her and we enjoyed each others company.

On weekends I spent time with the Etyemezian children. Anahid and I had a friend where we sometimes went and visited.

One day while at our friends' house, we saw Hussein, the king's son, come to see our friend in his sports car. Our friend a pretty girl with blue eyes and blond hair, enjoyed being with him. We promised the mother not to tell anyone about the king's son's visit.

We left them alone. Later our friend told us that Hussein liked her enough to visit often. Her parents were concerned; although Hussein would be the next king, he was Muslim, while she was a Christian.

Anahid and I continued our adventures with King Abdullah's private driver, an Armenian and a friend of our families. He gave rides to us in the king's limousine, and we promised not to tell anyone. We pretended we were royalty, and enjoyed every minute of it.

After a two week stay at my sister's house, my mother felt that we overstayed our visit; also things were not quieting down in Jerusalem. We wanted to go back but the borders were closed.The war was becoming intense. The news was that the *Haganah* was killing people, raping women, and treating non-Jews badly. On the other hand, my sister's in-laws were not happy about us being there. They complained, constantly. We also had a truck full of household goods in their front yard.

We found a house close-by with three bedrooms, a living room, and a spacious kitchen, so we moved. During this time, Anahid Oshagan (the daughter of the famous writer and teacher, Hagop Oshagan,) who also was a neighbor in Jerusalem had our house key. My mother asked her to collect as many items from the house as she could fill a small truck, and send them to Amman. Sure enough she did. This included the Piano the most precious thing to me.

Both my sister Berjouhi and I, spent our time playing the piano. Our rented house was newly built, but unfortunately, the roof leaked. The landlord was out of the country, so we had buckets in every room to catch the rain water. Finally, after a few weeks, the rain subsided and the landlord came and fixed the roof. But because of this situation, I became very sick, with high fever.

My family realized that the political situation had worsened and it would take much longer to return to Jerusalem. I registered in the girl's British school. After many tests the principle assigned me to the first-secondary class, which is equivalent to ninth grade. It surprised me. All my age students were at least in one year lower grade than myself. The girls in my class were older, and they were more interested in boys than in their studies. Also they used make-up and wore expensive clothing. I did not associate with them. I must have seemed strange to them, all I did was study. I did not have a social life except with my family and their friends. I wanted to be with my age group. I excelled both in English and Math, for that reason the school put me at a higher level. I looked at the girls in the lower grades, and saw what a good time they were having, I wished I had been with them.

This was a very different environment for me. Although I lived amongst the Arabs in Jerusalem, they were more liberal. Amman presented a different world for women. For the first time I saw women cover their faces when in public.

In Jerusalem, only older, very religious Muslim women covered

Artemis, Vicky, Garabed, Berjouhi, and Mary in Amman, Trans-Jordan 1947

their faces. In Amman most of my classmates covered their faces. Some only covered their hair. I was introduced to Muslim culture where women are second to men. They are to bring children into the world, take care of men and cook for them. Some men marry more than one wife with many children from each. Muslim religion allows a man to marry as many women as he wants, but is not allowed to have more than four wives at one time. They tend to have large families with many children.

Women cooked all day. At dinner time they took care of their husbands first, and then fed the children, and whatever is left of the food they ate. The first wife always governed the rest of the wives. There always was rivalry amongst the children. I found out that many educated families did not follow this Muslim custom of having more than one wife.

Amman was an experience. We believed that any day the roads will open, and we will be able to go back home to Jerusalem.

Most of my time was spent studying after school and doing homework. I spent almost two hours a day practicing the piano.

Politically, things were getting worse. Suddenly, my Uncle Stephan and family came from Jerusalem. We allocated the living room to them as a bedroom. A few months later, my uncle Pierre, with his wife and son, Hantz, came. They brought with them their big bulldog. We allocated one of the bedrooms to them. Thus we had one bedroom for us with four beds, and one bedroom for my Uncle Pierre and family. The living room became a bedroom for my Uncle Stephan and family, my brother slept in the den. Everyone did their share of housework and we all helped the maid. She was a blessing because my mother had a hard time with housework.

Artemis, my six year old little sister was always running out, she went to the neighbors house or down the field and vanished. I had to go and find her and bring her back. She was a cute and lovable little sister; it was hard to get mad at her.

Every so often my uncle's dog ran out of the house. My uncle always asked me to go find him. I used to have the hardest time in catching and bringing him back. You see, he only understood German.

There always was an excitement in our house. One day as I came from school my mother gave me a bunch of pictures.

"Here Victorig, take this package and burn everything!"

"Mom, what are they?"

"Don't ask questions; do as I told you - Now!" she ordered,

"Also, make sure you don't talk to anyone, only burn them in the bathroom. Fast!"

"But"

"Now you go in there and start burning, if anyone asks what you are doing, tell them you are heating the iron and preparing for ironing the cloths."

In 1947 we still used the kind of iron that you put coal in to heat it. When it's hot and ready, you do your ironing. Anyway I took the pictures. My mother was very disturbed and so was everyone else in the family, particularly my Uncle Pierre and his wife.

I went in the bathroom and after closing the door I looked at the pictures.

"Wow! What pictures!" Now I understood why they were upset.

Almost thirty or more pictures of dead bodies of naked women and children piled on top of each other in trucks. Some were pictures of a village, others were pictures of dead men scattered. I started burning one at a time. A wave of realization overtook me.

As I burned I could hear the voices of men coming from outside. I started to hurry not knowing what was happening. As I finished, I flushed the ashes into the toilet and put the iron on the window ledge. A sense of relief came over me.

Later I learned that these were the pictures of the massacre that the *Haganah* committed in the village of *Der Yasin*, Palestine. When I came out of the bathroom the whole house was in turmoil. Beds were turned upside down, some of the stuffing of the mattresses were out, and I saw the back of the men going out of the yard; My uncle Pierre was with them. Everyone was upset. We found out later that the men were from the secret police.

The reason they had come was that they had intercepted some pictures and writings that a journalist was sending to somewhere in the Middle East and the United States of America, from Palestine, via my Uncle's son Hantz, who, without opening the packages was mailing them out, using my brother-in-law Hovig's pharmacy as the postal stop.

Hantz had a friend who was a journalist, (Keshishian) he corresponded with him. When his friend asked him to mail these packages to another country, Hantz did it without opening and not knowing what was being mailed. The secret police intercepted one of these packages.

They took my Uncle Pierre and his son Hantz for questioning. Fortunately, both had no idea what was in the latest package. After a few hours, they let my uncle go. They detained Hantz for one more day. We heard that Levon Keshishian, the journalist, was also questioned and held for a short time. A lesson was learned by all.

Moving Again

There were no colleges or universities in Amman in 1947. My brother, who had graduated from high school, played the violin at night in restaurants, and at the prestigious Amman Club. My sister Berjouhi taught at the same girl's school I was attending. The war was getting worse making our return to Jerusalem impossible. The borders were closed and it was very dangerous to go back.

My mother had the foresight to take the family to the city of Beirut in Lebanon where there were Universities and colleges. My brother wanted to be a dentist like my Uncle Pierre.

We went to Beirut and I was enrolled at Central High School, one of the best high schools in the area. In *Ashrafieh*, we rented a second floor apartment. My brother registered in the dental school of the French University *Faculte Francais De Beirut*. Our apartment was roomy and comfortable with a large balcony.

In Beirut we continued practicing our piano; we each played for two hours every day. Eventually we took lessons from a famous French piano teacher, Madame Marie Rieu Langard.

We made our own bread. My sister Berjouhi and I took turns in kneading the dough. A friend told us that the dough will enhance and soften the skin of the hands. So we did this chore happily hoping to have healthy skin and graceful hands. We took the dough to the bakery across from our apartment, where they shaped and baked the bread. With joyful anticipation we waited at the balcony for the signal from the baker that the bread was ready. This was the best bread I ever ate. Also with the help of the bakery we prepared special dishes.

Our apartment was close to my school, and we could hear the morning roll call bell. Many times, I rushed at the last minute, and stood in line pretending I had arrived much earlier. Eleventh grade was the highest level in my high school. The school officials tested me and discovered that I was advanced for my age. Normally I belonged in the eighth grade, but because of my high scores the teachers assigned me to the ninth grade. They stressed that I must apply more effort on learning the Armenian language and spelling. I felt elated, almost like being grown up! This meant I would graduate a year early!

My classmates looked upon me with cold detachment because

I was a foreigner. Since I excelled in English and math, their resentment became painfully obvious.

I'd like to take a moment now to thank my parents for my success as a young student. By virtue of my mother's guidance, and her insistence that learning should be foremost in my life, I became a good student.

However, that ideal upbringing came with a heavy price.

Yes, I did well in school. Nevertheless, It grieved me to realize that if I had been just an ordinary student, my classmates might have welcomed me into their inner circle.

Nonetheless, fortune again smiled at me. That very same year, the school principal considered me worthy to advance yet another grade. And this time, my classmates turned out to be more mature than those I left behind. They welcomed me graciously, and before long I felt happy in their society. The warm bond of friendship which I established with some of them remains as strong today as it was then.

Our class had only twelve students, but we worked together in harmony.

In my last year of high school I started playing the piano for the whole school during the worship hour. Also, I became the pianist for the Protestant Sunday school and church choir.

After that service, Laurice and I, one of my classmates and a close friend, ran to our Apostolic church, and listened to the priest and enjoyed the Orthodox mass. My mother felt joy to see me at her church.

I excelled in reading and reciting poetry and participated in various competitions. One time, after practicing and doing well during rehearsals, I went home and kept on reciting over and over. Then to my horror, I realized that I was losing my voice. Even though I stayed quiet and drank hot liquids, when the hour came for the competition, the judges, sitting in the back of the vast hall, had a hard time hearing me. The people in front heard me and were sure I'd win. When I did not win, they all protested saying that the judges were not being fair.

Teen Life in Beirut

For my graduation ceremony, which took place during my sixteenth year, I was chosen to recite a poem titled "To a Skylark" by Shelley. A poem of special significance to young people on the threshold of becoming responsible adults. As I nervously stood on the edge of the stage, I remembered my past experience with the judges who could not hear me, and I projected my voice all the way back to the last seat of the hall.

The ceremony also included a rendition of Beethoven's Fifth Symphony, arranged as a piece for piano using four hands. A friend of mine and I performed that much loved music. At the end, the look of pride on my mother's face, as she applauded vigorously through a torrent of joyful tears, will remain forever in my heart!

My mother insisted that all her children get educated; she also insisted that all of us study music. My sisters and I always practiced at least two hours a day. We all played the piano on stage for different functions. My sister Berjouhi always accompanied my brother Garabed, who was very good playing the violin.

Financially, it was difficult; we did not have the luxuries that we had in Jerusalem. My brother played at night in nightclubs, my sister Berjouhi gave English lessons.

When my mother was offered land in a very sought after location, she refused, saying that we had lost everything, our house and all our lands in Jerusalem, she did not want to lose again. She said she would rather invest in her children's education, where they will have a profession and a better future. In Beirut there were no free schools, we had to pay a large sum of money every year for our education.

I remember going with my mother and sisters to audition for piano lessons from Madame Marie Rieu Langard. At first Artemis was going to stay at home, but she protested and wanted to come along. When we arrived at Madame's studio we were greeted by a tall sophisticated woman in a flowing gown. The smell of wood polish was suffocating, and I was nervous. She asked my older sister Berjouhi to play on one of the two pianos in the room. She listened intently as my sister played and when she was done, she asked me to play. I can't remember what we played, but when we were done, my little sister insisted on playing. We all chuckled, since she was only eight years old, but she would not take no for an answer. So Madame Rieu said, "Let's see what you can do."

My sister attacked the piano with so much energy as she played her little piece, that the Madame fell in love with her. She told us she would teach us without charge, only if Artemis could also be her student. The Madam saw in Artemis a great musical talent.

I enjoyed playing Bach, so she always made me play Bach for recitals. One of these recitals was in a large movie theater, this time I played The Music Box and my sister Artemis played Beethoven's Fur Elise, she could hardly reach the pedals. The audience stood up and went crazy clapping. Both my mother and I were crying. My mother kept saying to the people next to her,

"She is my daughter! She is my daughter!"

My sister Artemis was too young to go on her own to her piano lessons. So besides going to my own class, I accompanied her and brought her back home. Sometimes I waited inside in the reception room, and other times outside, sitting on the stairs. We used the tram for travel, there was a stop right outside Madam Rieu's apartment.

Next door to the apartment, shops sold cosmetics. I used to imagine myself buying all the cosmetics and being a ballerina. I loved dancing and wanted to study ballet but financially it was not possible. One day someone from one of the shops came and tapped on my shoulder. Suddenly I realized that I was so deep in my thoughts and imagination that unconsciously I was dancing in the middle of the sidewalk. I was terribly embarrassed and ran away.

In 1950, at the age of sixteen, I graduated from high school. I registered in the Evangelical College of Beirut, and majored in science. My family moved from Ashrafiyeh region, into an apartment right across from the main tram station. Our doors and windows constantly rattled from the use of machinery at the station. We felt it the first few months but after that, we got used to the vibration.

College was fun but I had to commute to school every day. I made good friends and here again my best subjects were math, english, and physics. It was a happy year.

I also studied and played the piano for two hours every day. My older sister, Berjouhi practiced during the day, Artemis practiced after school, and I practiced last. My poor mother, I can imagine how she endured this constant piano playing and practicing. When we asked her she would say,

"It's a pleasure to hear you practice."

My brother practiced the violin in the bedroom.

We had three bedrooms, a living room and a dining room. We converted one of the rooms into a dining room because it was closer to the kitchen.

My mother unfortunately had a heart problem, she was not getting better. All of us took care of the chores in the house. Many times when my mother was ill, I cooked for the family. I cleaned once a week on Saturdays. Laundry was done by hand; someone came and did the heavy laundry.

The nice part of this apartment was that it was built on top of shops. So our piano playing did not bother them much.

There was a grocery store right below our apartment. One day we asked my sister Artemis to go to the store and buy cheese and *halva.* (a sweet made with sesame seed) She took a long time to return. The next day she itched all over. Right away my mother knew that she had eaten too much *halva*. She got a good scolding from my mother. But her sweet tooth was her master. Every time she went to buy something, she bought *halva* and ate it. The red marks that appeared all over her face and body were witness to her 'sin'.

I had many happy memories during the first year we moved to this apartment. Friends dropped in all the time; we played instruments, sang, acted and told stories. One of our friends was John Agulian, we called him Agul, he had a beautiful voice. He wanted to become an opera singer. He imitated famous singers. One of us played the piano, my brother played the accordion, or the violin, the rest of us used kitchen utensils as instruments, and Agul sang.

Yervant Tavitian, another family friend was famous for telling fortunes, so we were always drinking coffee and asking him to look for mysterious clues in our cups.

About mid 1951, my sister Berjouhi started having headaches. Doctors gave her all kinds of medication but nothing helped. One day she lost consciousness, we were petrified, since we did not have a telephone; someone had to go to the doctor's house to bring him. My mother sent me to Doctor Markarian to ask him to come. I had no option but to take the tram.

As I boarded it, I saw a man with a face which was extremely distorted, many layers of skin hanging from his puffed up face.

Being late night he was the only one in the tram. I was horrified! Started shivering. I thought he might attack me. I kept on moving as far away from him as possible. As soon as I arrived to my station I jumped and ran as fast as I could to the doctor's house. I thought he was chasing me. I rang the bell a few times. I was shivering and my heart was pounding so hard, I thought it will come out of my chest. As the doctor's wife opened the door, she had one look at me and she thought I was going to faint. I must have been terribly pale. She made me sit down and gave me a glass of water. I told the doctor what was happening to my sister.

"I will come right away. You sit and rest, while I get ready."

The glass of water did the trick and I felt much better.

The doctor drove me back home, and after examining my sister, he recommended that we take her to the hospital, and go through different tests. He will check with the hospital and will let us know when this could be done.

During this time, my mother was also having heart problems. There were days where my mother was in one bed and my sister Berjouhi in the other. My sister used to call me 'pussy cat', because I used to curl up on her bed near her feet doing my homework or studying, this way I was able to watch her as well as my mother. Every day I stayed with them until my brother came from playing the violin, about two or three in the morning. Then I went to bed and he took over. I had to get up early in the morning to go to school.

Teenage Vicky and practising on her favorite piano, 1952

We stopped having any kind of social life, by reason of my mother and my sister's illness.

After many tests, the doctors discovered that my sister had a brain tumor.The news came like a dagger into our hearts. Doctors, at the hospital wanted to operate to ease the pain and take her out of the coma. The operation was successful, they opened a hole in the skull where the tumor was located. They did not remove the tumor; they recommended that she be taken to London where there was a specialist.

For a while this stopped the terrible headaches that she was having.

After many sleepless nights, my brother and Berjouhi departed to London for an operation by a well known doctor, at one of the famous hospitals. There was nothing else we could do but pray.

It was during this time that we had a visitor from a theater group. Mrs. Zepure Shant, a great actress, and a well liked person, had heard about me from other young people, she also had heard me play the piano on stage. She asked my mother if she will allow me to join the theater group for the performance of Ancient Gods *(Hin Asdvadzner)* written by Levon Shant, her father in law. A story based upon the life of the great Armenian composer, Komitas, describing his emotional behavior after he was tortured by the Ottoman Turks, during the Armenian Genocide.

Levon Shant was one of the great Armenian writers of his time, he had written many books and plays. He was a young orphan, a devout humanist and a cultural icon. He had written this dramatic masterpiece play in 1909 which was later published in Constantinople in 1913. Shant was his nickname which meant thunderbolt.

My mother was reluctant to let me go, but Mrs. Shant was very persuasive, she promised that she will take good care of me and my mother should not worry. My mother looked at me and saw the eagerness and the shine in my eyes, she reluctantly allowed me to join the group. She also felt that after the difficult times we were having with my sister's condition, this would be a bright spot in my life. Needless to say, I was thrilled and in seventh heaven.

We rehearsed twice a week. My role as a lead fairy, gave me the chance to take ballet lessons from Ani Varjabedian who was a well known dancer. I was ecstatic. I felt that one of my dreams came true. She taught me how to run, jump and act like a fairy. But alas! They were very short lessons, and only for a specific role. But still it was something and I was very happy.

My second role was to be the leading actor's lady partner. The scene, a Roman dining hall, with plenty of fruits on the long tables, wine in gold goblets, and plenty of cheering and drinking. I was dressed like a queen in gold and silver tones; my long hair was piled on my head with all kinds of ribbons, my face covered with heavy makeup. I did not have a speaking part, but I played a haughty and self confident lady, like a princess performing an ancient ritual.

I also was part of the stage crew with Mrs. Shant, we pushed and pulled the backstage sea prop, making noises as though the wind was blowing.

The play was supposed to be only for two months, but it lasted for over a year to full house audiences. My mother was pleased and proud of my performance. She also noticed that many of the props with drawings of Venus resembled me. I told her that it was true, the artist made me sit for the paintings.

This same year, I completed my sophomore year of college, majoring in science. I made good friends and earned high grades. My brother came home from London. My sister also returned after recovering in a center in Surrey, England. She was gone for about one month and we were all shocked to see the tremendous amount of weight she had gained from her medication.

The operation to remove the tumor was successful, but she could only remember things that had happened to her in the past. She had trouble remembering the present, and she repeated the same things over and over without realizing that she had already said it before. This was very stressful for all of us, specially my mother. We all pampered my sister, took care of her and never left her alone.

After graduating from junior college, I wanted to go to the American University of Beirut (AUB), but it was expensive. I thought maybe I can work. There was an opening at a laboratory at United Nation's Relief World Association (UNRWA) they wanted a Palestinian. I applied. My brother's teacher was one of the admitting committee members.

When he saw my qualifications, he voted for me but unfortunately the rest of the committee was playing politics, they chose a Muslim who had just graduated from high school. I was crushed!

We found out later that even though I was better qualified for the job, I was discriminated against, I was Christian! And above all a female Armenian!

In Beirut most families in the summer went to the mountains for three months to get relief from the heat. They returned to the city just before the opening of the schools.

We always went to a mountain resort where my brother found a job for his band. At least once a week; the family visited the night-club to listen to him playing the violin with his band.

Most nightclubs were on a hill with breathtaking views. Many couples came and danced all night. I was a tomboy; I wore pants and pretended I was the man. My sister Artemis and I danced the evenings away.

While we were at the mountains in the resort village of Alley, Ben Yotnakhparian came from London to visit and stayed with us for one week. He had just graduated from London University, and was looking for a job. He was on his way to Trans-Jordan to visit his sister Aznive, who was married to my uncle Stephan. He also was going to Amman for an engineering position. My brother Garabed had just heard that the University of Beirut was looking for engineering professors, so Ben applied and was accepted.

Because he was a guest and a relative, my mother wanted us to entertain him, take him around, and keep him company. My sister Artemis was too young, my sister Berjouhi was not capable to entertain, therefore, I was the only one left to do the job.

I had known Ben from the time when my Uncle Stephan married his sister. He used to come to our house once in a while to play tennis with my brother and sister Berjouhi. He was handsome, athletic, and an excellent tennis player. A champion in table tennis. I entertained him as our guest, and eventually started to enjoy his company. We spent many memorable days, climbing mountains, taking walks, visiting other villages and dancing almost every evening at the night club where my brother's band played.

All throughout, I never stopped practicing piano every day for two hours. All that summer my family and I continued enjoying the beautiful resort. In the back of my mind I always worried about the future. I started practicing my typing hoping I could find a secretarial job.

It was during this time that my brother received the news that UNRWA needed teachers to teach in their schools, so I applied.

Since I was a science major they offered me to go and take teaching courses. I attended a girl's college- British Training College, later it was named "British Syrian Training College." Most of the girls came from outside of Beirut and from affluent families, almost all stayed in dorms. I was one of the few who commuted. For me it was an experience. I made few friends. It was difficult to mingle with these girls. They were cliquish and always friends with their dorm roommates.

One day the principle asked me if I would help the blind school nearby. I was thrilled. The first time I went to teach, I came back crying, I never realized how blind people learned and how they did their chores. Their dorm was clean and spacious; each bed had a small table next to it. The blind students said they made their own beds and did their assigned chores. I played the piano for them and

Two sisters in the mountains of Lebanon, 1952

they sang. Most of them were not only blind but also had other handicaps, many had facial distortions. They were gentle young boys and girls, when they heard my voice they always showed their joy by making loud noises, clapping and running to hug me. Every time I looked at them I had a hard time holding my tears.

Both my brother and I graduated from college and dental school on the same day. My mother and sisters attended his ceremony, while Ben, who was in Beirut and teaching at the American University, came to mine. After my graduation ceremonies, the two of us rushed to my brother's University arriving just in time to take pictures; unfortunately we did not see him receive his diploma. Never the less, it was a happy time for us, and we celebrated.

Both my brother and I were concerned about our future. Being Palestinian refugees of Christian Armenian origin, Lebanon did not accept us. Even though my brother had graduated from a Lebanese University, he was not allowed to open a clinic in Lebanon. We were not allowed to become Lebanese citizens. He decided to go to Jordan and open his dental clinic in Amman.

College graduation 1952 (left) and graduating British Training College (BTC) 1953

The family surrounding the graduates, Vicky and Garabed, 1953

Getting Married

My sister Mary, her husband Hovig, and their three children, came to Beirut on their way to the United States in 1952. Before they left we had a family get together at Ben's apartment, and celebrated an impromptu engagement. Everyone was excited, especially my little sister, Artemis. She drank a full glass of wine on an empty stomach and slept through the evening. She never remembered what happened on that day. My sister Mary's mother-in-law called this celebration "the day of exchanging handkerchiefs," our family had never heard of this custom. We exchanged handkerchiefs.

My brother found a casino in the village of *Souk-el-Kharb,* high in the mountains of Lebanon where he played with his band. We rented a house nearby for the summer. Ben and my family decided that our engagement would take place at the village in August 1953, and the wedding a year later. My Uncle Stephan's family came from Amman, and Ben's mother and youngest sister surprised us and came from Gaza for the engagement.

The engagement party was beautiful. I wore my eldest sister's engagement full length blue dress, made of taffeta with an overflow of tulle. I felt like a princess! Close relatives and friends honored us with their presence. The priest blessed our engagement, and we gave candy wrapped in tulle to all. There was plenty of food and drinks, my brother played the piano, and everyone danced.

Engagement photos: Opposite page exchanging rings. Below left: Ben's mother Vartouhi, Vicky, Ben, and Vicky's mother Haigouhi. Right: Vicky and Ben portrait. Bottom right: dancing at the engagement on the right, Vicky's Uncle Stephan and his wife, Aznive. Garabed playing the piano bottom left side of picture.

Ben's mother insisted that the wedding be held as soon as possible, because she did not know when she would have an opportunity to leave Gaza again.

Ben and I felt unhappy that his mother was putting pressure on us. Our preference was to save money so we could go to Vienna for our honeymoon! Nevertheless we gave in. The wedding date was set for September 20. We had only 40 days to prepare for the wedding.

Money was tight and the brunt of the work was on my mother. My cousin, Anahis, came to help with the sewing. We pulled some material, from my grandmother's large dowry chest and made a few dresses. I had seen a picture of Queen Elizabeth's wedding gown, I wanted the same design, it was stunning, pleated tulle covered the brocade top with rows and rows of pearls sewn horizontally. The skirt was full brocade except in the front. From an opening, layers of tulle pushed out as she walked. Ben's sister Araxi made the wedding dress: just the way I had seen it. My mother miraculously found time to even embroider a tablecloth.

We had a very stressful 40 days. We always had relatives visiting. Every time Ben and I wanted to go out, Ben's sister Aznive and his mother sent seven year old Paramtzem, his niece, to be with us. We were never left alone. This annoyed us. One time we snuck out from the back door, and thought we outsmarted her but with help, she found us. She had a lovable way of putting herself between Ben and I and holding our hands. We just couldn't say no to her non-stop questions.

On the wedding day, we traveled with a caravan of cars: honking through the village announcing the wedding party. Children ran toward the cars for a glimpse of the bride and groom. We slowly made our way down the mountains toward St. Neshan Church in the center of the city of Beirut.

My dress was gorgeous. Every time I walked the tulle swished around and I loved it, the veil was the same veil that my sister Mary had used for her wedding many years back. It was attached to a ...

Before entering the church: my mother, my sister, Berjouhi, myself and my brother.

hat made of straw-like material with the central part open. Many of Ben's colleagues from the American University of Beirut, attended the wedding.

My brother Garabed gave me away. Uncle Stephan was the best man and Aznive, Ben's sister, was the godmother. My sister Artemis, Ben's nieces; Paramtzem and Salpi were the flower girls. We rejoiced when my eldest uncle, Pierre, came from Amman and surprised us. My mother was very happy for having both of her brothers there.

Ben and I felt that the ceremony performed by the Archbishop and two other priests, was taking longer than usual, Ben murmured "How much longer?"

Once the congratulations were over family group pictures were taken in front of the church .

From my side of the family were my mother, my two sisters and my brother, Uncle Stephan, his wife Aznive and the children. Uncle Pierre, and my paternal grand uncle with his family. From
Ben's side of the family was his mother his two sisters, his uncle and his uncle's wife, his aunt and his *genkamire* (Godmother).

The church provided a room where I changed to my travel suit. We were going to our honeymoon right away. I wore a white cotton suit with green stripes and short sleeves. I had white gloves, white

Family group picture after the wedding.

purse and shoes. I wore the white hat without the long veil. I weighed 100 pounds and the suit fit me very well. We came down and joined the relatives where Ben waited for me. I was confused, and dazed, everything was like a dream.The tightness in the back of my throat was holding my tears at bay. As we moved towards the car, the family showered us with rice, accompanied by high pitched ululations which is customary in the middle east.

We went to Brumana Village, a resort in the hills. When we arrived the hotel did not have our room ready consequently they gave us a temporary room so we could rest. We entered the room and surprise! We were not alone. Five or six little kids found our window, and with wide

Wedding portrait September 20,1953

After the wedding on the way to honeymoon.

open eyes, they pushed each other to get a better look at the bride and groom.

Soon our second floor room was ready with fresh flowers. The view from the large window was spectacular with beautiful mountains covered with evergreens and a sprinkling of red from the roofs of private homes and villas.

The next day my brother paid a surprise visit. He was concerned and wanted us to go to Beirut so that we can finalize our passports for our travel to Cyprus. We also wanted to see my Uncle Pierre and spend some time with him before he left for Amman.

We went to Beirut and met my uncle and brother at a restaurant called *La Coupol.* My Uncle Pierre was very happy for us, I had not seen him for many years and it was just wonderful that he came by and we spent some time with him. We were so absorbed talking with each other that we suddenly realized that we were the only ones left in the restaurant and there was little time left to go and finalize our paperwork for our travel. Little did we know that many years later, my brother Garabed would marry the restaurant owner's daughter, Zabel.

At the resort, our hotel gave us the red carpet treatment. One night we decided to go to a nearby nightclub. Being a weekday there were few people in the nightclub but the music was beautiful. Ben and I loved dancing. After a few dances we noticed a couple at a nearby table, signaling us. At first we ignored them but after a while they asked us to join them.

We debated, but we decided why not, so we joined them. We found out that they were from Kuwait. The wife seemed to be much younger than her husband. He took permission from Ben to dance with me. As we danced, the band people were trying to attract my attention, they tried to tell me something, I could not understand. After going to the hotel Ben told me that the band wanted me to tell the gentleman I was dancing with, to give a large tip to the band. I am afraid I was too naive and inexperienced in things like that.

It was getting late about midnight, Ben and I wanted to leave. The husband of the other couple insisted that we go with them to their place. They said that they also were spending their vacation at this resort town, and they had rented an apartment. He was drinking heavily, we did not want to join them, but he became argumentative especially when he found out that this was our honeymoon, he wanted to treat us. The poor wife beckoned us to come just for a short time so he wouldn't create a scene and since we did not want to be rude, we went along.

This was a strange experience for us, and we were nervous. We left the nightclub with them and walked to their close-by apartment.

The apartment turned out to be a large room. Divided by a curtain. There was a table and chairs in one side of the room, the other side was the kitchen. Our surprise was greater when the gentleman's first wife greeted us with a little baby on her lap. She invited us in and said that she was happy that we came and it was time for the young mother to feed the baby. Confronted with this awkward situation, we wanted to leave, but he wouldn't let us, he was drunk, he kept on ordering and shouting to his first wife,

"*Idbah el jajah!*. (Kill the chicken) kill the chicken! Set the table for us!"

Both women realized the situation and tried to help us leave, but unfortunately in his drunken condition he did not know what he was doing. He locked the door.

"You cannot go! You must eat with us!" He continued turning to his wife, and kept saying.

"Wife! *Idbah el jajah!*

Somehow the women lured him to another part of the room behind the drape, and while he was distracted, the older wife helped us get out of the door.

We left. Soon he came out of the apartment and was running after us, he wanted us to come back, at the same time screaming at the top of his lungs. I was petrified! We both started running and tried to find a place to hide. I had high heels and was not able to run fast. Fortunately there were many cars parked on the lot so we hid behind one and hoped he would not see us. As he came closer we jumped onto the road and I took my shoes off and started running in the street, my heart was pounding, this was past midnight and there was no traffic, finally we saw a car coming, we went to the middle of the road and signaled him to stop, he felt sorry for us and gave us a ride to our hotel. We both collapsed in our room agitated, but eventually, couldn't stop laughing, recounting the crazy experience we just had.

After a few days my brother came with the papers for our departure. The next morning we went directly to the ferry. In a few hours we reached Larnaca, the port of Cyprus. Our destination was north of the island, on the beautiful hills which we reached at dusk. Aside from the hotel personnel, the place was deserted. We wondered where the rest of the guests were.

Honeymoon ship to Cyprus. September 1953.

We had a wonderful reception and a good meal with wine and a variety of fruits. In the morning we again realized that there were very few people in the hotel. When we asked, the receptionist told us that there was a big earthquake in the northwestern part of Cyprus and people were afraid to travel even though this was far from that area.

The hotel, perched on a hill covered with pine trees provided a spectacular view. We hiked all over the wooded area. It seemed that we were the only ones there. We enjoyed the isolation and the attention we received from the management and the personnel of the hotel. They cooked anything we wanted, helped with our sightseeing and gave us all the attention we needed. We were having such a good time that we did not want to leave.

We had made reservations to stay a few days in Nicosia, the capital of Cyprus. There we went to an Armenian church and met some wonderful people, they took us around and told us that a group of archeologists had just excavated an area in Famagusta and found an Armenian Church. The archeologists had suspected that the mound of dirt was very unusual in that area. They decided to excavate, and came upon a beautiful small Armenian church built about the fourteenth century. But unfortunately in the middle of the Turkish quarter where Muslim people lived. Our new friends were excited and eager to drive us there to show the excavation. As we drove, they showed us the sights, and told us how this church was discovered.

As we came closer to the location, we noticed a lot of Turks. Men were sitting outside the shops and playing backgammon. Others sat on the floor and smoked water pipes, a few exchanged heated conversations, and many children were running around.

The moment I entered the small round church, I fell in love with it. The writings were in Armenian, the ceiling and the walls were covered with murals, telling the story of Jesus Christ and the Apostles. Everyone was excited, all of us were eager to read the writings that were on the circular wall of the church. The government protected it, and the Armenians took care of it. It was very emotional to see this building and how, like a dear old relative, the faithful preserved it throughout the years. My emotions swelled up inside and I allowed my tears of joy to flow freely..

Another one of the highlights of our trip was climbing the mountain to visit the castle of Richard the Lion Heart. A Byzantine construction, built in the 14th century. This was where King Richard was married to Berengaria of Navarre. He was known for his great courage and strength. Due to his joining the third crusade, he was known as "the absent King." The Turks took over the castle in 1570 and increased the fortifications, using it as a jail. We wondered how they had built a castle like that on top of a steep mountain. From one side it looked as though it was part of the mountain rising into the sky, like a sheer cliff...

During our tour we saw a construction site and noticed that the women were the ones doing all the work. They were carrying bricks and buckets on their heads. A few men sat around and talked. One of them seemed to be directing the women.

We still have the pottery vase we bought from Cyprus with ancient figures of Gods. Our last stop was Larnaca where we again took the ferry and went back to Beirut.

Married Life

Our first home was a ground floor apartment in a four story building. We had one bedroom with a balcony overlooking the garden. The next door neighbor's enormous wooded garden gave us privacy. As you entered the apartment there was a small foyer which led to the kitchen, on the left there was the dining room. From the dining room you went into the living room with a glass folding door separating them.

My brother surprised us with a beautiful German made piano as our wedding gift, I was so thrilled, I shed tears of joy when I saw it. We had our bedroom furniture, the piano and two chairs in the living room. We bought a small dining room table with a matching cabinet and a small bookcase. We set our record player on top of the cabinet.

In the kitchen we had two pots and a pan with a few dishes and a gas burner. The apartment was close enough that Ben walked to the University. Sometimes he came for lunch. We were like two little children trying to find a life together. Ben started teaching me some of the foods he liked. I knew some cooking, but not everything. Many times I burned, or overcooked, or undercooked. He was very patient with me, he never got mad when I messed it up. So about a week later he wanted to invite one of his colleagues from the University for dinner. I prepared the meal and made a wonderful desert.

The guest arrived, we realized we needed lemon; Ben went to the corner grocer to pick up some lemons. About two minutes later I heard screaming from the hallway, at the same time heavy banging on the door. As I opened the door I was shocked to see Ben's mother with a taxi driver arguing and screaming. All the neighbors came out to see what was happening. I was so stunned that I did not know what to say or do.

"Do you have any money? I need to pay the driver!"

My heart was beating hard and I felt it would explode.

"Yes I have." I said, my hands trembled as I fumbled for some money, "Here." I said with a meek voice.

We were not expecting her, she was in Amman with Azniv, her daughter, she was going to stay there for a few months. We don't know what made her leave so early. At 19 years old, I was inexperienced and did not know how to handle a situation like this. Our guest was embarrassed. He wanted to leave.

"No, please stay, Ben will be here any minute, we'll have dinner together" I said with a trembling voice that sounded like someone else to me.

"Thank you, it is best that I leave." he left.

Ben came shortly and was equally surprised. We had our dinner in silence, without our guest.

We had only one bedroom, therefore we had to rush and buy a bed and set it up in the living room, needless to say that at this time, we lost our freedom and privacy.

Ben's mother took over the kitchen; she did not let me do any cooking or anything else in the kitchen. We had delicious meals. I had enough time to clean the house, dust, finish the daily chores, read a book and play the piano. I was an avid reader and being just out of school I was still in the habit of carrying a book everywhere.

I played the piano any time I found time. Ben's mother criticized me for this and for not cleaning the windows... I was learning.

Vicky on the apartment balcony 1953 and with her classmates; Esther Matossian, Laurice Jibelian, Haig DerKhorenian, Khajag Chakerian, and Vahram Karageozian.

After two weeks, Ben's sister Araxi came from Amman. Again we were surprised, we did not expect her; she was going to stay there for a few years. We did not know why she left as well. We assumed that they had trouble getting along with Azniv. No one wanted to talk about it.

Ben's mother left after three months. The return trip to Gaza was easier than when she first came due to some easing of the political situation. She was hoping that Ben's father and brother will be persuaded to come to Beirut. Araxi, Ben's sister, stayed with us, she did not want to go back to her sister's in Amman. Her mother instructed her that she should help me, and not let me do any kitchen work. After a few weeks Araxi found a job with the United Nations Relief World Association (UNRWA) and started working. I took over the chores.

My sister Berjouhi used to teach piano in a Catholic girls school, when she became ill her position was vacant, the Nuns asked if I will take her place. I gladly accepted, and started teaching.

I also was teaching privately at home. My first students were two nine and ten year old beautiful black children from Addis Ababa. Their father was Armenian married to an Addis Ababa ballet dancer. They spoke Armenian and were eager to play the piano.

I also started to take lessons from Cheskinoff, a famous and strict piano teacher. I did very well and was envied by some of the other students.

Whenever Ben and I went out, Araxi, his sister accompanied us. People always thought that I was Ben's sister and she was the wife. I looked like Ben, his sister had a lighter complexion.

Levon, our son, was born on February ninth of 1955. He was a beautiful baby. Ben's parents had instructed us that if the baby was a boy, we should send them a telegram; otherwise inform them by letter. So we sent them a telegram.

Ben was active in university life. Aside from teaching, he was the advisor and organizer of the students' variety shows of the engineering department. At that time, there were no girls in the engineering school; the boys acted the parts of the girls. It was hilarious to see boys with their hairy legs dancing the Can- Can. They were good. Ben was loved and respected by his students.

The first summer the Dean of the school suggested that Ben and I chaperone a group of students to Damascus, Syria. The ruling party's son, a student, invited his fellow students to Damascus. He also invited Ben and I personally to go. It was a great trip. At age nineteen I could not imagine myself a chaperone to girls who were about my age or older. But being the wife of the professor had its advantages, they respected me.

We had the red carpet treatment, many parties, receptions, and dinners. At one of the dinners, the table, which could seat twenty four people, was filled with all kinds of appetizing and unusual foods. The family took us and the group, to their summer house. It was in the middle of an enormous farmland. The building was not big but everything was operated by pushbutton. This was a rare thing for Syria in the 1950s.

Shopping in Damascus was fun, the old market (*souk*) had high covered arches, and shops lined on both sides of the street. You could find anything you wanted, from furniture, to groceries, to restaurants and coffee shops. The aroma of the spices dominated the market. We bought a beautiful embroidered tablecloth. We couldn't believe our eyes when we saw the famous pistachio ice cream hanging on a hook, we asked the vendor to give us some from the container where it was not exposed to air. He scoped up the thick ice cream and rolled it in shredded pistachio nuts, it was delicious. We returned to Beirut and everyone claimed a great time.

The first two summers of our marriage we stayed with my mother, brother and sisters in the mountains for one month. In 1956 they migrated to the United States. That summer we went to Jordan and visited my Uncle Stephan and his wife Azniv, Ben's sister.

At Amman Airport we found out that all the passengers had departed and we were the only ones left. We asked the security why they were holding us. They called Ben in and asked all kinds of questions. They finally admitted that they were holding us because of his name, Benjamin. They wanted to make sure that Ben was not Jewish and that he was not a spy. They asked him; "Why is your name Benjamin?"

"My parents gave this name to me when I was born." Ben said jokingly.

At first it seemed comical, but as they kept on asking questions, we realized things were getting more serious. Ben's sister and my Uncle Pierre were waiting on the other side of the meshed fence. We conversed with them; we informed the security people that these were our relatives. They started suspecting us more, because my uncle was standing there with blond hair and blue eyes. Ben's sister also with blond curly hair, green eyes and very light complexion. Ben is dark skinned with dark hair and dark brown eyes. They began to question if we were really related.

After two hours of interrogation, they received a phone call and let us go.

We almost did not recognize Amman, new buildings were everywhere. We were excited to see family and friends; Levon our two year old son, met for the first time his cousin Garabed who was one year older than him. While we were there, we christened Levon, my uncle was the godfather. After the ceremony Levon, was sitting on the priest's lap. He grabbed the priest's long beard and asked him,

"Why do you have this? People will be frightened from it!"

We were embarrassed! Everyone else thought it was cute.

We decided to visit Jerusalem to see my paternal uncle and family. Not knowing when we will have the opportunity to see them again. Since the old city of Jerusalem was in the hands of the Arabs, it was easy to travel between Amman and Jerusalem. But our own house was outside of the old city and was in the Jewish section so we could not visit there.

Our visit to the Armenian quarter brought back many childhood memories. The school in the convent that I attended seemed very small. As a child I used to think that it was an enormous place, with lots of stairs.

The churches were as beautiful, mysterious and exotic as ever. Entering the sanctuary, I tip-toed along, shivers running down my spine. Pictures and murals depicting the life of Jesus covered the walls. In the quiet atmosphere, feeling the ghosts of the pilgrims of the early centuries passing by, one by one, leaving an offering of gold or jewelry hanging on various religious pictures and icons. These surroundings created a mystical and spiritual atmosphere that I had never felt or seen in any other church.

Outside the church, navigating along the outer passageway, I came to the large cobblestone courtyard, where people living in the convent congregated. Their chatter echoed in my mind.

In the convent, aside from the Armenian Patriarchate, there is the famous Calouste Gulbenkian Library with over 100,000 volumes. The Helen Mardigian Museum of Armenian Art and Culture with historical and religious artifacts and the St. Tarkmanchats school (which I attended).

There is also evidence of the Xth Roman legion (*Legio X Fretensis*) and this is the home of the first printing press in Jerusalem. Here is recorded historical evidence that as early as 254 AD, bishops and the Armenian Church in co-operation with other bishops of the Middle East were actively engaged in the discovery and confirmation of Holy Places.

It was an emotional time for me, I could hardly hold my tears, it seemed that I was crying all the time.

We stayed for a short time, because we noticed that as we traveled we saw a large amount of troop movement.

We feared we would be trapped in Jerusalem. Sure enough, on our way back to Amman, we were stopped a few times. Some roads were blocked, and tanks were traveling in all directions.

We stayed a few more days in Amman, before going back home to Beirut to prepare ourselves to migrate to United States.

Already my mother, brother and two sisters were in Chicago, where my eldest sister Mary was living. My brother Garabed had read in the newspaper that a Chicago company called Harza Engineering was looking for Engineers. He met with their personnel officer and asked if they would sponsor Ben, who was teaching in the Engineering Department at the American University of Beirut.

They agreed and sent the papers to Beirut requesting Ben as a "professional immigrant."

We were told by the American Consulate that the quota for professional immigration was open, which prompted us to start selling our belongings, and we informed the University about our departure, which we thought will be in the immediate future.

Alas! Ben received the news that the quota for immigrating for Palestinians was full for 1957, since many of the Jewish people, who had relatives in the United States, were immigrating; they were running away from the war that they thought was going to happen between the Jews and the Arabs. They had more priority than professional applicants. This reduced our chances of emigrating from Beirut.

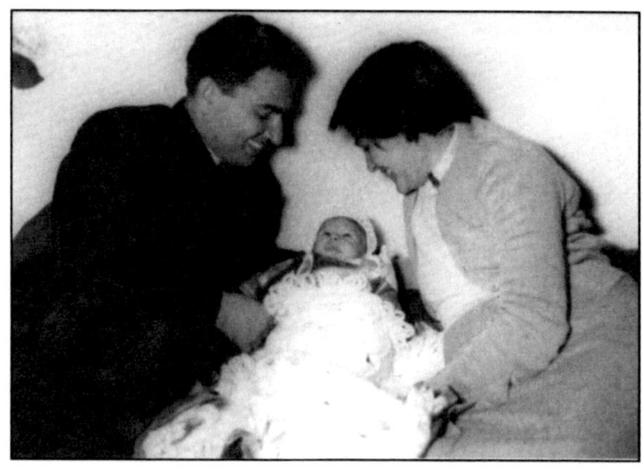

Clockwise from top: Dancing at an American University of Beruit function, Admiring our new baby- Levon. Vicky in Damascus, At King Hussein's reception.

Migration Problems

In 1947-1948, the Jordanian embassy in London had given all Palestinians, Jordanian passports. Ben's Jordanian passport was confiscated by the Jordanian embassy in Beirut. They would not renew it, saying that he received this passport in London, and this was a temporary passport. The reason for not renewing, they said, was because he was not of Arab origin and because his parents did not own property in Jordan, nor in Palestine in the area controlled by Jordan. His parents were in Gaza, which was controlled by Egypt at that time. Ben tried to explain that he was a student studying in England at the time of the Arab-Jewish war.

He asked them for a letter to show that they took his passport, and refused to renew it. But instead, they gave a letter saying that Ben had surrendered his passport.

Ben complained, "You confiscated it, I did not surrender it."

"This is all that we can give you." Was the reply from the Jordanian embassy.

We then tried to get an exit pass "*Lese Passé*" containing a return visa to Lebanon, as required by the USA immigration. This time the Lebanese government would not issue a return visa, saying that he was Jordanian. We were stuck in the middle again. This exemplified the reason we needed to emigrate to the United States to become American citizens.

Every day Ben went to the immigration office, they told him to come tomorrow; this went on for three to four months.

Suddenly, there was this Hungarian revolt, which the Soviet Union crushed. President Eisenhower decreed a law to allow 40,000 people to migrate to the United States. The American Embassy of Beirut included Ben and I into this quota.

We were elated. But in order to stamp the American visa, the US government required a passport or some paper from the Lebanese Government with a return visa.

We were terribly frustrated! Where shall we go? What shall we do? We turned over every stone possible with no results.

The United States Immigration office informed us, that within a month the visa will expire. Yet we had no passport or any official paper to stamp the visa on. We were desperate! We sold our furniture, informed the University, and the landlord, thinking that we will leave in a month. The University was very helpful, they gave us temporary furniture. The Dean of the Engineering school asked Ben to continue teaching, until all arrangements were done, and we were ready to leave. The landlord allowed us to stay until everything was settled.

We explained our dilemma to one of our friends, Yervant Tavitian, who was teaching French privately to a young boy, who was the son of a famous lawyer, who later we found out was the brother-in-law of the immigration officer. The same officer, who kept telling Ben to "come tomorrow."

We had only two weeks left before the visa permit expired. So our friend, seeing our desperate situation, said that he will try to talk to his student's father, and see what he could do for us. The next day both Ben and Yervant went to the lawyer's office. After hearing what was happening, the lawyer picked up the phone and called "the Chief" and asked him, "Why are you standing in the way of this young man's migration to the United States?"

After a short conversation, he asked Ben to go back the next day to the immigration office, his papers will be ready. Unbelievable! Though we thought the same thing will happen again, there was new hope. The next day as Ben entered, they welcomed him and greeted him with smiles. Ben thought what a reversal of attitude.

"*Ustaz* (teacher) we are greatly happy you came, we will do our best to get you the pass, come tomorrow."

Ben gave a quizzical look at the man and asked,"Is this the real tomorrow or are there other tomorrows?"

With a smile on his face, he said "Hah! This is the real tomorrow."

Sure enough, the next day when Ben went, his pass was ready. Joy of joys! We could not believe that it really happened. Ben went to the American Embassy and had the visa stamped on the *"Lese Passé"*

We thanked our friend profusely and wondered what would have happened to us if he had not helped.

Three years before, we had bought a plot of land for building a house on *Jabal El Mitten,* a suburb of Beirut. The lot was on top of the hill and had a beautiful view of the city of Beirut, the sea port, and the airport. We made the final payment; before leaving Beirut, we needed to transfer the title to our name. Ben went to the registration office. The officer was reading the newspaper; Ben tried to explain to him the urgency of our situation.

"Can't you see I am busy!"

"But sir, I'm leaving the country in two days."

"Sorry, I'm busy."

Ben went for help to the company we bought the lot from. They started laughing. "Come Ben, give me a five Lebanese pound note." said one of them.

He accompanied Ben to the Title Recording Office.

"*Sayed* (Sir), this Professor really needs to have that title."

As he was talking he slipped the five Lebanese pounds under a piece of paper that was on the desk. The officer took the money and with a warm smile and with great respect he executed and gave Ben the new title paper.

Vicky with Yervant Tavitian at a University dance, (right) Visiting our land in Beirut, 1957, (below)

Migrating To the United States

On November 1957 Ben and I with our two and a half year old son, Levon, left Beirut by ship and landed in Alexandria, Egypt.

The few days we stayed in Alexandria thrilled all of us. Only a few years had passed that the Egyptians had deposed King Farouk. Everywhere we went we heard nationalistic songs. The nightclubs where only the elite used to go, now were open to the public.

We visited the king's palace, which was like a vision in a fairy tale. It had never ending rooms with ceramic tiled walls, luxurious chandeliers, and finely crafted furniture. Alexandria exhibits a cosmopolitan elegance with wide boulevards lined with palm trees. We fell in love with that city.

We had never seen the Pyramids and the Sphinx so we wanted to visit Cairo on our way to Gaza to visit Ben's parents.

We hired a taxi in Alexandria, without knowing that it was customary that they fill the taxi with other travelers as well. The driver placed our luggage on top of the taxi and with a full load of people we started our journey from Alexandria toward Cairo.

It was late afternoon. Only one single road led to Cairo. All around us we could see the shimmering sand of the flat Sinai dessert. In some areas the wind blew the sand onto the road. The taxi sped on in silence as everyone in it nurtured deep thoughts. I sat in the front seat and watched the sandy surroundings go by, feeling drowsy.

After an hour of travel, we suddenly heard a big thump! The driver pulled over and got out to see what had happened. He asked us not to get out.

From nowhere, two tall men with long flowing garments ran toward the taxi. We had not seen them in that flat desert area before. In Alexandria, they had cautioned us about highway robbers. These men were coming like wildfire! We were concerned and hoped that nothing would happen.

The driver came back to tell us that our large suitcase slipped and fell-off the top of the taxi on the road. He cautioned us again to be very quiet and not to get out. Amazingly, as he was lifting the suitcase, the two Egyptians helped him set it back on the roof of the car and bound it tightly. Moments later the driver came back and started the car. We looked out of the window. To our relief the two men vanished as quickly as they had appeared! Where did they disappear to? There were no trees, or hills, or rocks to hide them.

As we continued our journey, we asked the taxi driver, "What would you have done if those two men attacked us?"

"I have a gun." He replied.

Wow! I could just imagine a gun fight and us in the middle of it!

After four hours we finally reached Cairo and booked into the Sheraton, by the Nile River. We were eager to see the sights! Our relatives, the Kavoukians came and picked us up.

In that North African ocean of sand, there stood one of the Seven Wonders of the World. The most imposing man-made ancient building still standing. The largest pyramid at Giza built by Egyptians for Pharaoh Khufu.

According to Egyptologists, the ancient Egyptians believed the shape of the pyramid mimicked Benben- a pyramid shaped stone found in earliest temples, which symbolized the primeval mound from which life emerged as the Sun God *"RE"*, who rose to create life.

We spent some time admiring the pyramids. As we walked toward our car, I saw tourists enjoying themselves on camelback, traveling toward the Sphinx. Right then the local people started to scream and point toward a black twisting cloud in the horizon.

"Take cover! Take cover!"

"Look! It's a black cloud far away." I said.

"It's a sandstorm! It's traveling fast!" said our host.

"The car is right here. We have enough time." I replied.

"No! Run! Run!" someone screamed.

"Levon get in the car. Hurry! Oh my goodness! The sand is almost here!" I said surprised.

"Get in and close the door!" Ben shouted,

"I can't close the door, help! The wind is pushing the door toward the apposite side." I screamed.

"Here... I'll help you" said Ben.

"Pull hard! Pull hard!"

"Now! Finally we did it!"

"Oh! What a disaster, sand all over! Look at my hair! It's covered with sand." I complained.

The car was engulfed with sand.

It was pitch dark.

"I have never seen anything like this." I said.

"I wonder how those poor tourists riding the camels are doing." I said, in a pitiful voice.

"I can't see anything, it's so dark Mommy." cried Levon.

"Oh, look! The sun is shining again." We said simultaneously.

"This was fast, how long did it take?" I asked.

"I think less than a minute, but it felt like an hour." Ben said.

We opened the car doors and stepped outside. Everything looked so shiny and peaceful as though nothing had happened. But we're all covered with sand.

We continued our sightseeing and admired the Sphinx: a statue of a reclining mythical creature with a lion's body and a human head, built by the pharaoh Khafra about 2558 BC. We questioned why it was built and why it's nose was broken?

A tall guide with long flowing garb approached us. He wanted to take us to a newly excavated place. He told us that no one was allowed to go in yet. But with a little money, he would give us a tour of the place.

"Do you think we should trust him? I asked our host

"He is a guide; he seems to know what he is talking about." He turned to the guide and said.

"We will give you the money after we have taken the tour."

"You won't be sorry." he replied.

Visiting the pyramids with the Kavoukians, 1957

At the beginning, the opening through the hill seemed creepy, very small and dark. But, once we went through we were pleasantly surprised.

"Wow! Look at the size of the enormous chambers with pillars." I exclaimed with surprise.

"The hieroglyphics tell about the life of the Pharaoh." the guide continued.

"Look closely at the colorful paintings, the frescos of the Pharaoh and his environment. Even after more than 3000 years, these pictures are as vibrant as if painted recently."

We could not believe our eyes. We thought the guide was worth the amount of money we had bargained for.

Our short visit with the Kavoukians will always be a joyful memory. We visited their photography studio. They insisted that we sit for a photo shoot.

At the house, my great-grandmother's sister Mayrenie, hugged and kissed me over and over. She remembered the old days and related the dangers she and the family had gone through during the genocide and She thanked God for our freedom and health. Unfortunately, that was the last time we saw her, she passed away after a few years.

We took the train from Cairo. For about eight hours we traveled the Sinai Desert toward Gaza to see Ben's parents. On the way, we saw the ravages of war. Destroyed vehicles such as tanks, military cars, and trucks were scattered all over. We arrived in Gaza, exhausted and cov-

Taken at Cavouk's studio

ered with sand from head to toe. At the end of our journey, I looked at Ben and began to laugh. Yes, I could laugh, even while exhausted.

"Ben! You look like an old man with white hair."

"Hah! Look at the mirror, yours is not any better."

Sure enough we all had white hair, and, the worst part of it was that it was getting into our mouths. It made us miserable.

We met Ben's parents at the station. It made them happy to see Levon their first grandchild destined to carry their family name.

Krikor, Ben's brother, greeted us with open arms. During our visit, Ben helped his brother with his photographic studio.

Ben's father loved to talk to his grandson. His pride had no bounds that we named his grandson after him. He pointed to himself and said "I'm Levon, You're Levon." Two and a half year old Levon repeated his grandfather's words and giggled.

They also loved to see their son, Ben. But were not too happy with me. They felt I had taken their son away from them. Their plan was to have Ben come back and work in Gaza. Ben tried, but he did not find employment in that city.

We visited Gaza's beautiful public gardens, with its unusual tropical plants, colorful flowers and pleasantly manicured lawns. We loved the stately palm farms. Hundreds of palm trees were lined up like soldiers. I fell in love with the shimmering sandy beaches. Levon loved to chase the sand crabs running every which-way.

After two weeks we left Gaza by bus. The bus was faster, and with tightly shut windows, sand from the Sinai desert did not penetrate through. But it was not as comfortable as the train.

When we were entering Egypt, a stranger came and told us he will help us go through customs without difficulty, especially with a two and a half year old child. We thought it was a good idea. He made it very easy for us, within a few minutes we went through customs without any problem. We gladly paid him what he asked.

On our return, we thought *we can easily get out this time without someone helping us*. As the man approached, we told him we can handle it, and thanked him. We had a surprise waiting for us. We hardly reached the customs section; they opened everything we had, dispersed all over the place, then they separated us and did a body search on both of us. They pulled apart my hand luggage and the baby's bag. They examined every single paper. They turned my coat pockets inside out. They turned my purse upside down spilling everything I had. By the time they finished with me I was livid, especially when I found out that they did the same to Ben in the men's section. We now realized how important it was to pay off someone to take us through Egyptian customs.

In Alexandria we picked up a ship to go to Naples. The seaport buzzed with activity. Porters carried large boxes up and down the ramps: confusion everywhere. It reminded me of the pictures I had seen of ancient ships with porters carrying their wares over their backs, climbing the ramps and the hustle-bustle of surrounding areas. As we reached the ship, the porters picked up our suitcases. When we reached our cabin, they decided to put them in a storage area. We told them that we had a baby and that we needed the diapers and other items from the suitcase. After a little argument, having learned our lesson, we paid them some money. They became as sweet and helpful as can be. Our suitcases stayed in our cabin.

Experiences in Italy

We disembarked in Naples and took the train for Rome. There a horse and buggy driver met us at the train station, we gave him the pension's address.

"I know this place, I can take you there and on the way show you some of the sights."

We thought it would be fun, so we accepted...That was a big mistake. He kept going on, and on, and on, we got tired. Levon began to cry, we told the driver to take us directly to our pension, but he pretended he did not understand. Meantime, the meter was running Liras and it was getting extremely expensive.

Finally we screamed at him, we told him to STOP. He stopped. We paid him and we came down from the carriage, of course not knowing where we were and how to go to our destination.

We had a map, but he took us in so many circles that we lost our direction. The place we stopped was a residential area. All walled in houses and no one was around. After walking and looking for signs, we saw a large walled establishment. We thought, "It looks like a pension." It was late and darkness was setting. Besides, we were exhausted and hopelessly lost.

We knocked on the gate and a rough looking guard with an old barrette, opened the gate a little.

"What do you want?" He said in an angry tone.

"We are lost, could you help us?" Ben asked.

"This is a convent. You can't come in."

We asked "Can we stay for one night?"

At first, he was reluctant to take us. He consulted with someone and they felt sorry for us.

"Come in.You can stay one night."

The nuns led Ben to a section where the guards slept. They took me with tiny Levon tightly holding my hand, to a different building. The room was plain with one single bed and a cot for Levon. The light bulb hanging from a string reflected blue walls. The bed and cot were covered with blue blankets. There was a cross on the wall and a picture of virgin Mary. It was so quiet that one could hear a pin drop at the end of the hall. It was a strange experience, though we were happy to have a place to stay, we really felt out of place.

In the morning, we had a good breakfast, they bade us goodbye and locked the gate behind us. We were happy to leave.

With daylight and with the help of the map, we found the pension we were looking for. The manager was happy.

"I expected you yesterday, I almost gave up. I was about to give your room to someone else."

Ben thanked her.

What a difference from the convent! We had a gorgeous room with a balcony. Once we opened the door of the balcony, the sun's rays rushed in. We saw the neighborhood and the apartments that surrounded us.Clothes hung to dry from one side of the building to the other side. We heard people singing from their open windows, with operatic voices as they went about their morning routine. We felt as though we were in an opera.

It was better than what we expected, hospitable and friendly people everywhere! But, it surprised us to see that we had to share the bathrooms with other tenants.

We could not contain our excitement. Immediately we got out and started sightseeing.

"Ben, St Peters and the Vatican is gorgeous. It's beyond my imagination." I said excitedly.

"Look at the stained glass, so big and colorful." Ben said.

"Levon don't talk, listen to the singing of the monks." I told our son.

We stopped to listen momentarily to the melodic voices of the monks chanting. It was ethereal, but since our time was limited, we had to hurry and go toward the Sistine Chapel.

"I can't imagine how long they worked on these huge tapestries that are hanging in the hallways. They are outstanding." I commented. The hall was long and both sides were covered with exquisite and delicate tapestries of full length portraits of royal scenes.

We had to walk fast in order to be able to see everything and reach the Sistine Chapel.

Finally, we came to a wide open ornate door. "This is the entry to the Sistine Chapel." said Ben and stopped to catch his breath.

As we stepped into the long chapel we were overwhelmed by the volume of vibrant paintings; the walls, ceiling and every inch covered with images depicting religious scenes.

We spent a whole day in the Vatican, but still, we were not able to see everything. We climbed the stairs of St. Peters, all the way up, but we had to stop a few times to catch our breath. "I don't know how the monks climbed all those stairs everyday." I wondered.

The Cathedral was enormous. It was impressive and mysterious.There were so many places to go and see we did not have enough time to see everything. But we did take a tour of the Pantheon. A temple dedicated to all the gods of ancient Rome. A circular building with a *portico* (porch) of large granite Corinthian columns. All around niches contained statues of ancient gods. The dome with a central opening, the *oculus*, is known as the worlds largest unreinforced concrete dome.

I'd seen pictures of the Trevi fountain. But, seeing it in person, took my breath away! We threw a few coins and sat to enjoy the outstanding marble statues surrounding the spouting water.

"Mom, so many steps." Levon exclaimed.

"Yes, Levon. It's the Spanish steps." I explained.

"Listen. Someone is playing the guitar." Ben said in a whisper.

We sat down and listened to the haunting music.

We visited the Forum and the Coliseum. My imagination took flight. I could see, in my minds eye, the fight of the slaves/ gladiators with the hungry lions. As the guide described the different sections of the Coliseum, and how the combatants played out their violent confrontations, I felt a sickening feeling come over me.

We went places where tourists do not visit, we did not speak Italian but we conversed with our hands and body movements.

We were very proud of our two and a half year old son, he was well behaved and always ready to go wherever we wanted to go.

We returned to the railway station to pick up the train to go to Naples. At the station I wanted to buy a small knife as a souvenir, it was sixty Liras, I did not have change so I gave the sales person one thousand Liras. He took the money and wouldn't give me any change. I started arguing with him but it was no use, with my language barrier I was at a loss. I started panicking and calling for the police. Ben had gone to arrange for our luggage, he heard my voice shouting, he came by and said that the train was leaving; I had to forget about the money. I was furious and that incident left a very bad taste. I did not want to leave Rome angry.

We had only two days in Naples. We stayed at the local YMCA in a nice room, but there was a curfew. So we had to be back by 11 pm. We made the best of each day; sightseeing and enjoying lunch by the sea. We met some very nice people, visited with them, and had lunch at places where locals ate. One of the restaurants had a beautiful view of Mt. Vesuvius. We wished we had more time to visit the city of Pompeii (We visited Pompeii in 2011).

This was the first time I had seen pizza being made. They had huge silver colored cauldrons, each containing different items that you chose to put on the pizza base. One contained a tomato mixture, another cheese, another pepperoni. The red cheeked server in white uniform with a white cap poured first tomato mixture on the dough with a huge ladle, then he asked what you wanted on it. We followed and watched how the locals ordered it and we did the same, for us it was fun and unusual. After covering the dough with tomato sauce from one of the cauldrons, he then sprinkled shredded cheese, and finally topped it with pepperoni. I wish I knew what was in the other two cauldrons, but we never found out what they contained, even though we loved the taste of the new found food: pizza.

Sailing

We boarded our ship, *Julio Ceasare*, we settled in our narrow cabin with bunk beds. Within a short time the sea became turbulent. The ship was rolling from side to side. In the hallways, we were being thrown from wall to wall. I had to hold tight the railing of the hallway in order not to fall. Little Levon enjoyed it. He thought it was fun to roll from one side of the hallway to the other.

Levon and I were doing well, but Ben was seasick, he could not get out of his bed. The two of us went to the dinning rooms, the crew laughed and said "Eat! Food will keep you from getting sick." They gave us a plateful of food to eat. They were right, as we ate we felt good and energetic. Ben still could not eat or get up.

Finally we reached Gibraltar. I had seen pictures of the rock but seeing it in real life was an awesome sight. It was huge; some areas were green with vegetation, other areas were sheer steep rock. We saw deer munching on grass. What surprised us were the monkeys called Barbary macaque apes, jumping about. Houses were scattered on the back side of the rock. (In 2011 we revisited Gibraltar and explored the caves, tunnels, and sandy beaches.)

The ship stopped there for formalities.We were not allowed to get off, but because the dock was multileveled, we could trade directly from the ship with the hundreds of vendors on shore.The vendors were so close we could exchange money and goods directly over the side. Ben was able to get out of bed and enjoy the beauty of the place. We heard that many robberies happen at this place, so we were careful. I fell in love with a life size doll dressed in a Spanish costume and bought it. That doll stayed with us for many years, always reminding us of Gibraltar, and the crossing of the Atlantic.

Back on our way, we hardly had crossed the Strait of Gibraltar, and were enjoying the calm Atlantic Ocean, when we heard the captain of the ship on the loudspeaker announcing; "A volcano just erupted on the Azure Islands. For that reason we will be changing direction."

Everyone went up on deck to see the volcano. It was a breathtaking sight. I had only seen volcanoes in movies, how spectacular! Red lava spurted out bursting high into the air with an extreme force. It turned into a mixture of smoke and became a huge cloud. The captain was moving the ship away from the island to avoid the turbulence of the high waves it was generating.

I ran down to get Ben and the camera to take some pictures, leaving Levon with one of the crew members. Ben had heard the announcement and gone to the deck locking up the cabin with everything including the camera. Finding myself locked out, I rushed back up to the deck to find him and get the keys. I rushed back down, unlocked the door and the closet, picked up the camera and directly went up. I was frustrated, angry and tired of going up and down the stairs. By the time I took a few pictures the ship had moved further away from the islands for a good shot. When we arrived in New York all the newspapers had articles and pictures of the Azure island volcano.

In seven days of crossing the Atlantic, Ben rarely got out of bed. Levon and I toured the ship, but it was not as much fun without Ben, I missed him and wanted him to be with me and enjoy the musical and romantic evenings on deck.

I met nice people. I enjoyed playing table tennis with members of the crew under the angry, and watchful eyes of a very conservative Armenian family. To them being a woman, and a mother, it was shameful to play table tennis, especially with someone from the crew. Whenever I met them on the ship, they criticized me and my two and a half year old child. When I told this to Ben, he started laughing, "Oh, don't pay any attention to them, enjoy yourself."

All throughout our sailing the Italians were singing and dancing. One of the songs that you heard all over the ship was *Arrivederci-a-Roma.* Sometimes they made a variation *Arrivederci-a-Napoli.* I heard beautiful operatic voices singing in the moonlight. It was exciting, nostalgic and romantic.

Our first stop was Nova Scotia. The Armenian family disembarked there, for which I was grateful.

Ben, Vicky and Levon with Armenian family on the way to the United States.

Arriving in the United States of America

There was excitement in the air. The crew was running around preparing for arrival to New York. The passengers sang and prayed more fervently.

There! I see the skyline of New York! The arrival to New York was announced on the loudspeaker. I also heard the voices of the people.

"Look! Look! The Statue of Liberty!"

"It's miraculous that we made it!" I exclaimed. I started crying and laughing at the same time!

Almost everyone was crying. People singing, praying and praising God. To see the majestic Statue of Liberty was emotional. It was spiritual, a welcoming beacon to the promised land. As though saying "come to these shores" to the people who were running away from persecution. It was exciting. It created a sense of deep feeling of freedom. We thanked God for our safe arrival.

It took some time for the ship to dock. We all prepared to disembark and lined up to go through immigration. Even though we were on land, I still felt the movement of the ship, it took a long time until I got used to standing straight. The familiar face of our relative greeted us on the other side of the barricade. We hurried and crossed the bridge and rushed to hug Nubar Karakashian, who welcomed us with open arms. He had a taxi waiting for us.

Our first impression of New York was disappointing. A cold and cloudy November greeted us. The trees were bare and the tall buildings covered with soot looked dark and foreboding. There was nothing bright around the city. A gloomy feeling settled on all of us.

When we arrived to Sahag and Louise Ounjian's apartment in New Jersey, their warmth and happy atmosphere created a better feeling.

We were hypnotized with the TV, which we had never seen before. It took us a long time to get over being on land and getting used to being in a strange country. The cultural shock lasted longer than we expected.

The skyscrapers fascinated us. We visited the top of the Empire State building. We loved going to the United Nations building. One incident happened there which I will never forget. Levon our baby started having diarrhea. In the old country eating yogurt helped the stomach to calm down. We looked all over and couldn't find yogurt in the markets. While we were in the cafeteria of the United Nations, we saw they were selling yogurt in small containers. We were excited and asked the lady at the counter to give us one of the yogurt cups. She looked at us and was shocked.

"Why do you want something like this?"

"We want it for our child," I said.

She looked at the child in puzzlement and said, "I refuse to sell you the yogurt."

"Why?"

"How can you feed your child this ungodly food?"

"It's alright, he loves it and it's nutritious."

"Poor child!"

"We insist, we want to buy the yogurt."

She was taken aback as we insisted, she had no choice but to begrudgingly sell it to us. She felt very sorry for our child and thought we were abusing him. We were surprised at her attitude. As for us we still were in shock and dizzy from the entire new environment.

After one week we left New Jersey and took a train to Chicago, our final destination. At the train station, my brother Garabed met us and took us to their apartment. My mother and sisters were glad to see us and they had prepared one of the bedrooms for us.

Settling in Chicago

A few days later after our arrival to Chicago, Ben started working with Harza Engineering Company. He commuted by train. From the train station, he walked across the Chicago river on an open bridge, to go to his office. In winter fierce winds from Lake Michigan would gust over the bridge and would often catch an unsuspecting hat off of a commuter's head and fling it up into the air. It would fly high above as if waving and saying good by and then fall like a frisbee into the river. Ben lost quite a few hats to that bridge.

Those were memorable and happy days. Almost every evening we played games. One of the games was called "donkey," where at the count of one, you had to pass a card to the person next to you. As you passed the card you banged on the table. With the new card you discarded the doubles until you did not have any cards left in your hand. The person left with the joker becomes the donkey.

The downstairs neighbors started complaining about the funny noise. They could not figure out what we were doing to create a synchronized sound. They instructed my brother to stop "bouncing that ball."

We were introduced to some of my mother's favorite shows on television. She loved and was mesmerized with Liberace's superb piano playing. She always commented on the candelabrum that he placed on the piano. I also enjoyed the show and would never miss it.

A month later we finally found a second story apartment and moved. After a few days we heard a thump from downstairs. We thought they were fixing something. As two and a half year old Levon continued playing in the apartment, we heard another thump from downstairs. A few minutes later a knock on the door. The downstairs neighbor, in an ugly manner informed us that we were making too much noise. Every time Levon climbed the stairs of the apartment, the woman of the first floor came out and scolded him. One day as we were on the stairs, their door was open and we saw both of their children roller skating inside! That angered me! When I questioned, I was told; "No one lives below us".

At this time my brother was accepted into the Dental School of the University of Detroit. He was thrilled. So my mother and sister Berjouhi joined him in Detroit. My younger sister Artemis stayed with us for a while and then went to Detroit as well.

Since both Ben and I come from Palestine during the time it was a British mandate, language was not a barrier; it was easy to adjust to the American way. But it took us almost a year to get over our culture shock. Being new immigrants, many were surprised to hear us speak good English, without any grammatical mistakes and with proper pronunciation.

One day I was at a dentist's clinic. He said,

"How lucky you are to live in an apartment with hot and cold running water, with electricity, a bathroom and not an outhouse."

I was flabbergasted!

"What's an outhouse?" I asked

"Ah, don't pretend you don't know."

"The apartment I lived in Beirut was much better than the one I am living in now." I continued. "We even controlled the temperature of our water at the desired degree. We also had a washer and dryer right in the apartment and we didn't need to go elsewhere to wash our cloths."

"I don't believe you!"

I was angry; I did not go back to this dentist again. Many had the impression that in the Middle East people lived in tents and traveled on camels. They had seen this type of living in the movies.

We quickly became tired of living in an apartment and wanted to complete the American dream and live in our own house. We looked and found an advertisement for an affordable housing development in Villa Park that offered brand new houses, close to a train station for commuting to downtown Chicago.

Living in the United States

We loved our new home in Villa Park, a suburb of Chicago, Illinois. It was a dream come true. The first day we moved in, Levon started jumping up and down non-stop.

"What are you doing? Why are you jumping so vigorously?" I asked.

"But Mom, there's no one living below us."

We laughed and joined him in making noise. We had good neighbors; many had children close to Levon's age. He made good friends and enjoyed the tranquil suburban life.

Vicky in front of the new house in Villa Park, Illinois

From the large living room with floor to ceiling windows we watched the snow fall, admired the icicles that formed on the branches and showed off my baby-grand piano.

Our children loved doing their homework on the sturdy antique dining table and chairs in the well lit dining room. We had the good luck of seeing a 'for sale' sign in the paper for this table. We traveled half an hour to see it. The owner said it was a family heirloom. They brought the table and chairs from Europe and won't sell it to just anyone. They had many offers but they looked for a loving family who would take good care of it. Both Ben and I were surprised to see such a beautiful oak table. We fell in love with it and offered to buy. They lowered the price on condition that we promise to take good care of it. They even gave us a handmade lace covering to put on the table. Indeed it lasted us for a long time.

The kitchen was large enough to accommodate a table and four chairs by the window. The side door from the kitchen led to the front yard and the garage.

The hallway that led to three spacious bedrooms and a bathroom upstairs became like a viewing balcony to all the activities that went on in the living room and dining area.

A finished basement with a bathroom became the entertaining center. Children watched TV and entertained their friends. It also became a popular location with our bridge playing group. Later served as a display area for our artifacts that we collected from other countries. It also doubled as a guest room with a comfortable sofa bed.

An accordion door set apart the laundry and the work room where Ben kept all his tools separate from the rest of the basement.

We surrounded our house with fruit trees in the backyard and spruce trees in the front. We planted an apple tree which was grafted to give three different kinds of apples. The neighborhood children loved to play ball on our yard. Every winter Ben vowed that he'll never buy a corner lot house again. It was back breaking cleaning the snow from the sidewalk along the length of the yard from both sides.

Ben commuted to work. He parked the car at the train station, a five minutes drive from the house, and took the train to Chicago Union Station. He walked the covered walkway at the station to his office building. It was very convenient, especially during heavy snow days. This way he never lost his hat to the river.

Every day about five o'clock in the afternoon, when we heard the train passing nearby our home, Levon our four year old son got excited knowing that his father would be home soon.

One day Ben took Levon to his downtown office on the train, he was thrilled. Levon thought his father was a train engineer. He didn't realize that there were other kinds; let alone an electrical engineer. When they arrived at the office, Levon demanded to know why his dad wasn't driving the train he rode on and was very disappointed. A female co-worker gave him pencils and paper to draw with and he drew the train and an engineer inside the train.

"What did you draw?" one of the co-workers asked.

"This is my father's train; he's the engineer of this train."

Ben's colleagues couldn't help but laugh. When they both came home and told me about it, I started laughing too. We realized that for Levon, at the time, his idea of an engineer was based around the character that he had seen in the commercial on TV. Where the young boy held a box of Good and Plenty candy and shook it toward the train driver, calling out 'Mr. En-gi-ne-er'."

We hardly had settled down in our new home, when our car, which was a Pontiac, stopped going backwards. To park we had to drive in circles until we found a parking place at a corner of a street, where we did not have to back it. It was frustrating!

We finally sold it to a dealer and bought another used car. After a few months, this car stopped in the middle of the road by the house, what a dilemma! This time the car will not go forward but it would go only backwards.

We decided that it was time to buy a new car. At the time it was not funny, later on, it became the joke of the neighborhood.

I began to give piano lessons. Many of our neighbors were thrilled. Within a month I had fifteen students taking lessons. I was always invited to play at different social events. Also I registered at Elmhurst College and started taking evening classes toward my bachelor's degree.

Both Ben and I became members of the local Home Owners Association of our city of Villa Park and became very active. We wanted our children to grow up in a good neighborhood. Ben was the treasurer. I was elected the hospitality chairperson of the ladies auxiliary of the city. I organized social events, met and greeted new neighbors. We became friends with couples living in the surrounding areas. Being avid bridge players we joined the contract bridge group. Once a month we played at different member's houses.

In 1959, I lost my beautiful mother, at age of 59, to a heart-attack. She believed in her children. She insisted that we get an education and be professionals. She made sure that we study music, and be the best in whatever we chose to do. It was too sudden. It was devastating! She was loved and respected by everyone she knew. She never deliberately wanted to hurt people. To wrongdoers she'd say "God will deal with them". Loosing my mother was very hard on me. She was the pillar of the family, the leader, the guide,

New Officers for Newcomers 1961

NEWLY ELECTED officers of the Villa Park Newcomers club who took office at a recent meeting in the village hall are: (Seated on floor) Mrs. John Kiely, corresponding secretary, and Mrs. William E. Schlehahn, publicity. Second row, left to right, Mrs. Walter Meissner, treasurer; Mrs. Gilbert Smith, recording secretary; Mrs. Ronald Angeles, social chairman; Mrs. Joseph J. Allen, president; Mrs. R. G. Wetzel, program chairman; Mrs. Benjamin Yotnakhparian, social chairman.

the advisor.

A year later in September of 1960, I gave birth to Sonia, the daughter we wanted so badly. She was tiny and a very cute baby, and became the darling of the neighborhood.

It was during this time that I developed hay fever. Being pregnant and sneezing constantly became a painful experience. After extensive testing the doctor found that I was allergic to ragweed, which grew wild all over the Midwest. Everyday during August and September the networks announced the ragweed pollen count and advised sufferers to stay indoors and to use their air conditioner. I took shots every

The family with newly born Sonia, 1960

five days during the high-season and tapered down to taking the shots once a month, for the rest of the year.

All this time I continued taking evening classes.

"Ben!" I said "Would you believe it? Finally I graduate with a Bachelor of Arts Degree in education."

"Yes. Levon, Sonia and I will be happy to have you home in the evenings." he said "And guess what! Next week we'll be sworn in as United States citizens."

"1962 is a lucky year for us," I said.

"Yes. We finally belong to the country we love."

It was during our becoming American citizens that we changed our name from Yotnakhparian to Parian.

What prompted the change was the behavior of our son, Levon. Yotnakhparian was a long and difficult name, but a very historic one. The origin of this according to my husband's father was that, three generations ago his forefather had seven sons. When people visited them they said, "We are going to the house of *Yot Eghpair*, seven brothers." *Yot*, in Armenian means Seven, *Ekhpair* means brother. As time went on, Yotnakhparian became the official name. It is a revered name- the name of an Armenian hero, Mgrdich a grand-cousin of my husband. During the genocide of the Armenians by the Ottoman Turks, in 1915, he courageously fought to the death to protect women and children from being massacred. Also Ben's own father and the namesake of our son, Levon Yotnakhparian, is also a national hero for going back into the deserts of Syria and saving thousands of stranded and orphaned Armenians.

Our son when he was about six years old always avoided giving his last name to his friends. We found out later that at school they teased him about his name with: "*Knock! Knock! - Who's there*?" jokes. His teacher told us that he was having a hard time with his last name.

It was not an easy decision, but we decided to make it shorter to "Parian", the second half of our last name, short enough but still kept the 'ian' ending of the Armenian name.

So our name became Parian which gave our son great pleasure and it made life simpler for all of us except, our Armenian friends, family and close relatives who did not like the change.

One day as I was standing in line at the checkout counter of the neighborhood grocery store, I heard my neighbor calling me; She was terribly excited, she called; "Vicky! Vicky! Guess What! I can pronounce your family name!"

I was pleased and smiled.

She in turn, with great dignity and pride announced, "*Yot nakh par ian*!"

Everyone around us clapped and I laughed, I was very impressed at the correct way she had pronounced it. At that moment I did not have the heart to tell her that we had just changed our name, but later I did inform her, she was a little disappointed but happy for the easier name.

It was difficult for me to go to school, take care of the family, entertain, and teach music. So when I graduated, everyone was happy; Ben put a complimentary statement in the local newspaper, congratulating me for my graduation, stating: "Vicky a mother of two, graduated with BA in Education."

A reporter from the paper wanted to interview me. My picture was all over the page with a beautiful long article. Immediately I was offered a teaching position on the phone, by the superintendent to teach fifth grade in the prestigious Elmhurst district. He said that he had checked the university records and that he was impressed with my diversified background. Needless to say I was honored, and thrilled to have an offer like this, but I did not have anyone to baby sit for my one and a half year old, Sonia. When a neighbor heard about my situation, she volunteered to baby sit for us. I also was delighted because someone had offered me a job without seeing or interviewing me.

Women in Profile

Armenian Mother Receives Degree After Five Years

Mrs. Benjamin Parlan

Born in Palestine, raised and educated in Beirut, Lebanon, Mrs. Benjamin Parian was graduated from Elmhurst college, Sunday, June 2.

I started teaching fifth grade in Elmhurst another near by suburb of Chicago. I suddenly found myself in an education oriented environment, with a very helpful principle, great teachers and a nice classroom. But I had to say goodbye to my piano students, I did not have enough time for them. With a heavy heart and a final recital I said goodbye to them and distributed them

to other piano teachers in the area.

We always had our meals at the kitchen table, by the window. One day, during dinner, a few of our neighbors were testing a motorbike. We watched them test-ride while their families cheered. The owner of the motorbike showed how strong and smooth the motorbike ran. Each man rode the motorbike along the length of the street, and with pride showed off how well he controlled it. When the tallest neighbor sat on the motorbike, instead of breaking he accelerated and lost control. He ended up on the lawn of the opposite neighbor. He hit his head on the sharp edge of the building, fell down, and the bike opened a hole in the wall of the house. I ran to the phone. By the time I finished calling the emergency operator, the neighborhood paramedic was there. Soon the ambulance arrived. Unfortunately, a wonderful young father, still in his twenties lost his life to an unnecessary accident. Father of three, ages four, two and six months old. We were terribly upset. I was sick to my stomach; the entire neighborhood was in shock. It happened so fast. This incident effected all of us. To this day I stay away from motorbikes.

Our Trip To Wisconsin

Summer vacations took us to various parts of the United States. One of them was to Wisconsin. We rented a cabin at Star Lake.

We enjoyed swimming. Sonia, loved building castles with sand. Ben and Levon rented a boat and went fishing every day. One day Sonia and I joined them. The fish were not biting! Ben prepared the reel and gave it to me to try and fish. Suddenly I had a bite. I got excited and stood-up shouting "I got it! I got it!" The boat started rocking. Everyone was shouting. "Sit down, stop jumping!"

Ben was shouting "You'll capsize the boat... sit down."

As I sat down, I noticed the tiny fish dangling from my reel. Oh! What a disappointment!

One of the men from the lodge, fishing a short distance away, wanted to know how big the fish was. Ben released the minnow sized fish back into the lake and told the man, "It was a whopper!"

That evening on our way to dinner at the lodge, we saw the same person getting his picture taken, holding a large fish with a wide smile. The person taking the picture, told us that it was his fish, but his friend wanted a picture with it so he could brag to his friends and family about it. We could not believe it.

The next morning as we were about to leave for breakfast we saw a family of skunks heading toward our cabin. Sonia was excited, she thought they were so cute, and she started to run out to go and hug them. We caught her just in time, and explained to her why we did not allow her to go near them. They went under the cabin. For about fifteen minutes we were trapped inside the cabin. Gingerly we stepped out hoping not to disturb them. To our relief, they were gone.

On our way back home to Villa Park, we stopped and took a tour of the famous Wisconsin Dells. We sat in an amphibious vehicle called "the Duck" to tour the Dells. When we came to a river, the vehicle stopped and the guide started telling us about the gorgeous rock formations. Then the duck started moving toward the river and floated onto the water. I was scared. I thought that the duck will submerge but it didn't. As we dove in, I told the children, "hold tight!". We were all mesmerized at the beauty of the rock formations and the Duck made the adventure even more interesting.

After the tour we drove home. We had wonderful memories of a lovely vacation in Wisconsin.

Vacationing in Michigan and Canada

On another vacation we spent a few days with my brother and family in Detroit, then we drove north through Michigan. On our way, we stopped at almost every small town. We drove toward Mackinaw bridge. Before crossing the bridge we visited Mackinac Island. Cars were not allowed on the island. We parked our car by the ferry docks, and took the passenger boat. The island is set majestically between Michigan's Upper and Lower peninsula in the strait of Mackinac. The boat was going at a high speed. We welcomed the cool wind blowing on our faces. Soon we started to see the beautiful outline of the island. Than came the quaint homes and impressive buildings. When we arrived, I felt I was in the 19th Century. A horse-drawn carriage stood in front of us, it was so attractive that we took a tour of the island with it. There were beautiful mansions and well tended gardens. The majestic Grand Hotel, with its slanted red roof and all white walls surrounded with manicured lawns and colorful flowers had a magical, timeless, and romantic quality. After a few hours of sightseeing, we took the boat back to the main land and to our parked car.

We continued our drive north toward Canada. In one of the border towns there was a fair where a variety of handicrafts were displayed. We spent some time watching a person blow glass. It was fascinating to see him heat the glass and shape it into a vase with a long curved rod. At one of the stores, I fell in love with an unusual basket completely made of peach seeds. Ahh! How can I resist it, of course I bought it.

We continued our drive arriving Sault Ste. Marie locks. We went to the Soo Locks. We had never seen locks before, all four of us were brimming with curiosity. Two people were directing traffic, one of them told us to follow the car in front, which was about to enter into the cavernous belly of a ship. We drove at a snails pace toward the opening. We couldn't see the inside, it was dark, but once we entered the ship they had strong lights and there were other men directing us toward a parking slot. After parking the car, we climbed to the top deck of the ship. Going from high level Lake Superior to a lower Lake Huron via locks.

Shortly the ship moved slightly toward the huge closed gate. The back gate from where we entered closed. The front gate opened slowly allowing the water to drain into a huge box like container which showed twenty one feet depth. The boat went down with the water until it became level with the lower lock. It moved forward allowing the back gate to close. This process was repeated until the water and the boat arrived to the lowest level. Once the boat docked, we rushed to our car and when our turn came, we drove out of the boat and headed towards Canada.

In Canada we started driving on the Queen's highway. At the time the highway was all covered with pebbles. At high speed the car started sliding right and left, WOW! We slowed down. It seemed like we were the only ones traveling on that route. We enjoyed the vegetation, the tall trees, and the wild flowers. We encountered deer and moose crossing the highway. The first town we came to, we decided to rest and look around. We needed to fill our tank with gas. There was only one gas station and one shop in this village. We asked for accommodations but there were no hotels or motels. Finally after half an hour of asking around some one offered a Bed and Breakfast in their home. We were delighted. It was a quaint little house with comfortable beds but one bathroom. The owners were very pleasant and helpful.

In the morning we woke up to an unwelcome, rancid smell- as though the sewage had overflowed. We were embarrassed to ask the lady why there was such an awful smell. We checked the bathroom, every thing seemed clean and dry. WHY THE FOUL SMELL! We decided to step outside to breath some fresh air, the smell was WORSE! After a full American breakfast, we mastered the courage to ask the lady of the house about this odor, she said that it was the smell of the paper mill. Having lived in this village for a long time they don't smell it.

Indeed on our way as we neared the factory, it became unbearable. We decided to run away from this area as fast as we could. We also found out that the nearest gas station was 60 miles away.

On our way, we watched the lumbermen. It was interesting to see how they cut the trees, collected and threw the logs into the river, which carried them toward the mill. This was the cheapest way of transporting the wood.

After traveling on the Queens highway for two days, we reached Manitoba county. Our reservation was a cabin in one of the many parks near the lake. Everyday, with buckets in hand, we went out into the wilderness and collected blueberries for our breakfast.

We went fishing and horseback riding. It seemed that Ben, always ended up with a horse that wanted to wander around. The funny thing was that one day he rode a horse that was called Ben. The horse wanted to graze, no matter what he did it won't move. The leader had to go and pull the horse. At the end we all wished our vacation was longer.

Every holiday we siblings came together, my eldest sister Mary and family, my brother Garabed and his family, my sisters Artemis and Berjouhi and myself and family. Thanksgiving was always at my sister Mary's house in Tower Lakes. Christmas was at our house in Villa Park. Our get-togethers were always fun and exciting. We sang Christmas songs, each of us used a musical instrument. We had the best percussion orchestra accompanying the piano, the violin, the accordion, and the guitar.

Traveling Overseas

President Kennedy was shot!!

This was November 22, 1963; the principal called me out and informed me about it. I was shocked! I could not hold my tears. How will I tell this to my fifth grade students? I could hardly control my emotions. As I went in after a few minutes they felt my agitation and wanted to know what happened and why was I so upset. I had no choice but to inform in a gentle way.

This was also the year where Ben's company decided to send him to train engineers in the water and power division of the government of Pakistan. Harza Engineering Company, had a contract with the United State Government to send engineers to other countries for developing their utility systems. They wanted Ben to help in planning the electric power system of Pakistan. This was a five year plan and it was decided that the whole family should go and live there.

Visiting Pakistanis, who were in Chicago for electric power system studies, gave us some ideas about life in Lahore, Pakistan. One of them told Levon, our son, that there were wild animals all over, such as lions and leopards; "Buffaloes roam everywhere and come visit the houses; they even sit on your lap. Cobras visit your bathroom through your tub's drain."

The imagination of an eight year old soared and took wings. He believed everything that was said. He was scared but really curious and wanted to go to experience it for himself.

At first, we did not want to go, we had become accustomed to our lifestyle and though we were seasoned travelers, this seemed very different, but we realized financially, it was a lucrative decision. Levon had other concerns like our albino rabbit, Thumper.

"Mom, Dad, can we take Thumper with us?"

"No dear, we can't." I said.

"What shall we do?"

"We'll put an ad at the supermarket and ask for a loving family who'll take good care of our beloved Thumper."

Soon the ad at the local supermarket; attracted a young couple. They came to see Thumper. Our son Levon after half an hour of quizzing them, decided that Yes! He will let them take Thumper.

"Will you take care of our much loved rabbit?" asked Levon.

Sweden
Finland
Norway
Helsinki
Stockholm
Estonia
Russia
Baltic
Sea
Latvia
Denmark
Malmo
Lithuania
United Kingdom
Copenhagen
Ireland
Berlin
Poland
Belarus
London
Netherlands
Germany
Belgium
Frankfurt
Czech
Republic
Ukraine
Isle of Man
Paris
Luxembourg
Slovakia
Austria
France
Hungary
Moldova
Switzerland
Slovenia
Romania
Venice
Croatia
Italy
Bosnia
and
Herzegovina
Belgrade
Bucharest
Black
Sea
Marseille
Monaco
Vego
Nice
Serbia
Bulgaria
Rome
Dubrovnik
Barcelona
Albania
Macedonia
Madrid
Naples
Portugal
Istanbul
Spain
Capri
Island
Greece
Turkey
Athens
Seville
Malta
Tunisia
Algeria
Mediterranean Sea
Morocco
Libya

"Of course we will"

We all were sad and tears were running as we watched our dearly loved pet go.

Renting our house out was another situation. We had to leave most of our furniture, including the piano. Therefore we needed a family who will take good care of the house. Finally we rented to a nice family that came by. With a heavy heart we prepared to leave for Lahore, Pakistan in July of 1964.

It was hard to say goodbye to family and friends. There was a fear in us facing the unknown. We consulted our Pakistani friends and other expatriates, they reassured us that it will be a pleasant experience. But still there was an element of the unknown.

My farewell to my students was very traumatic. I had students crying and parents trying to persuade me to stay and not leave. I never forget the mother of one of my fifth grade unruly students, who gave me a travel kit and told me.

"Mrs. Parian, in all these years, you were the only teacher my son listened to and followed instructions from."

She was crying and asking me if it was possible not to go.

My departure from the school was very emotional. I had mixed feelings, I was happy to be able to go with my husband, yet, my heart was with the children. It was very hard to leave.

We had made arrangements with our friends to come and take us to the airport. As we were getting ready to leave, our friend coming down the stairs with a suitcase, slipped and hit his head on the banister, blood everywhere!!

"Oh No! Here's some ice." I put ice into a paper towel and applied it to his head...

"Oh dear! Why did this happen?" I groaned.

Finally the bleeding stopped.

"How do you feel? Will you be able to drive?" Ben asked.

"I feel well, don't worry I am ok! Load the suitcases."

On our route to the airport there was a railroad crossing, **just our luck!** As we approached the crossing, the railway gates came down, and there was a freight train crossing with a never-ending amount of cars.

"This is the longest freight train I've ever seen." I said.

"Look, another one from the opposite side." Levon informed.

"Unbelievable! For sure we'll be late." Ben said.

"I hope we don't miss the plane. With all these cars lined up, we'll never be able to make it!" I moaned.

"We're stuck!"

I wonder if someone up there is trying to tell us something. I thought.

"Only a miracle will save us."

That miracle came in the form of my sister Mary. She and her husband Hovig had gone to the airport to send us off. As the time of departure came, and she did not see us, she started worrying and talking with the airline personnel. Being four of us in the first class cabin, the airline held the plane for us until we arrived. We were ten minutes late.

The moment she saw us she ran out to us.

"Hurry! Hurry! They're holding the plane for you."

"Really? Miracle of miracles!" I said.

We had traveled using a bus, a car, a ship, and a train, but this was the first time any of us had been in a plane and we were flying first class with TWA.

After emotional goodbyes from friends and especially my sister, we boarded the plane.

"Vicky, Ben don't forget to write" my sister reminded as we were boarding the plane.

I was an emotional wreck, thankfully the stewardess greeted us with smiles and a welcome champagne drink. The children were in seventh heaven, they were given toys, comic books, crayons. Each of us received a bag with toiletries, with our names engraved on each bag.

"Mom, look at this bag it has my name on it, there is a toothbrush, toothpaste, eye cover, comb and even a match box with my name printed on it." Levon screamed excitedly.

We each had the same contents, with our names engraved on a bag.

The drinks helped calm our nerves. We were wined and dined and slept for the rest of our flight.

On the way, we had planned on staying in New York for a week to see the Worlds Fair. We stayed at one of the biggest hotels at the time, it covered a whole block. I think it was the Plaza Hotel.

We spent a few days sightseeing in New York and were ready to go to the Worlds fair, Sonia our three and a half year old daughter, came down with a high temperature. What a dilemma! We called the house doctor of the hotel and he gave her some medicine. The hotel personnel were very accommodating and pleasant; they suggested an older babysitter and assured us that she is reliable. After a lot of hesitation we hired her.

The three of us went to see the World's Fair, but it wasn't much fun, we were worried about Sonia and were calling her every few minutes. Also we did not know how much we could trust the babysitter. Feeling guilty for leaving Sonia alone with a babysitter, we were unable to enjoy the fair. So after a short time, we decided to go back to the hotel and be with her.

One day before our departure from New York, as we were looking out over the balcony of our hotel room, we noticed a sign with the name Yotnakhparian Art Gallery.

"Look Ben, an Art Gallery with our name." I said.

We were surprised and excited!

"Let's go and see who they are."

We immediately went and were pleasantly surprised to meet Ben's cousin, who had come to Chicago a few years back for the wedding of another cousin, Vartkes and Mary Najarian. We were greeted with hugs and welcomes. The gallery was huge and it had several rooms, each room had many original art pieces painted by the old masters hanging on the walls. We realized that this was one of the prestigious art galleries in New York.

"I'd like you to come tomorrow to the house and meet the rest of the family." Ben's cousin said.

"We're so sorry we can't, we're leaving tomorrow." Ben answered.

We wished we had noticed the gallery earlier.

London

Our next stop was London. Ben talked so much about his school friends that I was eager to meet the Bandahans and the Fishers.

From the airport we took a taxi and everything felt odd because they drove on the opposite side of the street.

"Mom! Dad! Look at those two deck buses." Levon cried out.

"They're called double-decker." I stated.

"Can we ride on one?"

"Yes dear, we'll sightsee on one. It'll be fun." I replied.

The children were fascinated, especially Levon. He wanted to experience everything. Sonia was only three years old, so she was not aware of many things except, the colorful buses and the attention she was getting from passers by calling her "Hi cutie" or "Hi beauty" and other endearing words.

After settling in at the Hilton Hotel. Ben got in touch with his friends, and we were invited to their houses. First, we went to the Bandahan's house. I was a little shocked! He was a wonderful person; his wife was very nice as well. However, they were rude to each other. We could feel the tension between them. The house was not kept; things were all over the place. The yard was overgrown with weeds. We did not stay very long. Although we enjoyed their company individually, we did not feel comfortable. It was sad to see them so unhappy.

A few days later we went to the Fisher's suburban house. Ben's friend picked us up in his car. What a difference from the Bandahans! This family had children, and the house was in tip top condition. We were welcomed and were invited to a sumptuous dinner.

As we stepped into the dinning room, it felt like we entered into a different era. The dinning room was decorated in the early fifteenth century British style. It had a huge fireplace with a pot hanging from the center. The fireplace mantle displayed British emblems and pewter plates. The windows had hand-blown glass in separate squares. There was a huge oak table with thick ornate legs and the chairs were old British straight back woven chairs. The floor was stone and covered with a hand woven, earth colored oval rug. We truly felt that we were in an authentic fifteenth century room! The first course served on pewter plates, really set the mood.

When I went to the kitchen to help with the dishes, I was surprised to see an all modern kitchen with push button appliances, and bright counter tops. Here I felt I stepped into the future. They had appliances I had never seen in the United States.

I commented to Sam, "Your garden looks so beautiful."

"Come, I'll give you a tour of our garden and the greenhouse."

"I love these exotic plants they're so pretty."

"We import them from different countries, we even import these vegetable plants, you can't find them in London." he said

We had a lovely time. Sam drove us back to our hotel.

We were saddened to see the contrast between these two friends, the Fishers and the Bandahans.

London was fascinating. We visited the wax museum and took pictures of ourselves standing next to the Queen and with Elvis.

We were enthralled with the tower of London.

"Was this really a torture chamber?" asked Levon.

"Yes." Ben said

Both Levon and Sonia were terrified and disgusted.

"Mom, did they actually use these things to torture people?" Asked Sonia.

"Unfortunately, yes. They did." replied Ben sadly.

The children enjoyed the ride on the double-decker bus.

After eating and enjoying the popular fish-and-chips wrapped in newspaper, we realized why Ben, as a student in England, disliked the dorm food, sneaked out, and bought fish and chips for his dinner.

We were intrigued and captivated seeing and listening to all these unusual people lecturing at the speakers corner in Hyde Park. At one corner, a tall man, stood on an empty wooden crate. As he gestured, his well tailored suit, kept moving up and down. We listened to his political speech for a short time. Suddenly we heard a noise. We turned toward the commotion and saw a short man a few feet away, standing on a chair. His paint stained overalls made us think that he must be a painter. With the British flag in his hand, and with deep baritone voice, he was lecturing about patriotism. As we located ourselves near him, we saw that with his uproarious voice and movements, he was attracting more people from the surrounding area. There was one more group of people surrounding a speaker. It was interesting to note that people stood and listened to these men. No one argued or antagonized them. Unfortunately, our time was limited and we had to leave.

We visited the Parliament building, listened to Big Ben and watched the changing of the guards. We continued our sightseeing. Ben was very excited and was showing off to us. He took us to all the restaurants, shops, and sites he used to visit. He was reliving his student days.

During this time, my brother Garabed was also visiting London but we could not connect with him, and had made plans to see him at our next stop, Greece.

Greece

In Athens we met my brother Garabed who was staying in the same hotel as we were. Both children were excited seeing their uncle. His room being two stories above ours gave them an excuse to use the elevator more than they should. The three of them went swimming and were having a good time.

We were fascinated with Greek archeology. We went to the Acropolis and visited the Parthenon, a temple dedicated to the maiden goddess Athena.

We were mesmerized by the national Archaeological Museum. At the Agora, the ancient market-place and civic center where people gathered, Levon and Sonia started running from one pedestal to another.

We toured the winding narrow streets of the Plaka; the historic neighborhood.

We visited the shops at Sintagma square, where we saw carpets, fur coats, and a variety of clothing stores. At a later visit we bought a *flocati* rug made of lamb's wool, white and fluffy. We went crazy shopping at the flea market called Monasteraki.

In the open air theater of Dionyasus, we were amazed how clearly we could hear without loud speakers.

A few days later my Brother left. We rented a cabin by the sea in Astor Beach. A luxurious tent city, where a butler brought breakfast, lunch, and dinner into the tent. He had dark clothes with white gloves and brought us anything we desired.

The table was always filled with fruits and snacks for the children; we felt both Levon and Sonia will be terribly spoiled after such a trip. But we were enjoying every minute of it, swimming, resting, sleeping, and sightseeing.We loved their food and *moussaka* was our favorite.

MOUSSAKA

3 medium eggplants
Dash of ground cinnamon
1 lb. ground beef
3 tbsp. butter
1cup chopped onions
3 tbsp. Flour
¼ cup red wine
1 ½ cups milk
¼ cup water
½ tsp. salt
2 tbsp. parsley
Dash pepper
1 tbsp. tomato paste
Dash ground nutmeg
1 tsp. Salt
1 beaten egg
1 slice bread, torn into crumbs
¼ cup American processed - cheese, shredded
2 beaten eggs

Slice eggplant and sprinkle with salt. Set aside. In skillet, brown meat and onions. Drain off excess fat. Add wine, water, parsley, tomato paste, salt and dash of pepper. Simmer until liquid is nearly absorbed. Cool, stir in half of bread crumbs, the 2 beaten eggs, ¼ cup cheese and cinnamon.

In saucepan melt butter, stir in flour. Add milk. Cook until thick. Add ½ teaspoon salt, dash of pepper and nutmeg. Add a small amount of hot sauce to the beaten egg. Return to hot mixture. Cook over low heat for 2 minutes.

Brown eggplant in a little hot oil. Sprinkle bottom of baking dish (12 x 7 1/2 x 2) with remaining bread crumbs. Cover with layer of eggplant. Spoon onto meat mixture. Add rest of eggplant. Pour milk-egg sauce over all. Top with shredded cheese. Bake at 350 degree for about 45 minutes.

In the evening, we visited the seashore cafes in nearby Athens, where they were famous for their fish. This was where we were introduced to octopus. *E-e-e-ck how can you eat octopus!*

"Try it, you'll like it." I was coaxed by the restaurant owner,

I tasted, "Mmmmm it's good."

"Why don't you try these sardines as well, they're very fresh." The restaurant owner brought a dish filled with small sardines. They were out of this world.

We kept on coming back for more sardines. The week went so fast that we did not realize that our trip to Greece was over.

Beirut

In Beirut, the Paris of the Middle East, we stayed by the beach at the beautiful hotel Phoenicia. In seven years, the city had changed. The streets seemed narrower and crowded, the trams were removed and electric buses were operating. Many new high-rises had taken over the small quaint houses of old. Shopping was fabulous.

Our aim was to see all our relatives. Almost everyday we were invited out. We asked Maro, Ben's cousin from his mother's side to meet us at a restaurant, and we asked Vrej, his cousin from his father's side, to meet us at the same restaurant. They were both single and in their early twenties. We introduced them, and enjoyed reminiscing about old times.

We left Beirut the next day. It was a year later when we received their wedding invitation.

From Beirut we flew Pakistan International Airlines to Karachi. They spoiled us with gifts and served us food on real china. It was midday when we landed. Stepping out of the air conditioned airplane into the 115 degree humid heat of the day was like walking into an oven. After climbing down the steep stairs of the airplane, you could feel the tar of the asphalt stick to your shoes. The distance from the plane to the building was about one hundred fifty yards, we all followed each other in a single file. As we were nearing the building we turned around and saw Levon going back to the plane.

"Levon, where are you going?" I asked

He kept on going,

"What's the matter? Are you okay? I continued.

In a disgusting way he said.

"You can have Pakistan, I'm going back home!"

He could hardly breathe. We ran after him.

"Look Levon, come into the building, it'll be cooler inside" I tried to convince him.

"You're just saying that, if its not cool I'll go back to the plane"

It was comparatively cooler in the building and Levon, though unhappy, calmed down. The airport was a long big room. There were ceiling fans all the way from one end of the hall to the other.

After going through customs, we went to board a local flight; it was a Fokker Friendship airplane. We were now headed to our final destination; Lahore, Pakistan.

Lahore, Pakistan

As we approached Lahore, we saw a greener country than the Karachi area. Similar to the Karachi Airport but smaller, visitors could almost come up to the airplane. We were greeted by many of the Harza Engineering Company expatriates. Of course after a long journey we were tired and dazed. People were standing behind the 4 foot chain linked fence. Hands were reaching out over the fence.

"Give us your bags."

What a wonderful welcome. We were all ushered into a car.

"We will taking you to an apartment to give you some time to rest, and we'll be back to see you at dinner time." stated one of the Harza company women.

We were excited but a bit disappointed. We thought we will be in a hotel for a few days. The apartment had a living room, two bedrooms with a bathroom in each. The kitchen had a refrigerator and a stove. But everything was old fashioned. The floor of the kitchen was concrete. All the rooms were painted in white. The drapes were old and they were hung quickly and haphazardly. Many of the company people came and brought food and other items for us.

Dinner at Voiklander's house (Ben's new boss) gave us an idea about life in Lahore. There, as we were dining, we saw a few lizards scampering on the walls; we watched and followed their movements. I was afraid that one of them might jump on us. Mr Voiklander and his wife realized my hesitation.

"Don't worry, those are friendly lizards, they eat all the bugs and

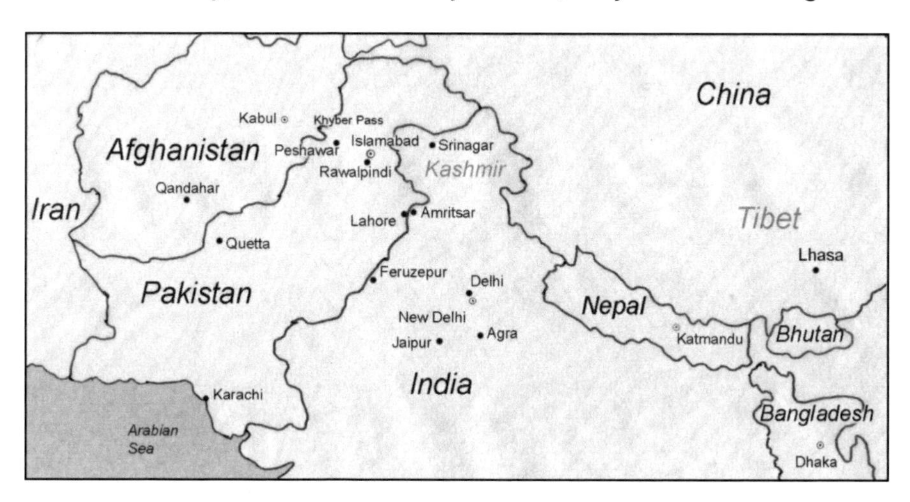

mosquitoes." said Mrs. Voiklander.

"Won't they fall or jump on us from the ceiling?" asked Levon like he was reading my mind.

"We never had that experience, this is very natural for Pakistan, after a while you get used to them." Her words assured me.

At the apartment, the refrigerator had all kinds of food; the generosity of the company wives was obvious. They brought in anything they could spare so that we could be comfortable.

"You're the first family that we are assigning to an apartment, we always assigned newcomers to a hotel, but we felt this is better for children, they'll be free to do anything they want, and we want you to be happy." Said one of the ladies.

Little did they know that we loved staying in hotels, being the first day and suffering from jet lag; tired, we wanted to go to bed early.

As we were getting ready to go to bed we felt that we were not alone. As I looked up, I screamed, "Look Ben! There are kids peaking into our window."

I ran to the window and drew the drapes which were long and heavy. As I was pulling them, there jumped a cockroach out of the drape, almost hitting me. This time I really screamed.

"Sonia, Levon come here!"

Our first apartment at WAPDA Flats- bottom right of building.

“What is it mom?” They asked in unison, wanting to know more.

“Don’t unpack your suitcases!”

“Why?” again they responded in unison.

“Look at the cockroach, they must be all over.”

But we did not finish there. I wanted to put something in the chest of drawers. When I pulled opened a drawer, a cricket jumped out. Wow!! This made me cringe. “Ben I am not unpacking! We are leaving tomorrow! I **will not** stay here!”

Finally after a lot of angry talk and arguments we went to bed. I could not sleep I was constantly thinking about these little creepers all over the apartment. My gaze wandered toward the ceiling and what do I see a lizard exactly above me. This was the last straw. I jumped!

“Ben! Wake up! Wake up!” I started crying. It was a miserable evening. But we were all tired and eventually we fell asleep.

The next morning we were pleasantly surprised because one of the company ladies had sent her servant to come and make breakfast for us.

“*Memsab* (madam) I am frying eggs for the children, shall I do the same for you and *Saab* (Master)”

“Yes please, thank you.”We were pleased by his politeness.

We again had visitors helping us to understand life in Pakistan to minimize the cultural shock. Eventually we started settling down and trying to get our own apartment. I did not like this apartment. We requested another one that had a balcony with three bedrooms. For that we had to wait until one was vacated. We had ordered a new VW ‘bug’, from Germany, which had arrived.

Hardly a month went by before the monsoon rains came and our apartment complex was flooded. The water started seeping in from the backdoor of our apartment. The front section was a little higher and had four steps; the water came and covered the third step. The Water & Power Department (WAPDA) who owned the apartment complex was pumping out water furiously.

Overnight our beautiful new VW ‘bug’ and other parked cars were flooded. The water level was very high and we were worried that the car would not work. Many people came and helped pull the cars on to higher ground. It took a long time for the water to subside even though they broke holes in the outside walls and pumped water out of the basement. It took months for the basement to dry and over a year to get rid of the musty smell.

We found out that the reason all the water accumulated was because the builders walled in the complex, without allowing for water drainage to lower ground. The record breaking rainfall filled the apartment grounds like a lake. The lower basement offices and furniture storage rooms became completely flooded and resembled a bathtub filled with water; furniture and paper floating in it. We were supposed to go down to this storage and chose furniture for our apartment. So much for the new furniture.

Ben and Vicky talking with Mr. Voiklander.

Harza Engineering group gathering

For the first three months we were in culture shock. The women of Harza engineering group were helpful, they too had the same experience so they knew how we were feeling. They showed us how to get around, how to buy food, how to make sure we did not get sick. For example we needed to boil our water and milk for 20 minutes to kill the stubborn germs. We also needed to iodine tincture our vegetables, and to make sure that everything was rinsed with boiled water. We had one rule of thumb; once in the apartment everyone washed their hands before they touched anything.

One day we were taken to the fruit and grocery market. I could smell an unpleasant odor in the air. I was shy and did not say anything; I thought I might be the only one.

"Ben are you smelling something bad?" I whispered, making sure I was not the only one who was flustered by the rancid smell.

"Yes."

"Where is it coming from?"

"I don't know."

Our friend did not seem to smell it. Finally we were standing at a beautifully displayed counter with gorgeous fruits, as I was filling a bag the smell got worse. I looked around and did not see anything that could smell that bad. I finally asked our lady friend.

"Do you smell something... bad?"

She pointed at where I was standing, which was a wooden board, "You are standing on an open sewer."

I was astounded; I left the fruit and started to leave. Our friend explained that the entire city had open sewers and the odor I smelled was from them. Eventually, after a few months, we became used to the smell and did not smell it any more. Later, we too brought newcomers to these same places and they too had the same reaction.

Our next stop was the meat market. The smell there was worse. This was a learning process. Each shopkeeper had his own cubicle, the meat, a whole cow or part of a cow or buffalo, was hung from an iron hook; our friend pointed to a part, "Please give me this undercut."

"Yes *memsab* (madam)."

"What is an undercut?" I asked our friend.

"It is the most tender meat, it is the fillet, this is the part you make fillet mignon with."

The butcher cut the undercut, weighed it and gave it to her. We had never seen where the fillet came from until we went to this meat market. We were shocked to see the butcher sitting on the floor, hands free, with the knife handle between his toes, cutting the meat.

Our next stop was the fish market which was next to the meat market. Most of the fish came from Karachi. They had the best shrimp. Here again, men were sitting in cubicles with fish baskets around them.There were so many varieties that I did not know which kind to buy. I asked our friend and she said,

"We usually have this flat and wide fish, why don't you try it."

"Fine, please give me four of these fish,"

"*Memsab*, you made a good choice, these are the best tasting fish, I will fillet them for you."

He cleaned and filleted it beautifully on his sharp knife which was between his toes. We were amazed! All the men in each cubicle were experts in cutting the fish into very thin slices using their hands and toes.

Lahore, Pakistan had many exotic markets; we were taken to a cloth market, where you could buy yards and yards of good quality material. Also sold was fabric from used women's clothing from the United States. They unraveled the seams of these dresses and sold them as cut material.

There were no markets for ready made clothes for women, you bought the material and you had a *durzi,* (tailor) stay in your veranda and sew the dress the way you wanted it. Men's used clothing, mostly from United States, was available in the bazaar. One of Harza Engineering employees recognized a custom made suit he had donated to the Salvation Army before coming to Lahore.

They had cottage industries where you bought wonderful embroidered tablecloths, bed covers, crocheted dresses, and many other items.

The basic dress for Pakistani women was the *shalwar kameez*. The *shalwar* is a baggy pants narrowed at the anklets with a wide waste gathered with a ribbon or band. The *kameez* is a straight cut top with long sleeves usually made with thin cotton. The *kurta*, another variety of the *kameez,* also straight-cut with a square material under the arm pits to allow more freedom of movement. Some of these *kurtas* were unbelievably beautiful with plenty of embroidery. In the hot weather it kept you cool at all times. The temperature in Lahore got up to 115 degrees (F) in the shade.

We loved going to the jewelry market. You could find gold at

Ben, Levon and Sonia in front of brass and copper shop.

Vicky modeling in a promotional photo for a local pharmacy.

very good prices and find fascinating items: bangles, rings, bracelets, brooches, earrings; you could even draw a design and have it custom made for a low price.

Right next to the jewelry market there was the precious stone market with diamonds, rubies, agates and a variety of stones. One could spend a whole day in these markets.

The most fascinating was the trinket market. I found all kinds of antiques there; old copper or brass vases, old *paan* boxes, brass and huge copper vases, carved plates and many other items.

A *paan* box is an ornate box made of copper or brass designed to hold the ingredients for making betel nut chew. In it there are smaller boxes with covers, and a tray. *Pan* is betel leaf a tropical creeper belonging to the family of plants named *piper betle*. Chewing this stimulant sweetens the breath and gives color (crimson) to the lips and tongue of a person. On the plate/tray (*pandari*) the preparer spreads the shell lime paste (*chun*) on the leaf, adds betel nut (*supari*), coriander-seed, cinnamon, cardamom, and flavored dusts, then rolls the leaf with its stuffing into a cone. After meals it is customary to chew *paan and* spit the juice out. There were special spittoons in houses where they spat out the juice. Outside, people spat on the ground. Many of the streets and sidewalks were red from people spitting paan juice. Actually at first we were disgusted seeing people spitting red something. Later we learned to accept the custom and got used to seeing the red juice stains on the sidewalks.

One day we were at a wedding, our hostess offered *paan* "No thank you," the hostess insisted.

"You must try it, it's very good, I'll be unhappy if you didn't." So I had no choice, when I tried, it tasted good. That was the only time I tried *paan.*

Paan is used by people in South Asia, Southeast Asia, Gulf states and Pacific Islands; it is chewed by all classes, sometimes as an item of ritual, etiquette and manners. At dinners and festivals, offering *paan* signaled the time for departure. During the aristocratic age *paan* preparation and the style of garnishing was a recognized folk art.

Going back to the trinket market. We were fascinated with the wax and wood design artwork. On wood the artisan puts layers of different color wax and the last layer he chooses mostly red. With a sharp object, he draws on this wood, creating a beautiful art work with multi-color design.

We went to the market where they made tablecloths. The shops looked like caves. Arched ceilings, dark inside with a very small window in the back, the floors of the shops were mostly hardened mud. The shops reminded me of the ancient construction of shops in the old city of Jerusalem. A smooth protective surface was laid on the floor and a white cotton cloth was laid on top.

We watched the artisan chose a wooden block carved with a design on one side, "Look mom the wooden block has a small handle" said Levon, who was intrigued with the procedure.

The artisan dipped the block into a dye made with natural plants, he systematically started stamping on the material by pressing this small wooden block in such a way that the design was continuous. "Do you mix the dye? I asked.

"No *memsab,* this dye is made with plants that grow on the mountains in the north of Pakistan, they make it there and we buy the dye from them."

Some wood blocks were about a foot long, some were shorter. They started with the outer edge of the cloth, with one color, usually black. Once the base color was printed they laid the cloth and let it dry. Once dry, with another carved wooden block, they started the second color, a design that complimented and filled in the first design. The process kept going on until all the desired colors were printed. At each level the cloth dries thus creating the most beautiful table cloth with rich natural steadfast color designs. After final touches they washed the cloth by hand and dried it in the sun, thus making it ready for sale.

They custom made different sizes and shapes of tablecloths. Some were round, others rectangular. They also made bedcovers, drapes, and material for dresses. You could choose the design and the size of the material and order whatever you wanted.

They were stamping fast and it looked so easy. They gave me a sample of material and a block. I thought, *surely I can produce a nice design in no time.*

"Oh boy! Did I prove myself wrong. What a mess! It looked so easy; I thought I could print just like they do!"

In order to create a continuous design, you had to know exactly where to stamp with just the right amount of pressure to look uniform. After watching and experiencing the process, I began to value these tablecloths and treated them with respect.

In summer, the weather in Pakistan is hot and dry, The houses are built with high ceilings. Since few homes have central air conditioning, most have window air conditioners except the Water and Power Division (WAPDA) flats where we lived, an apartment complex specially built for the expatriate community.

Some preferred to live in individual houses. These houses had desert coolers as air conditioners. For this type of weather it was appropriate. Most of the expatriate houses were large and all had big gardens and a bathroom in every bedroom.

We found out later that the houses were designed similar to the style of the ancient Muhanjedaro period homes. Archeological excavations found in the Indus Valley built as early as 2000 BC. It seemed the Indians of that period traveled and were in contact with other civilizations, such as the Sumerians, Assyrians and Egyptians.

WAPDA flats had apartment units each with their own central air conditioning units. Outdoor balconies surrounding each unit. There were seperate units adjacent to the building for the servants and their families, The basement had offices and a warehouse where they kept new furniture for newcomers. There were two gates one for occupants and their guests and the other for vendors.

Our apartment had three bedrooms three baths, a living room, dining area, a long hallway, and a kitchen with a little "go-down" (a pantry) which we used as a storage room. The living room opened onto a large balcony, this was where the *durzi* (tailor) sat on a mat on the floor with his hand cranked Singer sewing machine, and sewed clothing for the family. All I had to do was give him the material, show him a design, and next thing you knew he had matched the dress or shirt to the exact style that was in the picture. This was done within one day. I was fascinated, and surprised. He charged the equivalent of twenty dollars per day. Every so often, we asked him to come and stay a few days, until all the material that we had accumulated was sewn.

Chawkidars (guards) patrolled the apartment complex making sure that solicitors or strangers would not enter without permission. But now and then local entertainers were allowed to perform for the children of the flats.

"*Memsab*, come, bring the children, the snake *walla* (charmer) is here."

Sure enough there was a man with a large bag and a flute like instrument made with a gourd sitting on the ground outside the gate. He took a cobra out of his jute bag and set it curled in front of him, all of us took a step back. As the charmer started playing the flute, the cobra stood up out of it's coil and enlarged its hood. facing the flute player it started to sway side to side with the movement of the instrument. "*Memsab.* the cobra cannot see well but hears and feels the music."

There were other snakes that did similar movements but the scariest was the tiny snake.

"Children! Move back. This tiny snake is very poisonous. It can jump on you." When it was brought out of its bag, we again took a few steps backwards.

Other entertainers visited our apartments with trained birds and other animals, but I think the kids liked the monkey *wallas* best of all. The monkeys jumped around and did all kinds of tricks. They would snatch money from your hand and take it to the *walla* after the show. They were great entertainment for the children.

I always worried about the stories that I heard about the monkeys having rabies and I was nervous about them getting too close, but I would just bite my tongue and smile.

We received the news from Harza that it is time to go to a certain clinic and get some shots. Well, in the United States it was easy to go and get your shots so we assumed that it will be the same. They said it was live serum gamma globulin and it will be given on a certain day only. This was to prevent Hepatitis, which was rampant in Pakistan. We had no idea what we were getting into. The entire company was there waiting in line. First each had to be weighed. Unfortunately we had a big meal before coming so we weighed a few pounds more, we explained this to the Doctor, but he wouldn't listen. After writing how much we weighed, he produced this huge needle and counted the ccs. He said you get the amount according to how much you weigh and since it was so much serum, it had to be injected in the buttocks. The fear settled in our hearts. Levon and Sonia started to jump up and down thinking maybe they will loose some weight. Of course it did not help! One look at that huge needle was enough to make you scream. I felt the shot was never-ending, it was painful because they had to inject the serum very slowly. You could feel it flowing into your body.

This had to be repeated every six months. So, in preparation, we started dieting a few weeks before the shots were due. Always anticipating the needle with dread.

Teaching in Lahore, Pakistan

Eventually, we began to adapt to the local life. We registered Sonia in the Montessori pre-school, where another Harza engineering family had their son. Sonia enjoyed going to school, and she made friends. We hired a nanny (*ayah*) who took care of her after school. The *ayah* took her to the sandbox, which was inside the walled garden of our apartment complex; the sandbox was a center where all the apartment children congregated. While the children played, the *ayahs* gossiped and got all their news about the expatriate families. The *chowkidar*s also communicated with the *ayahs* and got their news as well.

The *ayah* gave Sonia her bath everyday, washed and ironed her clothes- ready for the next school day. Then she fed her and put her to bed. Sonia loved the attention! The *ayah* took care of Levon's clothes, as well, and made sure that the children's room was well kept and everything in its right place.

We hired a "sweeper" to come everyday, to clean the balconies and bathrooms. The old Indian cast system, to a lesser extent carried over to Pakistan. He was a poor Christian, who did nothing else, and all for a few dollars. He loved whenever we voiced our appreciation for his efforts. He was a proud young man and he did his work well. He had a happy disposition and did not know any other life. When we gave him food, for his family, he refused saying:

"I have my own food. If I eat your food, my family and I will become spoiled. We'll not like what we have anymore and become unhappy. We can't afford your kind of food."

He was right. We understood.

We also had a laundry man (*dobi*) who came twice a week, washed all the clothes, hung them in the sun, and then ironed everything- including the underwear. Once he finished ironing, he neatly displayed everything on our bed for my inspection. I would remove and put them into their respective hangers or chest of drawers.

Peter, was our cook/ butler, he organized the rooms, made the beds, and supervised the other helpers.

He was trained by the British.

"Peter, this salad is sweet. What do you have in it?" I asked.

"*Memsab*. I always put a sprinkle of sugar- it gives taste. The British people like it that way."

"From now on please do not put sugar in our salad."

"Fine, *memsab*, I'll not."

We had a few favorite dishes. One of them was chicken curry with a side of mango *chutney*.

CHICKEN CURRY

¾ cup butter
2 large onions, sliced
4-5 whole cardamoms
1" piece cinnamon stick
6 cloves garlic, ground
1 tsp. -green ginger, ground
1 tbsp cumin seed, ground
1½ tsp coriander, ground
1 tsp. ground red pepper
2 tomatoes, sliced
1 chicken, cut into pieces

Melt butter; add sliced onion, cardamom and cinnamon. Cook until onions are brown. Add garlic, ginger, cumin, coriander, turmeric, red pepper and tomatoes. Heat and stir until tomatoes are cooked. Add chicken and ½ cup lukewarm water. Cook on slow fire. When chicken reaches desired tenderness. If not enough gravy remains, add a bit more water and cook slowly for 2 or 3 minutes.

MANGO CHUTNEY

25 green mangoes
½ lb raisins
5 ripe mangoes
2 lbs tamarinds
Salt
½ lb ginger root peeled and chopped fine
1 tsp cinnamon
2 pts Vinegar
1 pt water
12 small hot peppers
2½ lbs brown sugar

Peel and slice mangoes; sprinkle lightly with salt. Cover and leave in refrigerator 24 hours. Peel tamarinds and wash well. Let simmer in small amount of water 5 minutes. Strain out puree.
Make syrup of brown sugar and one half of the vinegar and water. Add mangoes, tamarind puree, and all other ingredients with the exception of remaining half of vinegar and water. Boil ½ hour. Add remaining vinegar and water. Cook slowly until thick.

Pakora, *Samosas* and chicken curry are some of our favorite appetizers served with drinks.

PAKORA

½ lbs chickpea flour
1 bunch scallions
2 green chilies
1 tbsp ground spices (cumin, black pepper, cloves & cinnamon)
1 tbsp cumin seed
1 tsp baking powder
Salt to taste

Chop onions and chilies and mix all ingredients with water to make a thick batter. Keep for about 20 minutes before frying. Heat shortening in a deep pan, drop the batter with a spoon in small bits and fry until brown. To make Vegetable Pakoras, dip slices of boiled potatoes, onion rings, or whole spinach leaves in batter and fry. – Delicious!

SAMOSAS

1 1/2 lbs. ground beef
1 teaspoon salt
1 cup water
½ cup chopped onion
1 tablespoon ground ginger
Mint leaves
1 tablespoon ground garlic
Coriander leaf 1 teaspoon
Ground green chilies
3 to 4 chopped green chilies
1 tsp chili powder
Juice of 1 lime

Ground beef, add next six ingredients. Cook until tender, and water completely evaporates. Remove from heat. Add remaining ingredients and allow to cool. Seal in small pastry rounds or squares, and fry in deep fat.

SHRIMP CURRY

1½ lbs fresh shrimp
2½ cups milk
¼ cup margarine/butter
1 teaspoon salt
2 tbsp. finely chopped onion
1 tbsp. lemon juice
2 teaspoons. Curry powder
1 tsp finely chopped ginger root
¼ cup flour

Cook the shrimp by dropping into boiling salted water using 1 teaspoon salt to 1 quart water, cover. In another pan, melt butter; add onion and sauté until golden brown. Stir in curry powder and flour and blend to form a smooth paste. Add milk, stirring until sauce thickens. Add salt, lemon juice and ginger root. Add shrimp and let stand in sauce over low heat for about 30 minutes to blend flavorings before serving over appetizer crackers.

Often served with the above appetizers was a refreshing alcoholic drink called Sangria.

SANGRIA

Slice 1 lemon, 1 lime, 1 orange and put in large pitcher. Add 4 ounces of brandy mixed with ¼ cup fine granulated sugar. Let stand at room temperature for one hour. Add 1 bottle wine (Spanish), 2 tablespoons lemon juice. Stir and let stand again. Just before serving, add ice and fill pitcher with soda water.

Living in Lahore had many advantages, I had time on my hands, so I volunteered my help at the hospital- folding bandages and knitting. We always took the medical equipment and facilities available in the United States for granted. So it came as a surprise to see that the hospital did not have ready-made bandages. They had to be folded by volunteers like us.

The hospital encouraged young mothers to bring their newly born babies once a month for weighing and for medical check ups. For incentive, the hospital offered them baby formula.

After nine-or- ten visits the hospital offered them a set of knitted clothing. I enjoy knitting, so I joined the knitting group. Once a week we met and knitted small jackets, hats, and cardigans. My bonus for volunteering was learning more about life in Lahore and making friends.

It was difficult to mingle with the Pakistanis because of the Muslim way of male and female separation. Wherever we went the men sat in one room and the women in another. At weddings they each had their own entertainment. Food was served first to the men, and then the women were invited into the dining room.

Aside from colleagues of Ben our friends were mainly Pakistanis married to Americans, or to foreign non-Pakistani women. In their homes they intermixed. But, outside their home, families had to follow the Muslim rule of separation of men and women.

About the end of our first summer, the United States Consul General invited us to his house for a cocktail party, where I met the superintendent of the American school. I asked him if there were any teaching positions available.

"Sorry. Vicky, all the teaching positions are filled."

"I was hoping to teach in Lahore." I said disappointed.

"Where did you teach in the States?"

"I graduated from Elmhurst College and taught in the same district in Illinois."

The next day he called me, "Hi Vicky. I want you to teach a divided sixth grade class. Please come and see me. I want a teacher, fresh from the States, with new ideas and approaches."

I was surprised, but he told me later that he was from Illinois, and was familiar with the University I graduated from, as well as the school district where I taught. Needless to say, I was thrilled. The next day he gave me a tour of the premises.

The school was a huge colonial two story building, with many classrooms. The main building housed both the high school and the library.

"In the back we added classrooms for the middle school children." He explained.

The administration occupied two of the rooms of the main building. "This room is for the faculty. And it has a nurse's station."

Huge trees covered the grounds. The high school had a separate area for sports. The school day ended at 2:30pm; I drove to school with Levon. This was ideal, but I had to learn how to drive the VW "bug" with a stick shift. Also, I had to learn to dodge the unbelievable number of bicycles and scooters.

My worst experience happened on a hill at a red light. I had to stop. The car rolled back ... and back! At first, I panicked but then I regained control of the car. After a few near misses, I became much better at negotiating the hills. It took time, but I eventually became an expert. My international license was an accordion-like booklet made of jute glued to cardboard.

"Ben, are you sure this is my driver's license?" I asked, astonished by what I saw in my hand.

"Yes. I had the same reaction." Ben said. "The police reassured me this is the real thing. I also checked with others in the office. They had the same kind of a driver's license. The jute was stamped with the necessary information."

This reminds me of an incident that happened on our return to the United States. We had just returned from Lahore. Ben was driving at night. The children were sleeping in the back. We were returning from a late evening activity. Suddenly, we saw a police car light blinking and asking us to stop. We both sat up and wondered why he was stopping us. As he came to the window both children woke up. And seeing the policeman they jumped up.

"Driver's license please."

When Ben presented his international license made of jute and cardboard to the policeman, you could see the shock on his face. He was speechless, he kept on opening each layer of the accordion-like license and reading. Then he looked at each one of us including the children, then looking back at the license and shook his head. Finally, like someone waking up from a dream he said,

"You didn't stop at the stop sign at that intersection."

"I'm sorry officer, it's dark and I didn't see it, this is the first time we have traveled on this route." Ben replied.

The officer, with a quizzical expression kept on looking at the license. Then looked at the children then at us. *I was worried that the policeman will reject this international driver's license and for sure will take us to the police station.* After a long pause, which felt like hours, he declared:

"I'll allow you to continue this time. Drive carefully."

What a relief! We both were shocked!

Teaching school in Lahore, Pakistan, was not easy- one had to be creative. We did not go to the market to buy school supplies. Everything had to be imported. We had limited supplies and not everything that I needed was available. Many of my students had been in Pakistan for a long time, some did not know any other life. One day, we were talking about a "hydrant". One of the students raised her hand and asked

"What is a hydrant?"

I showed the picture of a hydrant, and she asked,

"What does it do?"

I was constantly being reminded that we were living in a different culture. Our teaching had to be "geared" to the needs of the students and we had to be resourceful, inventive, and flexible. For example, I used *papier-mâché* in Geography, to construct a three dimensional map. Our library was limited. I went to engineer friends and collected magazines that described scientific discoveries. The students came from the United States and Canada. There were also children of foreign embassy personnel.

School was 8:00 am to 2:30pm. There were no television sets. For recreation we read and played music. I played the piano, and tried to teach both Levon and Sonia to play the piano too. Many of our children's friends visited. They sat around, talked and listened to music. There were many receptions and cocktail parties, but, because of the children, we went to only a few.

We loved playing bridge. We had many bridge parties.

In Lahore both Ben and I learned to play golf. We took lessons from a golf pro and, after a while, we played almost every afternoon. We formed foursomes with other couples, it was refreshing and good exercise. Levon took lessons from the pro as well. He joined golf groups for the youth.

The young people had intergroup tournaments. Levon became the Junior International golf champion, for which he received a trophy (an American program)- to this day, he displays it with pride.

Vicky's sixth grade class in Lahore American Society

Vicky's fourth grade class in Lahore American Society

Our travels to India and Afghanistan

We became good friends with the Nobes from the Harza Engineering group. They had three children about the same age as our two. During holidays we took off with two VW 'bugs' and went to see the country. We traveled all over Pakistan, Afghanistan, and India.

India was a twenty minute drive from Lahore. Our favorite trip was going to Amritsar to buy pork. Pakistan is a Muslim country so pork is forbidden. We always called to order pork chops before we crossed over to India. We stayed in a pension that belonged to Madam Bandari, a vivacious, outgoing person- who knew how to attract expatriates, inundate them with care, and help them in obtaining pork. The pork, in refrigerated containers, was delivered to us at the pension on the day of our departure.

The first time we went to Amritsar, we visited the Golden Temple of the Sikhs, the holiest shrine in Sikhism, which is a striking architectural masterpiece! A young man approached us;

"Welcome to our temple. Please allow me to show you around," he said. We thanked him and he became our guide. He was a devout person, and he narrated the history of the temple. We listened intently to the reading of their holy book by their high priest. The flowered garlands, around his neck, sent their aroma everywhere. The combination of the reading, the aroma of the flowers and the incense created an atmosphere of tranquility, transporting us into a peaceful world.

Our guide started narrating. "Around 1557, Sikhs were driven out by the Muslims. Many were massacred." He continued, "According to legend, their leader was captured by the Muslims. Upon being decapitated, he grabbed his own long hair and threw his head as far as he could, about two hundred yards. On the spot where his head landed, the Sikhs built their temple."

Construction of the Golden Temple began in 1574, and it was completed in 1601. 100 kg of gold were applied to the inverted lotus-shaped dome. Decorative marble covered the floors, giving a stunning picture. The sacred part of the Golden Temple complex is the *Hari Mandir* or Divine Temple- a golden structure at the center of a large body of water, reached by way of a bridge. The gold plated building features copper cupolas, and white marble walls, with precious stones arranged in a decorative Islamic-style floral pattern. At night, the golden dome shines.

"We vowed that we'll never forget our history. For that reason, the men let their hair grow. They collect their hair on the top of their heads, and bind it and cover it with a turban." Our guide continued, "We never shave; we comb our long beard and wrap it under our chin." The young man pulled a comb from inside his turban and showed it to us, saying. "We always carry a comb."

Levon was looking at the young man's bracelet. When the guide saw his curious look, he explained, "We wear this special kind of circular bracelet as a symbol of our bondage by the Muslims."

We found out that the Sikhs are very proud people and devoted to their religion.

We attended their religious ceremony and afterwards we noticed women in the back of the temple feeding people. Others were washing the utensils and metal bowls; they were using ash, instead of soap, to clean the dishes. They believe that ash cleans everything. At the end, we wanted to pay the young man but he refused.

"As a Sikh this is my religious duty." He explained.

We left the Temple satisfied; having learned more about the Sikh religion.

The kids enjoyed being on a *rickshaw*- a three wheeled tricycle that has a buggy behind it. The driver pedals the tricycle, riding and pulling the rickshaw, up and down the streets. The passengers sit in the buggy which is over the back two wheels. These were less expensive than taxis and very popular with the local people.

Also, the three wheeled motorbikes have been converted to small taxis for two or three passengers; racing along the narrow streets, avoiding pedestrians and bicycles and tricycles. A convenient way to travel in crowded areas, but frightening. We used them every now and then but with a lot of praying.

Pakistan has several official religious holidays. Coupled with our Christian holidays, we had many days where we were able to travel. We traveled in all directions with our friends the Nobes. Our trip to the *Khyber Pass* was one of the most memorable. Dr. Nobe is an agronomist, but he also collects antique guns. We knew there was a small town, in the *Khyber Pass*, where they made their own guns.

Once our two VW 'bugs' received permission, from the border patrol of the Khyber Pass, we started our journey. We had to go through checkpoints, manned by the tribal people. These people were tall, with weather beaten faces always wearing *shalwar* (baggy pants) and long shirts made with light brown cotton that blended with the mud and dirt of the surroundings. All the grown men had bullet belts criss-crossed on their chest with rifles on their shoulders. We were told not to talk with anyone. Only one person was to be our spokesman.

A few more checkpoints, and paper searches, and we were finally allowed to proceed to the village center, where the gun factories stood.

Unbelievably! There were no machines to do the work. Instead we discovered that everything was made by hand. People, squatting on the ground- worked on a part of a gun. Some banging with hammers. Some scraping. We did not dare say a word or speak to each other.

We were told "Do not take pictures" so, we hid our cameras. The smallest mistake could bring our life to an end. We knew them to be the sort of people who kill at even the slightest annoyance. Dr. Nobe did not agree to buy any of the guns the tribesmen showed. He did not find the specific gun he was looking for.

"Michael, tell everyone to get in the cars. Move slowly. Do not run," Dr Nobe whispered. "Don't do anything that might anger them."

To please them we distributed cigarettes as fast as we could, and drove out of the region without looking back. We prayed that they would not follow us.

We continued on the winding road between cliffs of shale and limestone passing through the tribal lands of the Kyber Pass. In the Pass there are a few flat areas where people have built their villages. Each village is encircled by a wall. The walls, as well as the houses, were made from clay mud. We saw old fortresses, adobe-walled and crumbling, set against the scenic snow capped Hindu-Kush Mountains to the north. The imposing mountains, held caves scattered along deep gorges and up unto jagged peaks. Most were still occupied.

"Mom. Look! People are in those caves," said Levon surprised.

The paved road was clear of traffic. The tribes recognized that the road belonged to Pakistan's central government, but beyond the main road, we were on tribal territory. The government was no longer responsible for our welfare. So we were very careful to stay on the road and not get off of it.

When the Nobe's car began having trouble, they pulled over onto the side of the road to make some adjustments. Our car came behind them. Within minutes we were surrounded by young tribal boys. We didn't know where they came from. They were not there a moment ago.

"*Saab.* Cigarette?" One of the boys asked Dr. Nobe.

"No, cigarette."

As he rushed back to his car the youth began pelting his car with rocks. I couldn't believe how fast we got out of there.

Phew! It was a close call!

In my minds eye I saw different tribes on their horses, congregating in the pass, preparing for games, contests, meetings and discussions, all with their rifles and bullets criss-crossing on their chest.

Traveling on the Kyber Pass, just before the boarder of Afghanistan, in no man's land- there is a market. We stopped to look at the small shops, next to each other. People went from shop to shop reminding me of a duty free flea market. Bargain, argue, buy.

People, from everywhere, come to buy or sell. Some dress in Pakistani style cloths, with white *shalwar* and long shirts, Afghanis wear woolen caps, or felt hats, and the tribal Pashtuns, with their reddish brown earth color *shalwars*, shirts and bullet-belts. Each blends into this environment, the colors are all earth tones and no bright colors catch the eye or bring attention to anyone in particular.

The hustle-and-bustle reminds me of Bible stories, and Biblical times, in the old city of Jerusalem, but with a twist. The goods they sell are modern 20th Century, mingled with antiques. People come by buses, by cars and on donkeys.

"Mom. Look at that bus," said Levon "Two people are hanging from the door. They'll fall if that bus makes a sharp turn."

"Oh, look! Three people are sitting on top of it." Chimed in Sonia.

More people sat at the windows.

"Look at that pickup truck it's filled with people too." We were worried about it turning over, and tumbling down the ravine. It was traveling fast around hairpin-curves.

It was also common to see rock slides on those mountains. We pulled off the road to watch one. The sound deafened us. We were lucky, our side of the road was the safe side.

After crossing the Afghan border, we felt the effect of the high elevation. Along mountain roads we saw more caves in the distance

Public transport preparing to travel through the Kyber Pass.

Landslide along the road of the Kyber Pass, a common event.

and people moving around in them. Further along we saw mud walls that were almost like fortresses. Some of the walls had cow dung cakes stuck on them to dry. These cakes are made with cow/ buffalo dung mixed with hay, shaped into round thin cakes and slapped onto the outside walls. Once dry they are collected and arranged into piles next to the house ready for use as fuel for cooking and heating.

Kabul, the capital of Afghanistan, is a city of contrasts. Next to a four-story building, we see mud huts. Beside a car, a man was using his donkey for transportation. Next to a truck, a man carried a bale of hay on his head.

Our hotel was one of the best. There were push button elevators, attractive candelabras, lovely sitting-areas and piped-in music everywhere. Its service was superb. The nightlife was entertaining. Our room was large, with one double bed and two single beds. Marble tiles covered with Persian carpets and red themed furniture decorated the room.

I told Ben "This reminds me of a Middle Eastern luxury hotel."

There were many foreigners, we thought we were in Europe. But one look outside brought back the reality of mud-huts, men carrying loads of wood (or hay) on their backs, and women covered from head to toe in their *burkas*.

Like Pakistan, Afghanistan had open sewers (*jubes*), but the smell was not as bad because of the high altitude and the cold weather. Michael, the Nobe's five year old son, accidentally stepped into one of these *jubes*. A water faucet near by helped to clean up the grime, but, it took many baths and scrubbings to get rid of the smell.

Miles and miles of poppies grew wild on the hillsides and were cultivated in the valleys.

"Mom. Look. My favorite color! All purple poppies." Sonia, our four year old said excitedly. She jumped, and ran amongst them. We could hardly see her head above their tall stems of purple poppies. At first, we just enjoyed the stunning view. We took pictures of her standing amongst the flowers. Strange to think that they were planted for the opium trade.

We learned how they harvested the poppies we had seen growing all over. The men sliced the head of the matured poppies, thus allowing the juice to ooze out. They wore leather vests and walked between the rows of the sliced heads of the poppies. The juice stuck to the leather vest. Once the vest is fully covered with the juice they let it dry, and later scrape the leather vest, thus collecting the pure powder to process it. This opium was easy to buy in the market.

Because of the inexpensive drugs, we saw many young Europeans traveling to Kabul. It was sad to see so many young people in tattered clothes, sitting on the corners of the streets in a daze, some were even begging. This really was shocking for us. I wondered, "**How can so many young people get into this condition?**"

Away from home, in a strange country, they must have spent all their money buying drugs. We learned from others that at first their embassies tried to help by giving them plane tickets to go home. The drug addicts sold the tickets and used the money to buy more drugs. The embassies tried to use other methods to help them get out of there, but did not succeed. Eventually, they gave up. It was a good lesson for our children to see how people can end up.

While we were eating in a restaurant, we heard a commotion at the door. There was a group of young Germans and the doorman of the restaurant stopped some of the group from coming in. *We wondered why?* Apparently the restaurant did not allow people to come in without shoes. So a few with shoes did come in and when the doorman wasn't looking, one of the group threw his sandals out. The sandals were put on and the next German walked in and he in turn threw them out to the next person! This went on until all the Germans had found a seat in the restaurant. It was hilarious!

Afghanistan was a paradise for antique collectors. We bought antique guns with ivory inlay, oil lamps made of soapstone, and old musical instruments. We had to register every antique we bought with the government office before taking them out of the country.

The shops, like the environment, were full of contrasts. You could buy makeup, nylons, dresses, and anything you wanted for a low price. These were things we could not buy in Lahore, Pakistan. Marks and Spencer of London had a division in Kabul; we were so excited that we shopped to our hearts content. The local people were also buying. We realized that underneath those *burkas*, the women wore the latest fashions.

Good Lapis Lazuli is mined in Afghanistan. We bought jewelry with lapis stones. Most Afghanis wore sheepskin jackets and coats to stay warm. The outside skin of these jackets were covered with embroidery and were fashionable in the West at the time.

"Mom, I'd like to have one of these sheepskin vests" said Levon. Indeed it was an intricately embroidered vest. We could not resist and bought one for him. We also bought long winter coats for each one of us hoping to use them during the cold Chicago winters.

The Afghan people we met were tall good looking and healthy. They were proud people and very hospitable.

In order to go back to Pakistan, we got up very early, and drove through the Khyber Pass in daylight. The road in places was frightening, one side a straight ravine, and the other side rocky mountains with caves.

After driving a few miles, we saw this bus coming at us with a great speed. Ben pulled over to the side to allow the bus to pass. Goods were piled up on the roof as well as people sitting on top of the goods. The bus was so full that people were hanging out of both doors! We sat in fear and amazement as the bus zoomed past us and left us in a cloud of dust with absolutely no concern for the cliff ledge on their side of the road. We couldn't believe our eyes.

We continued our journey back home with awe at the surrounding vibrant, lively and dangerous mountains. Not realizing how many more times we would return to this treacherous and picturesque pass.

War and Evacuation

The conflict between Pakistan and India was over the province of Kashmir. Pakistan tried to seize the Northern part of Kashmir, in April 1965. Fighting broke out in Ramu and Kachchh, along West Pakistan and the Indian border. It spread to the Kashmir and Punjab regions. By September, Pakistani and Indian troops crossed the partition lines and started assaults on each other's cities.

The history of the conflict began during partition. Maharaja Hari Singh, a Sikh, was the reigning monarch of Kashmir in 1947. At the conclusion of the British rule they divided the subcontinent and partitioned the British Indian Empire into the newly independent Union of India and the Dominion of Pakistan.

Kashmir's population, in 1947, was 77 percent Muslim, hence, the people anticipated that the Maharaja would accede to Muslim Pakistan. The Maharaja chose India and the British decided to divide Kashmir between India and Pakistan. They have been in dispute ever since.

There we were in the middle of it with no way to leave. At night we watched as the Indian planes crossed the border, drop their bombs, and made a U turn over our building and returned to India. By the time the air raid sirens were activated, the Indian planes had already disappeared.

We were not afraid for our safety, since we knew that the Indians were bombing only the military installations and the airport. One day the company gave us small American flags because there was a rumor of Indian paratroopers dropping into the Lahore area. We were told to show the flags if we found ourselves confronted by them.

The Nobes lived on the third floor of our apartment building. We'd visit them at night to watch the artillery flashes and calculate the time the sound traveled to us. The first flash from the shelling compared to the length of time of the first sound of the explosion indicated the proximity of the bombardment. When the shelling started getting close, we knew it was time to run down to the basement.

During the day the men went to work while the rest of us stayed in the apartments.

Sundown was curfew time. We had to be careful not to allow

light to filter out of our windows. We drew the curtains tightly. We had to use candles. Even lighting a cigarette outside could be seen as an act of treason.

Shortly after the paratrooper scare, we received a message for a meeting of the company people. At the meeting, the company administrators informed us that the next day, all women and children will be taken to the airport. We will have one night with the family. No one knew where they were taking us. They said the American government kept the destination a secret.

We felt uneasy. The situation became unbearably tense. Some women protested loudly! "We will not leave our husbands!"

Those with children knew they had no choice but to leave. The school had closed and we were cooped-up inside of our homes. I was expecting our third child. But I was not afraid. Just concerned.

The Pakistan government would not allow the American men to leave the country, but they did make an agreement to allow for the evacuation of women and children. Pakistan and India agreed with the United States on a short truce, at which time American military planes were allowed to land at Lahore airport.

We were apprehensive because none of the men were allowed to come with us. "Start packing your suitcases, Sonia, Levon."

"Where are we going, Mom?" asked Sonia

"No one knows! ... Pack both summer and winter clothes. Coats will take too much space. Carry them!"

The next morning, we went to the airport where huge American military transport planes had landed. The airport runway had potholes from the bombing.

Our company people were ushered into one of these enormous planes, where we sat in cloth bucket seats. We had never been on a plane like this before: all of the interior insulation as on commercial passenger airlines had been stripped bare and we could see all the color-coded wires and levers moving in every direction. One of the crew members said, "This is how we transport soldiers." We were handed cotton to put in our ears to protect us from the noise. Levon, our ten year old son, was fascinated with the instruments, he was allowed to go to the cockpit and watch the pilot. I did not see him until it was time for the plane to land.

On the other hand, Sonia, our four and a half year old was miserable. She was scared and she wanted to sit on my lap. She wasn't the only one: many young children were clinging to their mothers.

I comforted her, but her weight on my lap during that crowded noisy flight left us both miserable. Others acted brave; they thought of it as a big adventure.

Once out of Pakistan's air-space, we were told: "Our destination will be either Turkey, or Iran!" We were very close to Tehran. The pilot announced that we will land in Tehran, Iran, this made most of us happy.

The moment we landed the American embassy personnel welcomed us. We had to go through "red tape" which included taking some kind of pills. Unfortunately, at this time being three months pregnant, I did not have the courage to speak up. I also took the pills, which, I think, resulted in my loosing my baby within the next two months.

We were taken to hotels. Our room was cheerful and it had a view of the swimming pool with greenery around it.

The children were enrolled into the American school. A bus picked them up from the hotel everyday. Sonia was too young to attend the American school, so I found a Montessori school and a separate bus transported her back and forth to it.

People in Tehran were very hospitable. After the initial shock, we got out of the hotel to investigate our surroundings. We found good restaurants and wonderful places to shop. We met Armenians, with whom we made friends.

So far, I had not seen a doctor. "I need to see a doctor." I informed our company leader. She directed me to the military hospital and made an appointment for me.

The doctor assured me, "Everything is normal."

On my second visit to the doctor, I told the nurse: "I'm not feeling well, my body is not functioning as it should be, I've never felt like this before. This is my fifth month, and the baby is not moving. Something is not right!"

"Ha! Ha! This is your third pregnancy. You should know how it feels."

"I know how it feels. Please tell the doctor to come and check."

"The doctor is busy!"

"I'll wait."

"No! You can't wait... I told you she is busy!"

After sitting for some time, I realized she did not tell the doctor, when I went to find her, or the doctor, they were nowhere to be found. I decided that I will tell the doctor on my next visit.

Living in a hotel was difficult for children who needed space to play, some were getting very rowdy. One day a young boy was misbehaving, and our son Levon stood on the side and watched. One of the waiters wanted to quiet the boy and started chasing him. He had a bucket and a dirty mop in his hand. When the waiter could not reach this rowdy youngster he saw Levon standing on the side, he attacked him with the dirty mop and wiped his face with it, he was covered with grime. When I saw this, I was enraged.

"Stop! Stop! "

"Madam, he was misbehaving."

"No! I was watching. He was standing and watching, the other boy was misbehaving!" I continued screaming.

"**How dare you brush his face with this dirty mop!**"

"I didn't mean to hurt him."

"**He'll get sick from it**." I continued "You could not catch the other boy, so you took it out on Levon! **Don't ever touch my children or go near them again!**" I screamed.

After shrieking at the waiter I gave Levon a bath, went to the Hotel management and complained but to no avail. The waiter was not punished or reprimanded. I was extremely upset and angry. I ordered the waiter not to serve meals to my children.

"Never go near them." I told him again.

This created stress and anxiety. That same night, I started hemorrhaging.

One of the Harza engineering wives was a nurse; she was staying in the same hotel. I called her and told her what was happening. Immediately, we got a car and went to the hospital.

The doctor checked, "You better stay in bed and not move at all."

For two weeks I was sick and, after two weeks, I rushed again to the hospital. It was at this time that I lost the baby. I was depressed, angry, and miserable.

The whole group was upset and my children were disappointed, especially Levon. He wanted badly to have a brother.

At the hotel I had to stay in bed with the hotel management and the waiter tried to do everything to please me. I refused to have the waiter serve me or my children; I told him "If you come near my children I'll call the police."

One day he tried to bring my lunch order into my room, when I saw him I blew my top, I was furious and screamed "**Get out of**

my room! And don't you dare go near my children!"

About this time, the political situation was changing. Foreign nations intervened. Prime Minister Shri Lal Bahadur Shastri, of India, and President Ayub Khan, of Pakistan, met in Tashkent. In January 1966, they signed an agreement pledging continued negotiations and respect for the cease-fire conditions.

Back to Chicago

Because of the shortage of Pakistani currency, the Water and Power Department (WAPDA) and Harza Engineering Company, decided to send the consultants back to Chicago and work from there.

We received a letter from Ben:

Dear Vicky, Levon and Sonia,

The company needs me in Chicago. I will leave Lahore in one week. I need to sell or give away almost everything including our books, household furnishings, kitchen appliances and cloths.

Vicky, I am very sad about losing our baby, please take good care of yourself. Be strong. Sonia, Levon -take care of your mom. I will be there in about one week, and we will travel and make stops on our way to Chicago.

Love
Ben

On December 17, 1965, Ben, after three months apart, joined us in Tehran. It was a bitter-sweet reunion. Each of us were unhappy about my losing our baby. Poor Ben, all three of us tried to hug him at once, he didn't know where to turn.

We went to lunch at the American club where we were joined by other Harza colleagues. Ben had carried letters for a few of them.

At the hotel, we put the children to bed and joined our friends John and Pam Priest for a drink. After which, just the two of us went and had dinner at The Rainbow Cave.

Early the next morning, Ben went to the PAN AM office to buy our tickets. They were rude and gave us all sorts of difficulties. He had to go a few more times to their office to arrange our trip. We decided to go home via the enticing Far East.

In order to travel light, we packaged the clothes that we did not need, and sent them to the United States through A.P.O. (American Post Office Box) via the American Embassy.

The next day, Mr Farman Farmaian, Ben's college classmate and friend, arranged a guide to take us to Karaj Dam. Ben wanted to see the illumination of the Dam and the powerhouse he helped design. It was spectacular. A few months later, we heard Levon tell his friends, proudly, "I walked on the dam that my father built!"

We wanted to leave Tehran as soon as possible. But to make matters worse, we needed to renew my visa and get entry visas for Japan. After a lot of running around and frustration, Ben was able to retrieve the visas and pick up our airline tickets.

On December 20, we left Tehran. On our way to Cairo, we stopped in Beirut for three hours. We called a few friends and made appointments to meet them at the airport on our way back from Cairo.

The view from our room at Shepherds Hotel in Cairo was gorgeous. There was a river next to the hotel and beautiful manicured gardens surrounded it.

In the morning, we went to the pyramids. Levon was excited. He was very young the first time we visited them. Once we were there we found out that tourists were being allowed to go inside. They had removed one of the huge square slabs and made an opening for people to go in. We climbed, bent over, on wooden planks with tiny step-like sections on them. It was exhausting! The air in the shaft was warm and thick, but we were determined to reach the top. Fortunately, the burial chamber had a high ceiling and we could stand up straight. About ten people could stand in that room. The only opening was the door we came in. We saw a small vent on the side. The guide explained that this was for the spirit of the Pharaoh to travel in and out.

Our guide led us to the Sphinx and later to the newly excavated temples. In the afternoon we visited the Cairo Tower. The view was spectacular! We could see all of Cairo from the top. As it got darker we started hearing music and suddenly a burst of fireworks came up. What a marvelous sight! We were as high as the fireworks, we had never seen them so closely. Local people told us that they are celebrating Port Said day- an important port, located on the North of the Suez Canal.

On December 22 we flew from Cairo to Al-Arish with a stop at Port Said. At Al-Arish we took a taxi and reached Ben's parent's house in Gaza at 4:30 pm. At the house no one was waiting for us. *We wondered why?* We kept on knocking on the door. Finally Ben's mother came to the door. The moment she saw us she screamed! She rushed and started hugging everyone. We were afraid she would faint. She said, "You are early, we were expecting you on the 27th." They had not read the letter properly. Everyone was talking at the same time. Ben's father, his brother, Koko, Shakeh his wife and the two children. Everyone was emotional. There was plenty of hugging and crying.

The next morning we spent our day washing all the dirty clothes that we had accumulated throughout our journey. I don't know how the word got around, by afternoon we had non-stop visitors to welcome us. Ben and Koko, his brother, went with our passports to verify our return flights. Again problems! The airlines had reserved spaces from Cairo on, but not from Gaza to Cairo. The plane was full! This meant, again, that we would be busy with the airline's mistake instead of enjoying our stay with the family.

We were inundated with visitors. Many of Ben's childhood friends, classmates and their families came to see us.

On December 24th we decorated the Christmas tree. In the evening Santa came (Levon our 10 year old son) with a bagful of presents and candy. Both, five year olds, Levon Jr. and Sonia were excited. Levon Jr. did not move from his place, his whole attention was on Santa. Whereas Sonia was jumping up and down saying, "I was a good girl! I was a good girl!" Little one and a half year old Silva was screaming for the candy.

We distributed presents to each of the family and filled the children's bags with toys and candy.

On Christmas day Ben's mother, cooking like a hurricane, made all the food that Ben liked. I helped a little but she shooed me out of the kitchen.

It is our tradition that on Christmas day, after church, men visit friends and family. Women stay home and receive visitors, offering coffee and candy. Ben, Koko, and I went and visited old friends. Haig Bardakjian's mother was thrilled to see us. We had seen Haig in Pakistan so we gave the good news that he was well and working hard. Dr. Wahid-and his wife, also were pleased to see us. They were our first neighbors in Jerusalem. We had not seen them for a long time. On our return we were surprised to see a houseful of visitors.

The day after Christmas we went to the beach. The children had a great time making sand castles and running after crabs. In the afternoon Haig's brother took us around Gaza. It was tragic to see the Palestinian refugee camps and the few Arab soldiers protecting them. They lived in tin houses built haphazardly next to each other. Dirt roads surrounded them, children were playing in front of their houses. One of the families knew my mother-in-law. When she saw us, she greeted us with hugs and insisted that we go in and have coffee. The room was well arranged and clean. I found out that in order to make a living the women embroidered colorful designs on black cotton cloth and sold them to the visitors. We came close to the UN line between Gaza, Palestine and Israel and visited the newly planted orange groves.

Gaza had only eight Armenian families. Because of the Arab - Jewish war, they were isolated from the Armenian church for nine years. Up until now, the priests were unable to visit. But during this Christmas a group of Armenians came from the Jerusalem convent with a priest. There was jubilation in the air. All eight families went to church. An eight year old girl was baptized and all the families gathered at her parent's house with the visitors and the priest. Celebrating until the wee hours of the morning.

Unfortunately, the next day was our departure day. But, still no tickets! Finally, about ten at night, we received the news that the tickets were approved.

Our departure from Gaza was highly emotional. Hugs and crying was abundant. At the airport, Ben remembered that he left his coat at home. Koko promised that he would send it with someone. Sure enough, the next day, a man with Ben's coat came to our hotel in Cairo, right before we left to the airport. What joy! But our joy didn't last long. They stopped us at the airport. At passport control, it was revealed that while leaving Gaza, the officer at Al-Arish had forgotten to stamp Ben's passport. So Ben had to go from one office to another to explain the situation. The airport people were nice. They held the plane for ten minutes. Some employees were amazed how they let Ben go.

When the plane landed in Beirut we were met by our relatives the Najarians. We were greatly surprised to see Ben's colleague from the American university, Suleiman Deeb. He had come from England for Christmas vacation. We were not allowed to leave the transit area but we were able to converse through a barrier.

Our stay in Beirut was short, but we were happy to see our relatives and friends. We continued our flight and arrived in Tehran. Ben had to go and arrange our seating. We had first class tickets from Tehran to New Delhi, India. But again problems. The children and I sat in first class. Ben sat in the tourist class, because there was no space in the first class compartment. I could not imagine how these airlines could make such mistakes. Almost at every stop we confronted some problem.

Our next problem came when Pakistan did not allow PAN AM flights to cross their air space. So instead of four hours it took five and a half hours to fly from Tehran to New Delhi, In New Delhi, finally Ben came and joined us in the first class compartment. We had a comfortable journey. arriving in our final destination, Bangkok on Dec. 29th.

Bangkok

After resting a little at Hotel Oriental, we rushed out and took a tour of the city. Beautiful modern buildings, shopping centers and venders along the canals. We visited the Marble temple, where we saw Buddha in different positions made of bronze. Most of the temples had gold leaf on their walls and roofs. We were amazed seeing the twenty five ton reclining Buddha covered with a layer of gold leaf.

The highlight of our tour was visiting the golden Buddha, made of solid gold. The temple was small and the Buddha had many flower garlands around its neck. It was out of this world! Stunning! The temple was shining but once outside the temple, debris covered the surrounding area.

Near by there was a laughing Buddha, when Levon asked if someone will be angry if he rubbed the tummy of the Buddha?

"No, you are supposed to make a wish and rub his tummy. It brings good luck." Ben explained.

We noticed that every building had a tiny house next to it.

"Why does each house have a tiny pagoda-shaped mailbox by their yard?" asked Levon surprised.

"Are they for letters?" asked Sonia,

The guide explained that the Buddhists respect their elders and believe that the spirits of their ancestors live in these small houses and protect them from danger. "Everyday each family gives an offering of fruits, and flowers. They also light a candle for the soul of their ancestors."

Next morning, we went on a four hour tour by boat to see the floating market. Endless canals wind through the city and as we went from one to the other, we saw shops and houses built on stilts. Also the canals were full of sampans where mostly women did the rowing, selling and buying. The people who live there, bathe, wash their cloths, and swim right at their own doorsteps. Children were everywhere splashing around in the water.

Merchants had boats painted with their individual colorful logos. Each had a gong, a bell, a drum or a rattle that announced the type of wares they were selling as they approached.

"Look! Each monk has a bowl in his hand. Are they begging for food?" Asked Levon.

"No! It's tradition, the Buddha begged for his food." Said the guide, "It represents his begging. Feeding monks is a Buddhist tradition. Our people donate food and receive the blessings of the monks."

On our way we stopped at the Temple of Dawn. Climbing up those steep steps was tiring, I could see all of Bangkok from that height. Ben and the children climbed further up to the top.

On continuing our tour we reached the Royal Barge. What a spectacular view! It was Immense, beautiful, and colorful. Red and gold were the dominant colors. On the barge we met an American lady and two Spanish ladies who gave us some names and addresses to go to in Hong Kong, which was our next destination.

The afternoon tour took us to the Grand Palace. It reminded us of the musical "The King and I".

"Ben. Is this real or are we in a fairyland?'

The guide heard me and answered "This is real! This is where the king lived."

The palace and surrounding buildings dazzled in their red and golden colors. Bells were on the eaves of the temples and on some of the buildings; people believe that the ringing of the bells drives away the evil spirits. Hearing these tiny bells ring, ever so gently by the breeze mesmerized us. The whole visit felt like a beautiful dream. Surrealistic! There were people going around and preparing for the next days celebration for the visit of dignitaries.

We walked to the temple where the Emerald Buddha was kept. The temple was surrounded with all kinds of smaller temples, pagodas and statues.

"The Buddha is made of emerald. Every season the king dresses him with different clothes" explained our guide. We boarded a small van and continued to sightsee.

Suddenly, Levon screamed!

"Stop the car! Stop the car! Look at that elephant! It's carrying

Elephant loading a truck in Bangkok.

a log," Levon was fascinated! "Look! It's loading the truck." We stopped the car to watch the elephant load those heavy logs.

We got out of the car and walked down a path and came to an opening. Both Levon and Sonia signaled "Hurry! Come!" They had seen the elephants coming to this open space. We ran just in time and saw each elephant walking by, holding the tail of the elephant in front of it with its trunk: the last one to Sonia's delight was a tiny baby elephant. The elephants started dancing and doing all kinds of tricks. A small crowd of people had gathered and we all watched in amazement.

In between sightseeing, I went wild with shopping for all kinds of items made with batik and silk.

Bangkok is well known for its Arboretum. Since our time was short, we did not think it worth going there. I must say that we were wrong. I am glad that our guide persuaded us to go. It was the best thing that we did!

"I never realized that pepper came from such huge trees, like these," said Levon

"Neither did I." said Ben.

There were many unusual trees with exotic names.

"Look at those beautiful orchids" I said

"There are more than fifty varieties of orchids!" The guide told us. "Many grow wild."

I couldn't believe my eyes. So many! So unusual! So exotic!

That same night our guide took us to a Thai restaurant with entertainment. We sat on colorful mats, in front of low tables with gold

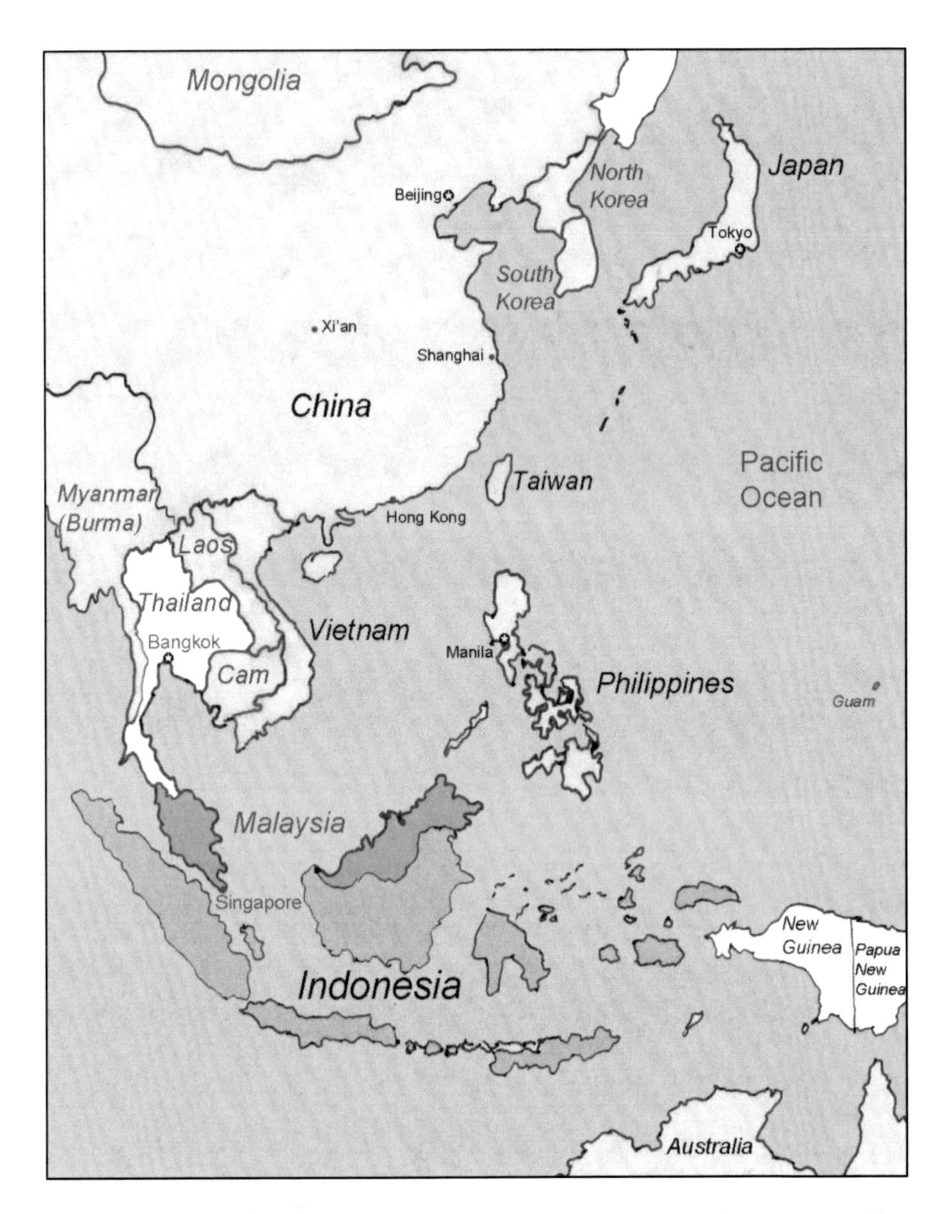

color tablecloths. The waiters gave us red pillows to lean on and be comfortable. The napkins were folded in a lotus flower shape. The show consisted of Thai dancers accompanied by a band with traditional instruments.

"I want to shape my napkin like your lotus flower." said Sonia

The waitress heard her "I'll show you how to fold the napkins."

Sonia was thrilled. With the help of the waitress, she folded the napkins and admired her handiwork.

"Why do we have so many small plates of food? asked Levon.

"Each has a differently spiced food, Take a little of each onto your plate, and mix them."

At first it felt strange, but, after mixing and tasting it, we really liked the results.

"M-m-m-m. It's good." We all agreed

We watched, spellbound at the floor show of girls dancing in traditional Thai costumes with long artificial nails and graceful hand movements. One of the acts was a sword dance by men dressed in warrior costumes. To protect the audience, a wire barrier was set-up on the stage. Levon tried to go as close as possible.

"Levon! Don't go so close to the stage" Ben said in Armenian.

"I want to see"

"Come here!"

At that moment, I noticed that someone, sitting at a distance, looked to be an American soldier in uniform.

"Look. The young man sitting across from us looks familiar, maybe he's Armenian." I said.

"He could be Italian," Ben replied.

Levon, fascinated was inching his way towards the stage.

"Levon! Didn't we tell you not to go by the stage?" I said in an angry tone.

At the end of the show, this same young man came to us and in perfect Armenian introduced himself.

We could not believe our ears. What a surprise! He was Ben's cousin, Azad Husnian. The young man was in the American army, and had taken time out for an R and R (rest-and-recreation) from service in Viet Nam. He was now visiting Thailand.

A few years ago he stayed a couple of days with us, in our Villa Park home. "You were younger then... and not in a military uniform." Ben said.

"No wonder we didn't recognize you," I exclaimed.

He agreed. "I didn't recognize you, either... not at first, until we started talking."

What a small world! We hugged. Then we reminisced about old times and shared our own experiences with him until closing time.

The next morning December 31, we were awakened by a call from PAN AM letting us know that the flight to Hong Kong was delayed until one o'clock in the afternoon. This gave us enough time to indulge in a leisurely breakfast before hiring a car to go to the airport. Everything went well until the driver decided to take a short cut and drive through town. We ended up in the middle of a traffic jam. What a mess! It took us one hour to go to the other end of the city center. To top it all the taxi suddenly broke down. We had no choice but find another taxi. We were sure we would miss the plane. By the time we arrived to the airport we only had twenty minutes before take off. What a mad rush! Check baggage, verify passport, and run toward the gate. We finally made it! Once on the plane, Ben ordered a martini, and all of us had lunch fit for a president.

Hong Kong

It was hard to leave Bangkok, but we were looking forward to our next stop of Hong Kong: another exotic city. We arrived on New Year's Eve. The hotel was having a New Year's Eve party. We put the children to bed and went down where they were celebrating the New Year. "We want to join the party" we told the management.

"Sorry. It's sold out."

"But we just arrived." I said disappointed.

"Wait here. Let me see what we can do." His words lifted our spirits immediately.

After fifteen minutes the manager came back, he said "Come in, since you're staying here we have arranged a table just for you."

To our surprise, they put us at a small two person table, in the front, as though we were dignitaries. Soon, we received all kinds of presents, including a bottle of champagne. Many curious eyes were directed toward us, no doubt wondering who we were and what country we represented. After dancing and having a good time, we left with the bottle of champagne.

"Now. What will we do with a huge bottle of champagne when we're traveling?" Ben found the idea amusing.

"Oh! I know! My Birthday's on the second of January. Why not celebrate with dinner and the bottle of champagne?" I said excitedly.

Ben bought a beautiful pearl ring for me and we celebrated my birthday with a sumptuous dinner with plenty of champagne.

Hong Kong celebrates the New Year for six continuous days-and-nights. All the shops close for the Holidays. That disappointed us. But, fortunately we enjoyed sightseeing. We took the 'little train' to China's border. There, we conversed with the Chinese people.

They wore hats that resembled a flamingo dancer's with pompoms hanging from them. They wore them while they worked in the fields.

We saw them shouting messages back-and-forth with the people on the other side of the border fence.

Field workers with tools were crossing the border.

We asked, "Where are they going?'

We were told, "They work on the 'no man's' land." The strip of land between the two borders.

During our return trip we were surprised to see an American on the train coming from China. How can that be? We wondered. *An American coming from Communist China?*

At that time, the United States had no diplomatic relations with China. Our ten year old son Levon, seeing an American, rushed over to him to strike up a conversation.

"Are you an American?" asked Levon

"Yes. I am .... What's your name?"

"My name is Levon, I'm an American too... Where are you coming from?"

"Beijing, Levon."

"Where's Beijing?"

"In China."

"Why did you go to China?"

"To bring mail. I'm with the American diplomatic mission."

"What's that?" Levon asked surprised, he had never heard of the American Diplomatic Mission before.

"I work with the American Government."

Our hotel was in Kawloon, on the mainland. In order to go to Hong Kong Island, we took the ferry, which Levon and Sonia loved. Crossing took eight minutes. The bundle-carrying passengers looked as impatient as New Yorkers at rush-hour. As we looked across the water, we saw that we were surrounded by an assortment of boats. There were little ships, freighters, junks with reddish sails, ocean liners, tubs pieced-together from rusty scrap iron, sampans of all shapes and sizes: all traversing the water way. As we approached the island we saw the sprawl of houses and hotels.

We followed the holiday crowd, and we found ourselves in a *dim sum* restaurant.

The food was served in round bamboo baskets with lids. Waitress's with trays that hung around their neck would call out and sell the baskets, like cigarette girls used to sell in the United States.

We stood at the door confused-obviously looking very foreign.

A waiter led us to a table. Girls passed by announcing, in Chinese, the contents of each basket. The local people selected by yelling out to the girls what they wanted and the girls responded by yelling out what they were offering. The noise was deafening, and we had no inkling as to what they were saying.

"Levon. Pick one please." I said.

"Vicky," Ben requested, "I want one from that girl's basket."

We kept picking baskets. We enjoyed every bite. Upon leaving the restaurant, I asked Ben, "Did you notice the shape of the meat? It didn't look like chicken or even taste like chicken. ...Didn't it taste more like fish?"

"Yes." Ben replied thoughtfully. "It was round... more like eel."

None of us knew what we had just eaten.

We decided to take a bus to visit the other side of Hong Kong Island. Houses and gardens leaned perilously on both sides of the hillside. The frangipani, the flowerpots, and the clusters of honeysuckle wafted a delicious fragrance. Dense jungle growth overflowed the steep gullies, carved into the hillside. The view was breath-taking from the peak. A beautiful church, with its high steeple, gave the impression that this must surely be the center of the island. Across the harbor, the Dragon Hills seemed to rise above other ranges, beautiful blue, gray and gold colored highlights, contrasted against pink and magenta shadows, all surrounded by the peacock blue and gold sea.

On the other side of the island, we saw a market where all kinds of snakes were being sold.

"Look! Just look at those snakes... You know, the meat we just ate looked exactly like those snakes." I announced worrisome..

"Oh No!" Levon spoke up. "What we ate must have been snake meat... but it was delicious."

"None of us are sick." I said with a relieved voice., "Not so far anyway, it must have been ok."

One of the highlights of our stay in Hong Kong was having a meal at a floating restaurant. We had to take a small boat to get there. In the restaurant they had a huge tank where fish swam. Both Levon and Sonia watched the fish with fascination. We chose the fish we wanted; the restaurant people caught it for us and cooked it. Levon had difficulty eating his fish, because he knew the fish in front of him had been happily swimming just a while ago.

I had been admiring the Chinese brocade material. I wanted to have a dress made from it before we left Hong Kong. Ben insisted that I have the dress made. I couldn't believe, the dressmaker brought it to the hotel completely finished one day after I ordered it. We also bought a tape recorder and a transistor radio.

At the hotel we found out our flight was delayed.

Japan

In exotic Tokyo, our first stop, sightseeing took us to the snow covered Mt. Fuji. Sonia did not remember the snow in Chicago, she was very young when we left and was a little nervous. The rest of us were excited, we had lived in a warm climate and had not seen snow, for a long time.

"How Majestic!" I said, I was overwhelmed.

"Look, Mom! Dad! Sonia! Come. Let's play in the snow," said Levon, jumping up and down all the while.

Gingerly, Sonia took one step from the bus and stopped.

"I can't move! I'm stuck!" Sonia had stepped in a bank of snow.

"No you're not! Come on! Give me your hand. ... follow me," Levon wanted Sonia to enjoy her first contact with snow.

"HELP! I'M STUCK!" She shrieked dramatically. Sonia took another step, cautiously

"Good! Take another!" Levon coaxed her again. He was determined to help her enjoy the experience.

"Come on, Sonia. Don't be a 'scaredy cat'." Levon had gathered snow to make her a snow ball. "Here! Throw this snowball!"

After throwing it – her first snowball- Sonia felt more at ease and continued to play in the snow.

Levon started pelting Sonia with snowballs and, before we knew it, she made her own to throw back, laughing at the same time.

She overcame her fear and started enjoying the snow.

. People climbed toward the heavy mist coming from the snow covered mountain. The crispness of the air, and the magnificent beauty of Mount Fuji- silhouetted against the cerulean blue sky- gave me a sense of freedom and happiness.

We found a vacant summer recreation area, a mile away from Mt. Fuji, empty sailboats were lined up like soldiers on the lake, it evoked the feeling of a ghost-town, but had a very Japanese quality. The culture fascinated us-their simple life, their temples, their daily rituals and their ceremonies-evolved over thousands of years.

We gazed with profound respect at the imposing copper Buddha at Hakone. Levon and Sonia went inside the monument and climbed the steep stairway to the top of Buddha's head.

"Hi, mom! Dad! Look up. We're up here," they shouted. Proud of where they had gone. We were surprised. They had managed the climb to the top.

The next stop was the underground ammunition, and aircraft factory, that the Japanese built during the war. As we approached the entrance, I thought, we were entering a cave. We sat in open mining carts that were on railway tracks, which took us into a tunnel. We took a bone cracking sudden drop; much like a roller coaster would do. Upon going further into the deep, we saw an enormous room. Everything was underground; nothing could be seen from above.

The tour director explained: "This was where the workers assembled the ammunition and, with the help of carts like the one we're sitting in, transported the completed ammunition to airplanes."

I imagined thousands of people at work. Remembered Pearl Harbor being attacked with these same bombs and those same bullets that had been manufactured in this cave- and all underground!

We continued sightseeing, we boarded bullet trains- which we had never ridden before. At first, we were nervous. The train moved so fast that we could hardly see the view outside. The other passengers just relaxed. They seemed to be enjoying the ride. But not us, we were on the edge of our chairs. After a few minutes, we accustomed ourselves to the speed of the train and relaxed. It was an education.

At the Mikimoto pearl factory, we viewed the demonstration on how pearls were developed; and the guide told us:

"First, you open the shell of a live oyster; then insert a tiny round pearl and then close the shell. The oyster then tries to protect itself by covering the inserted object with layers of membrane, when hardened, creates a beautiful perfectly- round cultured pearl."

Levon, curious as ever, asked "What if you put a tiny flat or tiny square object in the oyster?"

"The shape of the pearl will take the shape of the object." the guide replied.

The high-rise stores were crowded with holiday shoppers and all the shops were decorated with colorful festive designs.

We visited the palace, Akazaki and the Olympic building, huge, modern and beautiful. This was where they had ice skating. The Japanese were also proud of their newly built highways.

Altars were built in designated sites, where incense spewed from caldrons. As people passed they purified themselves by drawing the fumes with their hands towards their faces.

While visiting some private homes, we admired the simple furnishings. Their homes and gardens are decorated according to nature. Each rock and tree in their garden represented something.

I remarked thoughtfully, "I don't know if I could live like this myself, it's too spartan for my taste."

"I could," came Sonia's little voice "I could run around without banging into tables or chairs."

We were not the only ones who laughed at her remarks; other visitors had heard her and joined in the laughter.

Ben and I were captivated by the nightlife, especially our visit to the Geisha House, where we listened to Japanese songs and watched their dances. Food and sake (an alcoholic rice wine) was plentiful. Coming from Pakistan, a culture where alcohol is prohibited, and having experienced the dangers of war, it was refreshing to see the lights, and the gaiety of Tokyo. People strolled along the streets! Shops were filled with all kinds of exotic items. Above many doorways hung lanterns of paper and bamboo: red, green, orange in color, with shapes like gourds, melons and pumpkins.

We realized how much we missed our home, the concerts, its theatre and other cultural diversions.

On our last day the hotel management invited us to a spectacular lunch. The staff set a table in the middle of the dining room with over fifty kinds of dishes. I had never seen such an attractive display of fish- some raw, others fried, boiled, or stuffed. Some plates were attractively embellished with fish, other plates had a large fish surrounded with small fish.We gorged on the gourmet delicious food. We had never eaten raw fish, so we did not even try them.

Our stay in Japan went so fast, that we wished we had more time to spend there.

Hawaii

We were having such a good time in Tokyo that we did not want to leave. We also were looking forward to our next stop, which was

Hawaii. We boarded the plane in Tokyo on Thursday January six, at 9:30 in the evening. We reached Honolulu on the same day at 9:30 in the morning!

Sonia learned and recognized all the airline logos, she liked to name them .

We don't know why but all the time she was thinking about Honolulu. She was unable to say Honolulu so she kept on asking, "Are we in Ho-lo-lu-lu?" We laughed at the cute way she pronounced it.

"Not yet." We told her.

Every time we landed in a country, she would ask, and received a negative answer each time. When we arrived in Honolulu, Sonia did not ask. We wondered why.

"Sonia. This is Honolulu"

"Are we really in Ho-lo-lu-lu?"

"Yes, Honolulu"

"O! Boy! She started jumping up and down like a little puppy.

We were greeted with open arms. Everyone said "Welcome Home"

Although this was not home, we were in the United States. It was home. It was emotional, as everyone was greeting and welcoming us, tears came to my eyes. We rejoiced but were very tired. We slept almost all the next day.

We were pleased that Pan Am had reserved a two room apartment hotel for us with a living room, dining room and kitchen. After a long journey, it felt like coming home, cozy and wonderful. We enjoyed walking by the beach and visiting the international market.

I got in touch with the family of my former student, John Studebaker. We had dinner at their house and reminisced about old times in Pakistan. John had grown and had become a handsome young man. We met his charming grandparents. Levon was having so much fun that he did not want to leave the house.

We also met up with the Minekiems with whom we were evacuated from Pakistan to Iran. She was the nurse who helped me during the time when I lost our baby. She was godsent at that time, I don't know what I would have done without her. We spent the whole day together. They were leaving for the mainland the next day.

We rented a car and explored the island, visited a pineapple plantation and tasted the delicious pineapple. We lost our way inside a sugar cane plantation. The plants were high, we were going in circles, every corner looked the same with high canes. No one was around nor any signs on the road. We knew we were lost and finally after some traumatic circling we found our way out. What a relief!

Waikiki did not have the high rises that we see today. Largely one or two story buildings, with wide open spaces, beautiful beaches, and very friendly people.

We always seemed to have some problem at the airport. This time it was our fault. We were too relaxed and we woke up late. After dropping us at the airport Ben had to return the rented car. We ran the long hallways toward the gate. I asked the captain to wait just a little for my husband. He gave a quizzical glance and started looking toward the hallway. Sure enough within five minutes Ben was running toward the gate. I will never forget when the captain turned around and in a funny and relieved way asked me "Is this your husband?" With a sigh of relief I said "Yes". I saw the relaxed expression on the stewardesses faces.

Our flight to San Francisco was unnerving, too many air pockets. The plane was constantly shaking. Finally after landing we relaxed. We searched our itinerary for the name of the hotel we had reserved but couldn't find it. The person in Lahore had forgotten to include it. What a dilemma! Confused, angry, tired. Now what do we do?! Right at that moment we saw my cousin Paul waving at us. What a miracle! He insisted that we stay with him and his mother, my father's aunt. This worked out very well. Paul's two story house was cozy and comfortable. Paul's mother was concerned that the children will act wild and disturb the furniture. We instructed them to be careful with the furniture and behave. Fortunately, neither one of the children misbehaved.

Ben had an interview. So Ben and Paul left the house early. Paul's brother Sarkis came in the afternoon and gave us a tour of the city. Both Levon and Sonia ran around at the Golden Gate park. I enjoyed viewing the interesting art at Le Young museum. On the way home cousin Sarkis dropped me at the hairdressers. She was a very sweet lady, but she styled my hair in such a way that I looked like an old lady! It was horrible! Sarkis felt bad that he took me to this hairdresser.

That evening, Araxi Soghomonian, an old friend we knew from Jordan, and her husband came to visit us. It was a treat for I had not seen her for a long time. We hugged and hugged and started talking at the same time. After they left, we went to the Omar

Khayam, the famous restaurant, to meet Mr. Mardigian, the owner, a good friend of my sister's family. He was entertaining an Egyptian journalist. He and his wife came and sat with us for a short time. As the custom was we "broke bread" together. Dinner was out of this world. We also met a friend, Mr Djanigian there. The night was young and we were too excited to settle down, so after dinner, Paul gave us a tour of a few nightclubs. We ended up at a Mexican night club with a homey and cozy atmosphere. We had a great time.

Upon our arrival, January thirteenth, we had called Ben's colleague from the America University of Beirut, Mr Abboud, informing him that we were in San Francisco and wanted to see him. He invited us but we never realized that he and his family lived in San Jose, which is about forty miles from San Francisco. Fortunately, Paul gave us his car, so we drove.

It was a lovely ride.

They had a large house with a well groomed yard. We reminisced about the good old days. They felt that the school their three children were attending had a higher standard than the schools in San Francisco.

We were having such a good time that the kids did not want to leave. Unfortunately, we had to say goodbye to our friends by three thirty in order to make it to Ben's next appointment for his company.

In the evening we went to Araxi's house for dinner. The road was precipitous and had many sharp turns, we were glad that Paul was driving. The house was on a steep hill, half of it built on stilts. The view was spectacular! We could see almost all of San Francisco. She had a sun room filled with gorgeous plants. I wondered, *what would she do if a strong earthquake hit the area.*

She must have slaved all day long for the table was filled with all kinds of Armenian sumptuous dishes.

The next day, Sarkis, Paul's brother took us to the Golden Gate bridge. Driving on it was exciting. We were mesmerized! Both children wanted to stay longer at a sightseeing location and watch the cars go by.

We stopped for lunch at a quaint restaurant in Sausalito, an artists colony, which is near the Golden Gate bridge.

On the morning of January fourteen- while Ben interviewed an engineer for Harza- I packed our suitcases for the next day departure from San Francisco. As soon as Paul and Ben came we went to our friend Azadouhi Janigian's house for lunch. Her sister, Araxi, who we had dinner with the night before, met us there. Azadouhi, also had prepared almost every Armenian food you can imagine. We ate nonstop.

At three thirty we decided to go downtown and bought a silver tea set for Paul. It was funny, as soon as we placed it on the table. Paul's mother wrapped each piece in plastic and displayed them in their cabinet.

That evening Paul took us to Bagdad, a topless nightclub, which had belly dancing and arabic folk music as a theme.

After nightclubbing it was hard to get up early. The kids were excited because in Los Angeles we were going to see my niece, their cousin, Arda. She married Luther Derian (who is related from my father's side) while we were in Pakistan.

When we landed in Los Angeles, we were surprised to see our friends the Hajians, (Hadjian was a former student of Ben, at the Engineering school of America University of Beirut) Ben's sister, Araxi, and my niece, Arda, and cousin Luther welcoming us at the airport. We found out later that my sister Mary had called all our friends and relatives about our arrival to Los Angeles.

My niece's house was too small to accommodate all four of us, so Luther had arranged for the children to stay with his brother Harry. His two children are about the same age as Levon. (I had not seen cousin Harry since he left Jerusalem. He was a dashing young man and a great artist, a sculptor.)

In Los Angeles, we were wined and dined by our friends and relatives; we visited Knotts Berry farm, walked down Hollywood Boulevard and visited the stars of famous actors. We were sad that Disneyland was closed.

California is beautiful, and inviting. But we missed our home in Chicago.

We did not know what awaited us! We were supposed to be in Pakistan for two years, the war between India and Pakistan cut short our stay. Before leaving Chicago, we rented our house to a family for two years and could not break the lease. Reality continued to sink in- school, home, and the uncertainty of direction became a worry.

My sister Mary was at the airport to greet us when we landed in Chicago. We stayed with her for a week. We looked for a house- or an apartment- to rent, and we found a quaint summer house in the back of a huge mansion in Barrington, next to the children's school, built in the early 1900s, with wood panels (inside and out) and surrounded with apple trees.

"Mom! Look at that red barn... Sonia. Let's go investigate!" hollered Levon

All the children had to do was to jump the shrub-fence to be on the school grounds. The view from the large window of the house was enchanting! In winter, icicles hung from the tree branches of the apple trees. In the spring, a view of white apple blossoms was enjoyable.

Ben continued his work with the Harza Engineering Company in Chicago. Levon started fifth grade. And Sonia began Kindergarten.

Levon came home excited. "Mom! Dad! The principle talked about me on the intercom! He said Levon lived in Pakistan. He has interesting stories to tell everyone at the school assembly"

"Fantastic!" clapped my hands with delight and I smiled at Levon to encourage him to continue his story.

"I need to take some things to class that I brought with me from Pakistan!"

"Sure, Levon, I'll help you," I volunteered to help gather them.

"We're proud of you, son," Ben exclaimed.

Levon became the center of attention by showing his souvenirs, and telling the exciting stories of living in Pakistan and of his travels in the Far East.

Sonia, on the other hand, was unhappy. She began to find excuses not to go to school. I went to see her teacher. I learned that Sonia had advanced far beyond her classmates, the other children were only beginning to learn the alphabet, while she was able to read and write.

"Sonia has been overseas in schools where they teach children to read and write at an early age." I explained.

"Sonia knows more than the other children of her age. She shouldn't have been taught so much so soon." The teacher said.

That comment flabbergasted me! From my perspective as a teacher, I tried to reason with her. I tried to explain why Sonia had learned so much at her young age, to no avail! This was the only school Sonia could go to in this small affluent town. I always encouraged Sonia in what she was doing. I stopped worrying when she did not want to attend school.

I was also having a depressing time. I mourned the loss of our baby. I regretted having to leave our household items behind. Although we had settled down, the past continued to haunt me.

I isolated myself. I slept longer hours. There were even times when I could not bring myself to prepare meals for the family.

After a short time, with the help of my loving husband and children, I came out of the depression. My sister Mary also tried to make things happy for us. She lived in the city of Tower Lakes, twenty minutes away from our house, in the middle of the woods, near the lakes.

Once a week, Mary and I visited a members only store. The store was called the 'Jewel' and, indeed, it was a jewel!

Her husband, Hovig (a chemist) worked with a company that specialized in scientific research. The members of the company and their families were able to buy the tested and approved items at reduced prices, at the company store.

Both of us, avid shoppers, bought and bought items, such as clothing, small kitchen appliances, and anything else we could use, or give away as gifts.

It was fun living in Barrington, and being near my sister Mary. But we needed more space. We missed our own home in Villa Park. Finally, our tenants bought the house next door. We moved at the end of the school year to our own spacious house in Villa Park. We realized that we had missed living there. The children renewed their friendships with the neighborhood boys and girls.

We resumed our normal life. Ben took the train to work everyday. Levon loved school; he became the well known international traveler. Sonia bloomed in first grade; her teacher knew how to motivate her, Sonia's grades went up, and it was a joy to see her go to school with great anticipation.

Levon started taking violin lessons. Unfortunately, his friends called him a 'sissy for carrying the violin. He joined the school orchestra but it became a struggle. Some of the neighborhood boys started picking on him. He often came home bruised and with torn clothes. One of our neighbors had six children. Two of the older boys always challenged him, I heard him shout at them, "Wait and see. When my big cousin comes he'll beat you up!"

We enrolled Levon in judo classes which gave him self confidence. He wrestled with one of the older boys and brought him down; this stopped the older boys and other neighbors from picking on him.

Sonia joined the Art Linkletter dance group. She tap danced, took acrobatics, and ballet.

Living in Pakistan made me forget the hay fever allergy I had in Chicago.

"Ben, I feel funny. There is no mirror in this shop. Look at my face, and tell me what's wrong"

"Your face... and the whites of your eyes are swollen," he said in a concerned voice.

"Oh No! The hay fever is back!"

Hardly five minutes had gone by when I started sneezing. So I began taking a series of shots, once a month throughout the year and every five days, during the high season.

Once, while I was waiting for Sonia's ballet class to finish, the person-sitting next to me- looked at my face and became alarmed.

"Are you alright?"

"Yes. Why do you ask?"

"Turn around....Look in the mirror,"

I turned around; **I thought I was looking at someone else! This couldn't be me!** My face was swollen like a balloon; you could hardly see my eyes. I was shocked! Fortunately Ben was returning that evening from one of his Central American business trips, from Tegucigalpa, Honduras. Sonia and I picked-up Levon from his Judo class and went back home to wait for Ben.

Meantime, I called the doctor. The doctor was worried, "Come to the office immediately!"

Fifteen minutes later Ben arrived in a taxi.

The moment he entered the house, I told him "Get in the car! Let's go to the doctor right away."

He stared at me and asked, "What happened to you?"

"I don't really know... We have to go to the doctor's office... I don't dare go by myself like this. I know you're tired, but you have to come with me."

Levon was old enough to babysit his sister by now.

By the time we arrived at the doctor's office, I could hardly breathe. There, we found out that the nurse injected an overdose shot for my hay fever. Right away the doctor prescribed an antidote; I had to lie still until the swelling subsided. It was almost two hours later that I was able to stand up. All that time, poor Ben, with jet-lag, waited for me, half asleep, in the reception room.

When we moved back into our home, the Superintendent of

Schools of Elmhurst District must have heard that I was back in town and after a few days I received a call from him.

"Hi! Vicky. Welcome home. I've a fifth grade class at Elmhurst for you to teach. Come for orientation on Friday,"

"How did you know we were home?" I asked surprised, "I can't believe this....only half an hour ago they installed the telephone for the house."

"I heard you'd come back. I called Ben at his office and got the phone number from him."

I was amazed. This was the third time someone offered me a job without my applying for it. Of course I felt honored. I could not refuse, and we needed the extra income.

Ben continued his work with Harza Engineering Company while training Pakistani and Iranian engineers to do Electric Power System planning. He also traveled to South America to train their engineers.

Being from a musical family, Ben and I always attended concerts. One day we received the news that Aram Khachaturian, the famous Armenian composer, was coming to Chicago and will be giving a concert.The telephones were ringing off the hook. Within days tickets were sold-out. My sister and I took out our sheet-music of Khachaturian compositions and went to the concert with our families and friends. It was such a thrill to see him on stage conducting. I had to pinch myself to realize that it is not a dream. It was an outstanding and memorable concert. At the end he signed our music. We were in seventh heaven.

We went to pick our six month old car from the valet parking. After waiting for more than an hour, our car came with the right front bumper smashed in. We were terribly upset and started complaining. As we were arguing, composer Khachaturian and his companion came down to request their car. Of course at that moment we forgot everything and started conversing with him. He has a great sense of humor, he was making a joke when he noticed the condition of our car. He remarked "Oh no! You see what happens when you come to see me perform!" His transport came and they took off.

We both came down to the harsh reality of our situation. After more than an hour of arguing back and forth the attendant finally admitted that it was their fault. At the end we were elated and yet depressed.

In 1965, when Ben left Pakistan- to come to Chicago- the Pakistan authorities requested that he prepare a report to cover the electric power development of Pakistan for the next 20 years. In 1968, upon completing the report, he was sent back to Pakistan to explain it.

As he was about to leave, the WAPDA (Water and Power Division) authorities requested that he come back to Pakistan, again to continue the training of their Engineers.

Ben remembered how we had bragged about the wonderful times we had the first time we were in Lahore, he gladly accepted the offer.

When he came home, he said “We’re going back to Pakistan!”

‘Nooo!” was the reply from all three of us in unison. “Not again?”

“But you’ve been bragging, saying what a good time you had!” Ben answered, surprised. Harza Engineering Company was contracted by the United States Government to send engineers to certain countries, like Pakistan, to help in the Electric Power development of these countries

Finally, we accepted the inevitable. In June of 1968, at the request of Pakistan Water and Power division, Harza Company decided to transfer us back to Pakistan.

At first, we were not very happy. But we realized this was a big promotion for Ben and another opportunity to live, and once more, experience the exotic life and culture of the far east.

Meeting composer Aram Khachaturian after a concert in Chicago 1968

Second Assignment to Pakistan

To start teaching, we needed a second car. We bought a new, 1967, dark blue Buick Special with tan interiors. I loved that car! The smell of the new upholstery uplifted my spirit! This car was luxurious, it ran smoothly-a joy to drive!

When Ben came back from Pakistan, he told us, "We are returning to Lahore."

"What will we do with our gorgeous new car?" I asked.

"We'll pack it up in a suitcase and take it with us." he said, jokingly. "Okay! We'll sell it."

I was sad; I did not want to part with my beautiful car.

About a month before the end of the school year, we put a 'For Sale' sign on the back window of the new car. Three days later, we received a phone call asking its price.

So soon! I was not ready to part with it so fast!

I asked "Where did you see our car?"

"I live a few doors away from the school parking lot and admired your car. It's always shining. So, I knew that the owner was taking good care of it."

He did not bargain about the price. He agreed to pay what I asked, and I was satisfied that we had found it a loving new home.

So, at the end of June of 1968- with a heavy heart- we sold the new car, rented out the house and at the end of the school year, we were ready to leave.

Having had the experience of evacuation at the time of war we decided to pack important items, such as: pictures, family mementos, antiques (bought in different countries), important books and other keepsakes in a metal chest - all locked and placed in the crawl space of the house.

While I was packing and getting ready, some of my students, called to wish me, "Happy journey."

One of them, Shelley, a well- mannered girl with dark hair and shy intelligent eyes, called me.

"Please, don't leave." She was attached to me. Shelley was under psychiatric care. She called at odd hours of the day, and talked long periods. She was unhappy. She told me that her family did not pay attention to her. She felt lonesome. Shelley loved her younger sister, but she did not want her to cling to her all the time.

In the second semester, Shelley's work had become sloppy. It distressed me to see an intelligent, hardworking and outgoing student with 'A's so unhappy. She would not complete her assignments. She stopped participating in class activities and her papers were nearly illegible.

I consulted with her parents.

"We're as baffled as you are," said her father.

Shelley's mother broke in, "We're so concerned. Shelley's been having seizures four to six times a day. And- during those times- she's not aware of her surroundings." The mother continued, "Once she started a fire in the living room. Fortunately, her sister came in, just in time, and called for help."

I too had noticed the staring spells, where she would roll the edge of her notebook paper in an unconscious movement with a frozen glare. Talking to her I discovered, calmed her down.

I consulted with her psychiatrist, told her about the situation. She reassured me that she was working with her and has seen progress.

My family and I were getting ready to leave the house, when Shelley called.

"Shelley. You know I am leaving the country, I do like you very much but must go."

"I don't want you to leave." She pleaded

"You have your family ......your friends. They love you," I tried to sound convincing.

"Please don't go. You're the only person I can talk with." She insisted.

"Oh, Shelley, Yes. I will be far away, but I'll write." I set the phone down thinking she was convinced.

Half an hour before our departure for the airport, I received another call from Shelley, she was crying she did not want me to leave. I felt traumatized by her call.

"Shelley, please talk with your psychiatrist. She'll help you."

"I want you! Please don't go!" She begged of me.

"I have no choice; my family is waiting." I told her.

"I'll do anything. I'll come and help you. Please don't go,"

"Shelley, your family loves you... and needs you. They'll help you. You must **stay** with them.

"They don't need me! I want to be with you!"

She was not willing to get off the phone. **Now it was my turn**

to beg.

"My family is waiting in the car. **I have** to leave," I pleaded. "Shelley! I have to go. I'm going to hang up," I heard in the background the voices of my family shouting. "We'll be late! Let's go!"

With a soft 'good by' and tears in my eyes, I hung-up the phone and rushed to the car. I was distressed.

So on our second assignment to Pakistan, we left in July 1968 with a heavy heart.

Again we traveled via Europe. In London, we visited our friends that we had met in Pakistan. The Cunninghams lived in Greenwich Village, which historically became known for giving its name to Meridian and Mean time. The town was also the site of a Royal Palace from the 15th Century. Many members from the House of Tudor (the British royal family), were born there-including Henry VIII and Elizabeth I. We took the riverboat and traveled on the Thames River, to go there. The small, quaint village had many parks. And homes built in the 1600s.

The picturesque and ornate original façade of our friend's house was unusual. As a historical monument they were not allowed to change the outside appearance of the building. Our friends were remodeling the inside.

After spending time with them, we went to The Clock that regulated the hours of the world- the Greenwich clock, it's an enormous clock with an intricate mechanism.

"Sonia. Look! I can see part of the clock from here. Let's go to the second floor and see the rest of it." said Levon excitedly.

"Look! All the parts are moving, I can hear them tick." said Sonia.

We followed every small movement that the marvelous clock made. Later, we playfully walked over the imaginary line which divided the time between East and West. The children were puzzled. How, by standing on the opposite sides of the line, could one be in different time zones?

"Sonia, you stand on that side of the line; I'll stand on this side. My time is 4:00 PM. And yours is 5:00 PM." said Levon.

"Amazing! Is it real?" asked Sonia.

"Yes. It is." I said.

As we continued our travel to Lahore, Pakistan- once more we stopped over in Greece. We visited the *Sintagma* Square, a large open space-Greek mall, where skilled craftsmen create beautiful lambskin carpets (*flocati*), which can be used as bedcovers.

It was while we were there that we discovered the place where consummate chefs prepared the best *souvlaki*- a Greek dish, wrapped in thin bread, with all kinds of condiments... we returned to it almost every day.

If you enjoy to experiment with new dishes, here is a recipe for *souvlaki*:

SOUVLAKI

1 lb of ground meat
One cup minced onion
One whole onion
½ tsp pepper

Mix ground meat with minced onions, and ground pepper. Squeeze the mixed meat around a long skewer until it is smooth, and properly stuck to the skewer (keeping the meat cold will help it stick), cook it over charcoal.

Meanwhile, slice the onion into thin slices add salt. Let it stand five minutes. Squeeze the onion well. Drain the liquid from it. Rinse with water to get all the salt out. Add sumac and mix. Optional:Add sliced tomato, and tzatziki sauce. Wrap the cooked meat with onion mix in grilled pita bread and serve.

TZATZIKI SAUCE

Strained yoghurt
Salt & Pepper
1 tsp.garlic.
Olive oil
Mint, dill, parsley, or lemon juice
One finely diced med. cucumber

Mix all ingredients and add to meat as desired.

Our visit to a nightclub was an education!

We jumped up surprised when other people started breaking plates next to the dancer's feet. This was the custom, we found out that if you enjoyed the performance, you asked for special plates and threw them to the ground.

We continued our travel toward Pakistan.

Our stop in Beirut, was too brief. We had a good time visiting with relatives and old friends in and around the city, enjoying the balmy weather and the seaside cafes. We also took time to check on our half-acre property, set on a gentle hill, and covered with scented pine. When we first bought it, we thought *"We'll build our dream house, and we'll retire midst attractive surroundings."*

Sitting on a rock on the property, listening to the chirping of the crickets-brought memories of the fun times we had while climbing the hills. We absorbed as much of this tranquil environment as possible, the beautiful view of the city, the harbor and the airport.

From Beirut, we flew to Karachi, Pakistan.

We found Karachi- as usual- humid and hot. The heat felt thick enough to touch-fortunately, we only had to change planes to continue our journey. When we landed in Lahore, our friends and colleagues- from Harza Engineering Company- met us. The weather was much better than that of Karachi. Our friends- and the happy atmosphere- made it feel like a home coming.

Our furnished apartment had three bedrooms, each, with its own, modern bathroom; in the wide hallway we placed a long table and its chairs. The large living room and dining area, opened to a spacious balcony -later we enclosed it with screens to avoid the flies and mosquitoes.

Looking for furniture was fun! We ordered stuffed chairs and matching draperies, with intricate designs. The two matching camel chests-we ordered-were made of Rosewood, with copper and brass inlay.

"Why are they called a camel chest?' I asked the vendor

"Camel chests are two matching chests-of-drawers- used by the bride to carry her dowry, one chest on each side of the camel."

The mixing of cultures was so fascinating. We felt that we were living in British colonial times, with many servants and help. It took a little time for us to accept these traditions but we eventually acclimated to this life style.

One of our friends recommended Joseph, our cook. He was conscientious and hard working. He loved the children and always looked after them. He knew what the children liked and wanted to please them.

We had a *doby* who came twice a week to do our washing and our ironing.

One person came every day to clean the bathrooms and the balconies. Each person had a designated job and they would not go beyond that specific requirement. The cook supervised them.

As our children grew, they started having many activities; thus, we needed to hire a driver, to drive our new Mazda, that we had ordered from Japan.

Lahore, West Pakistan had an American community that fluctuated in size and when school population increased, we needed more classrooms.

A few weeks after our arrival, I visited 'The Lahore American Society school'. I had previously worked with many of the teachers, who were very happy to see me. The Superintendent said. "I want you to teach again, and bring the new ideas from the United States to motivate the teachers who rarely have the opportunity to teach outside of Lahore."

He divided the sixth grade and, 'voila'! I had my own class. I drove to school with Levon and Sonia, and I came home with them also. Two of our neighbor's children rode with us, a five year old and a six year old.

One day, a bicyclist crossed in front of my car without looking. I slammed on my brakes! Barely missing him, I screamed "*A-boush*!" Stupid (in Armenian). Solvang, the older child, riding in the back seat, immediately said, "Aunt Vicky. I don't see a bush."

Levon, Sonia and I couldn't stop laughing.

The next year, I was assigned to teach the Junior High Math and Science classes. Most of my students came from homes where at least one parent was a university graduate-children of engineers, or of representatives of various international embassies. Fortunately, having an engineer husband and many engineer friends, I had access to science books from their personal libraries.

I had to study each math lesson before teaching it! Math was very challenging. The students tested me at every single step. Some children came back with an alternative way of solving a math problem. The students and I had healthy arguments and always ended with positive results.

Some parents told me how I motivated their children. "Every evening our family discusses what was done in class, and tried to find different methods of solving the math problems; many times we argue about it."

Science fascinated my students. The lack of books turned into a challenge for us all. To teach some classes, I had to improvise. Fortunately, the school had a good library, we used it extensively.

Students always would look forward to our science class. I used our surrounding environment for our experiments.

Once we took a few drops from one of the neighborhood ponds and dripped them into a large bucket of clean water. Every day the students checked to see if we had anything new in the water.

Within a short time, it developed life. Ecosystems were formed. I assigned two students to each microscope. With books from the library, we identified the life cycles and followed their growth.

Science became exciting! Our lack of textbooks did not stop us from following the United States middle school curriculum, as I created an outline based on books and magazines from the library as well as the nature around us. I was pleased to be told that the curriculum that I wrote, was used extensively and became a standard for teachers who came after me.

Levon joined the High School Science Club, and I joined them on some of their field trips. While on one of these field trips a student discovered something amazing, a prehistoric fossil, the large jaw bone of a mammoth's skull! Excited, the students excavated it, and we brought it to school.

The science club decided to take it to the museum in Lahore, to have it evaluated. At the Museum the Anthropology director and his staff were thrilled.

"We searched for this part of the Mammoth, a few years ago. We had already excavated the rest of the skull. Now, with this missing piece, we'll have the complete head," one of the managers said. "Can we keep it, so we can exhibit the whole reconstructed body?

Levon and science club member with the mammoth jaw bone- circa 1970

The students donated the jaw. They were proud that they contributed something important to the Lahore Museum. The experience had a lasting affect on all the students.

In Lahore, we did not have the curse of television. We had the blessing of experiencing real culture. The young people participated in sports. They read books. They listened to music. They explored their own imagination for entertainment. Levon took violin lessons and Sonia took piano lessons. Unfortunately the teacher who was a nun moved to Australia. As both Levon and Sonia were busy with school and needed time to practice, we stopped the lessons altogether.

One of the exciting events we went to watch was the yearly National Horse and Cattle show, which was held at the Fortress stadium in Lahore. It was an exciting and a wonderful experience. We saw men in colorful costumes on beautiful horses decorated with all kinds of ribbons marching. We applauded the "tent pegging" contestants and the polo players. We cheered the camels racing, we even screamed with delight at the donkey racing. The police motorcycle daredevils left us breathless. Nowhere else have we ever seen such an unusual and entertaining show.

Traveling Within Pakistan and India

We had a busy, happy life; Ben came home from work everyday at 2:00PM, and School was over at 2:30PM. This gave us time to play golf almost every day.

Driving in Lahore was always a challenge; dodging other traffic made up of bullock carts, three wheeled rickshaws, horse drawn tongas with bells, and an endless stream of bicycles with maybe a boy shepherd with his herd of goats, makes you an extremely patient and understanding driver.

During the evenings we played bridge or socialized with friends. The school closed for both American and Pakistani holidays. We took advantage of these days off and explored and traveled.

Our trip to Swat Valley, located in the North West Frontier Province of Pakistan, was memorable. The capital, Saidu Sharif, sits in great natural beauty with high mountains, green meadows, and clear lakes. The Valley was inhabited for over two thousand years. In ancient times, it was called Udyana and was thought to be the probable birthplace of Bajrayana Buddhism, known throughout the world as the holy land of Buddhist learning and piety.

Saidu Sharif, aside from its palace, was a quaint little town with small picturesque stone houses, clinging to the steep hills. Each house had its small cow dung cake pile, which the people used for fuel in the winter months.

On our way we passed many mud villages where families lived in crowded quarters near a water hole with water buffaloes cooling off in the mud.

We drove carefully on dirt roads in the high mountains. In the middle of dense forests sits the gorgeous marble palace of the valley's governor. The palace, constructed of white marble, had black color designs in it. The marble walkways meandered around manicured gardens. The sun shining on the palace, with the tall trees surrounding the area, made a stunning landscape!

The guide took us to a steep hill with sets of stairs, where the governor climbed three times a day for prayer. At the top of the hill was a platform, where he sat and prayed. We reached midway to the first platform, the view of the valley from there was magnificent. It felt as if one was nearer to God.

"Sonia, I can race you up the stairs!" said Levon

"Oh! Yeah! I can go faster!"

"Mom, Dad -come on up: What a view of the valley!"

Those children have the energy of mountain goats. It was too steep, we adults decided not to climb any further, I felt exhilarating peace and spiritual harmony with nature's beauty.

Mosquitoes seemed to have a gargantuan appetite for our daughter Sonia's sweet blood. She had bites all over her arms and legs. The small town had one lane with shops on both sides displaying daily necessities. When we saw a Pharmacy, we approached to see what we can find to relieve her painful itching.

It was a small shop made of stone, with a round roof and no windows; it reminded me of an open cave. It had bails of seeds and a variety of dried plants in each jute bag. An assortment of small boxed medication rested on shelves. A man, with a stern and serious look, dressed in Pakistani garb, was sitting cross-legged in the middle of the floor.

When we asked him "Do you have something for mosquito bites?" He reached for a small box of ointment,

"This is good for bee bites and mosquito bites."

Here in the middle of no-where, what do you find? *The best medicine I have ever come across*- it was an ointment made in England and it cured the itch and sting of insect bites almost instantly.

The mosquitoes were big and vicious, and they loved Sonia.

Mangla Dam, one of Ben's projects in Pakistan

Thanks to that little pharmacist and the magic ointment, poor Sonia was able to sleep at night.

During the day, we knew that the wild animals were in hiding, but at night we felt their presence, and heard the coyotes and the roars of the feral animals. We did not dare go out after sundown.

We spent many vacations in India. The Himalaya Mountains separate India from the rest of Asia with large bodies of water on three sides. The Bay of Bengal in the east, the Arabian Sea in the west, and the Indian Ocean in the south. This vast country, 2,000 miles long from north to south, included almost every type of landscape.

"I read somewhere that India is the largest democracy in the world with a population of more than one billion. Is it true? asked Levon, finding it hard to believe.

"Yes," I answered convinced it was true.

"While we were in the north of India, the locals were speaking a different language, it didn't sound like the language that they spoke in Delhi."

"There are twenty two major languages in India with seven hundred twenty dialects. English is spoken at almost all tourist centers."

India was only about twenty minutes from Lahore, where we lived. An exotic and memorable visit was the visit to Agra to see the Taj Mahal, one of the Seven Wonders of the World. As I walked in through the gate, the sun was shining, I had to stop and gaze with awe at this dazzling gorgeous mausoleum, considered to be the jewel of Muslim art, built by the Mughal Emperor Shah Jihan to his beloved wife, Mumtaz Mahal, who died during the birth of their daughter Guahara Begum, their fourteenth child.

In 1632, he commissioned the Taj Mahal and it was completed about 1648. The marble walls as well as the domed roof, are covered with various designs with inlays of semi-precious stones. It is surrounded by its four minarets. I went close to the marble walls and examined the various designs and inlays of the semi-precious stones. I couldn't believe how beautifully the craftsmen had designed the flowers, leaves and branches. We decided to visit the mausoleum at night. At the gate I had to stop, I felt my heart palpitating, I thought I was dreaming. I was afraid to close my eyes fearing it would go away. The beauty of the Taj Mahal is unsurpassed by any other monument, especially when viewed under the full moon. A masterpiece of the world heritage.

The beautifully manicured gardens, complimented the gorgeous structure.

A short distance away, we marveled at another mausoleum built for Emperor Akbar in the city of Sikandra, located 13 km from Agra Fort. The mausoleum was planned and started by Akbar himself in 1614, but he died before its completion; his son Mogul Jahangir completed it. This unique pyramid tomb structure as it was described to us, had a blend of Hindu, Islamic, Buddhist and Jain motifs, reflecting the spirit of religious tolerance that Akbar practiced during his reign.

Another location of interest is the sixteenth century Red Fort; this was the seat of great Moguls, who lived and governed from there. It contained the state treasury and mint. Presently it is a UNESCO World Heritage Site.

Inside the Fort was built the seventeenth century palace, where Shah Jehan lived with his wife. We enjoyed strolling through the well maintained beautiful gardens, where all kinds of monkeys roamed about.

"Sonia, Levon, stay away from the monkeys!"

"They're so cute!" the children said.

"They can jump on you and bite you.... They might be rabid."

The fort had so many rooms that it took us a long time to see them all. The room that impressed us most was the queen's bedroom. It was more spacious and colorful.

"As you can see, the walls are covered with half-inch circular mirrors." said the guide, pointing out at each as he gestured..

"Look at the dome-shaped ceiling... It has the same round-mirrors ...and so do the four walls." Levon pointed out.

Our guide closed all the doors and windows and lit a candle. A fascinating sight emerged!

"Mom! Look at the mirrors. The candle is reflected in every one of them." Said Levon excited.

It was dazzling, we all admired it.

"The whole place is shimmering and shining!" Sonia screamed excitedly.

"Stunning! ... How ro-ma-n-tic."

Delhi, the capital of India, was as exotic as the rest of the country: the bazaars were a shopper's paradise; the winding, narrow serpentine streets of the old city, where brass tables and goblets are made, held fascinating sights and sounds. We watched a person shaping a copper bowl on an iron shoe-shaped holder. We could hear banging from other sides of the street. The aroma of the spices filled the air. You see a blur of shades and textures as women in colorful *saris* with sequins, rhinestones, and metallic thread, seem to be asserting themselves against a pitiless life.

We visited the gold bazaar to find the most beautiful and ornate jewelry. India is known for its silver-filigree work and semi-precious stones, set in gold and silver. Stacks and stacks of gold bangles. Here also were authentic Indian goods and antiques.

Driving in New Delhi was a challenge: avoiding wooden carts loaded with rice, spices and flowers drawn by oxen; watching out for bicycle-drawn rickshaws tooting constantly, weaving through the market, circling the roundabouts, broad boulevards, and narrow, winding streets.

Alarmed I yelled "Watch for that little boy! He is trying to cross the street," (TOOT-TOOT) and Ben sounded the horn.

"Dad! Look-out for that mountain of hay. It's moving!" shouted Levon.

Ben pressed on his brakes! (SCREECH – TOOT-TOOT).
Indeed, We saw a large amount of hay, piled up on a cart and drawn by two oxen. It lumbered along the road as we slowly passed. From our side, we did not see anyone guiding the oxen.

"Dad! There's another one in front of it, WATCH OUT!"

"Oh! Look, there's a man lying on top. He is asleep."

"I saw this in Pakistan, a friend traveling with me said that oxen are trained to go home by themselves, they don't need guidance." Said Ben.

"I can't believe this! I'm not driving. But I'm a nervous wreck!" I exclaimed.

Suddenly, on the road we saw a beautiful wild peacock prancing along. Ben had to swerve the car in order to avoid the bird. Small birds were flying all over the area. While driving, every now and then one would hit the car. We always felt bad when that happened. But there was no way we could prevent it.

After sightseeing, it was always invigorating to go to a good restaurant and order a *tandoori*- chicken. We asked the waiter "Bring the chicken with less spice please, because the children can't eat it if it's too spicy. "

Once the meal came in, Levon- after a single bite started jumping. He became red and rushed for the Fanta.

We called the waiter, told him the situation, and he was surprised.

He said, "But *Saab,* we only put a drop. How can you eat food without spice?"

Another time, after biting a spicy chicken, Ben, pointed to his neck, "Look, look, do you see smoke coming from my neck?"

Another hot dish is the 'chicken tikka'.

CHICKEN TIKKA

Cut chicken into four pieces. Remove all skin. Slice each piece deeply in a waffle design, Apply chili powder over parts of chicken liberally. Before grilling over a slow fire squeeze ½ small lemon over each piece. While chicken is over fire, apply butter by dabbing -1/4 lb. of butter for one chicken. Broil until golden brown and tender. Eat while hot.

With the chicken tikka a common side dish would be the east indian lentils with rice.

EAST INDIAN LENTILS WITH RICE

1 cup lentils
2 Tbsp. butter
2 cloves garlic, minced
½ tsp. mixed spices(allspice)
6 cardamom seed, crush
½ tsp. pepper
hot, cooked rice
1 cup brown rice
1 large onion
2 tsp. salt
1 slice lemon

Soak lentils overnight. Drain, wash and simmer in salted water, until tender, about 2 hrs. Boil rice. Meantime, melt butter and fry onion and garlic. Add spices, cardamom seeds tied in cheesecloth and seasonings to lentils. Simmer 10 mins.
Remove cardamom. Serve on platter in a border of rice; garnish with lemon.

A well balanced Indian meal is to include the categories of six tastes: sweet, sour, salty, spicy bitter and astringent, side dishes such as chutneys, curries, daals, Indian pickles, often used as a way to add to the flavor, texture, and to provide the balance of the six tastes.

The skill for the best Indian food is the blending of the spices to enhance, not to overwhelm the flavor of the food. The spices also act as appetizers and aid in digestion.

Key spices used, include coriander, cumin, turmeric, red pepper, nutmeg, mustard, saffron, cinnamon, cardamom, ginger powder, paprika, mace, cloves and black pepper.

Hindu and Muslim traditions have influenced Indian cooking.

The Hindu tradition of vegetarian meals was prevalent in the country. The Muslim tradition has most influenced the cooking of meats, rich kormas (curries) tandoori murg (chicken). Food was usually eaten with fingers.

LAMB KORMA CURRY

3 ½ lb. butter *1/2 lb. onions, slice*
2 lbs leg of lamb meat-cubed *2 tsp fresh ginger, ground*
8 cloves garlic, ground
2 tsp. coriander seed (ground or powder)
¼ lb. blanched almonds *4 oz. yogurt*
2 tbsp. raisins *½ tsp. cumin seeds*
¼ tsp. whole cloves *½ tsp. whole black peppers*
6 whole cardamoms

Melt butter in saucepan and fry onions until light brown. Add meat, ginger, garlic, coriander and brown 5 minutes on low flame. Add yogurt and brown. Add almonds, raisins, cardamoms and 2 cups warm water. Cook on very slow fire for 20 minutes. Grind together coarsely cumin, cloves and peppers, add to meat and cook 4 minutes.

We learned that Delhi is the center of the astrological gardens. The gardens had a huge sun dial made of stone. It was surrounded with large columns of various shapes showing the signs of the skies.

"Look dad the sun beam is coming directly to the stone sundial from the middle of those two columns."

"Yes, in early times they used this method to study the movement of planets."

On our way back to Lahore, Pakistan, we suddenly saw a huge elephant walking in the middle of the highway. TOOT-TOOT. The children wanted to see the elephant, so we stopped on the side of the road, the elephant came and stopped right behind us.

"*Saab,* the children can ride the elephant."

"NOOO!" said Sonia.

"Dad, look, the elephant is twice the size of our VW bug!" said Levon with a curious look..

"Yes! It is humongous!" said Ben.

"Let's get out of here before the elephant turns vicious and decides to crush our car!" I said in a high pitched voice.

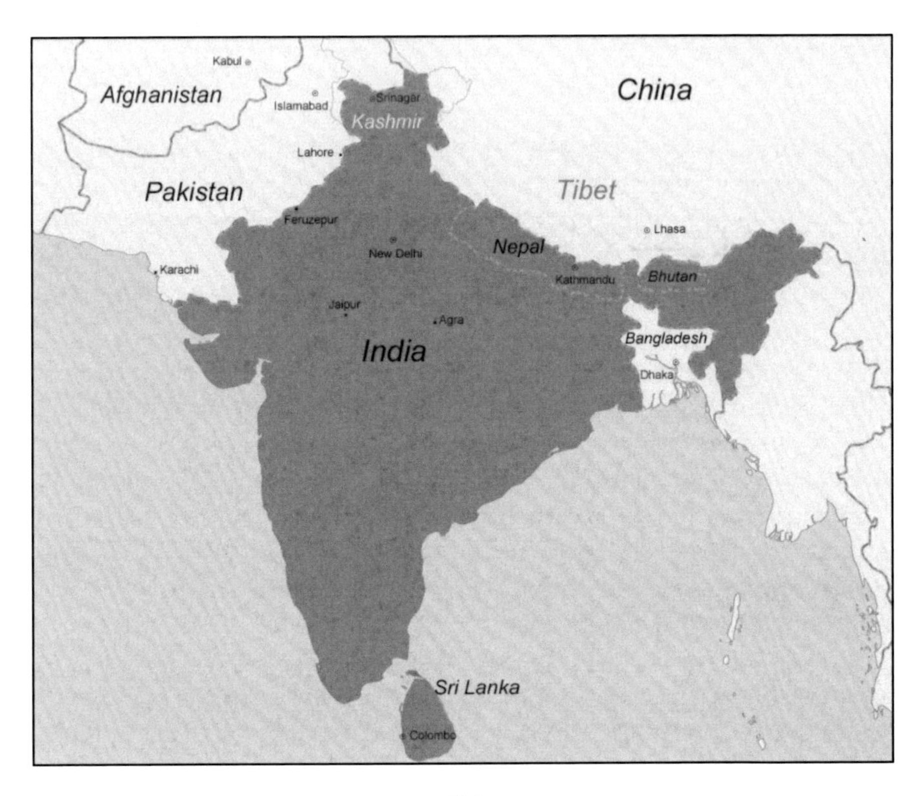

Sri Lanka (Ceylon1948-1972)

We took a special trip and visited Ceylon in 1969, an Island country in the Indian Ocean, off the southern coast of India. As the center of Buddhism where the Tooth of the Buddha is housed in the "Temple of the Tooth," it is considered the holiest place of worship. In 1815 it became part of the British Empire. In 1948 it became independent. The official name of the country was first changed to Sri Lanka in 1972 then to Democratic socialist Republic of Sri Lanka in 1978.

The forests, the terraced land, the inviting sandy beaches and beautiful landscapes promised an exciting vacation.

To Sonia's delight, a group of dancers greeted us when we landed in Colombo, the capital of Ceylon.

Men and women with baskets hanging on their shoulders, were collecting the famous Ceylonese tea leaves by hand from these terraced lands. The scene reminded me of paintings done by the masters, such as the three ladies harvesting by Paul Gaugin.

At the tea factory, the workers sorted the leaves according to size, by using graduated sieves. They spread them on metal nettings to dry, and made them ready to package and export.

"Now I know why Ceylonese tea tastes so good!" pointed out Ben.

"Look at that terrace; they are picking coffee beans by hand as well." I remarked.

We were amazed at the rubber plantation. "Mom! Look! They have buckets attached to each tree!" pointed out Levon

The guide explained, "The men make a slit on the rubber tree to let it bleed. The sap runs into the attached bucket."

The milky white sap looked sticky.

The rubber factory nearby was a simple one story building with wide open windows. Once inside the factory, the guide explained, "The rubber is coagulated by acid in tin containers."

"Dad! Look! Huge rollers!" Levon pointed to the huge rollers .

"Yes," continued the guide, "These wooden rollers compress the rubber and squeeze out the acidic water."

We went to another chamber where we saw sheets of compressed raw rubber hanging.

"It looks like washed white towels hanging to dry!" I exclaimed.

Our guide continued, "The raw rubber is hung to dry and then smoked over a wood burning fire. The smoking stabilizes the rubber and blackens it, then it's sold to manufacturers."

I never imagined how fascinating it would be to see the whole process from liquid sap, to hard rubber.

The country exports tea, coffee, coconuts, rubber and cinnamon.

We were intrigued with the bananas of the island. They came in all sizes; fat ones, thin ones, big ones, tiny ones. To Sonia's delight, the tiniest ones were the most delicious; the thin ones were the sweetest.

The city of Kandy built on a highland, fascinated us with its beauty. We visited a traditional Sinhalese temple built on a ledge that can only be reached via a long series of rock-cut steps.

"Breathtaking! **How can they build such an amazing temple?** Look at the walls! The ceiling! All covered with paintings of the Buddha amid colorful flowers!" I said.

E-E-E-CK! Iguanas everywhere!

While riding in a taxi, we suddenly saw a giant lizard run across the street. The taxi driver applied his breaks. We all screamed "What was that?" He stopped the car and the creature looked around before darting into the high brush.

"Did you see that?" screamed Levon excitedly.

"Yes! It was green with brown spots protruding from its back." I said equally excited.

"I'm scared!" screamed Sonia.

"The long thick tail was going right and left!" continued Levon.

"It's a dragon. They're all over Ceylon," Said the driver.

"O-NO! A Dra-go-n! Was fire coming out of its nose?" Screamed Sonia.

Ben tried to calm her down, "Sonia it's not the fantasy dragon you read about in books."

We had never seen anything like it! It almost looked like a giant iguana. Later we learned they are indigenous to Ceylon.

Aside from the tea and rubber plantations, Ceylon had forests of ebony, redwood and teak.

The Island was a shopper's paradise- shops were filled with ebony, teak artifacts and semi-precious jewelry.

Our guide invited us to go to a semi-precious stone mine while we were admiring their jewelry. We agreed to go, but we were a little skeptical – *I suspected this is a scam; maybe they want us to buy expensive jewelry.*

In a four- wheel drive we traveled for over an hour. Suddenly, we saw barren land- some distance away. There were no dwellings; the ground was almost white as the moon's surface- dry and deserted. The guide pointed to a spot.

He said, "There's one of the mines."

We were expecting an entrance to a cave, but instead we saw a hole in the ground, some metal sieves scattered around, men collected soil from the hole and passed it through the sieves. One of the men gave Levon a sieve; he dug some soil, emptied it shook it. All of a sudden; he started jumping.

"Levon! What happened?" I asked.

"Mom! Dad! Look at this big stone!"

Sure enough, there in the sieve a beautiful large brown agate, like a huge eye, staring at us.

Because the sun was strong, they ushered us to a shed where they offered refreshments and showed us many of their findings. There were impressive semi-precious stones, all named and categorized.

"Wow! Look at this large yellow quartz." I said.

With excitement we chose a few "stones" to take with us. Eight year- old Sonia was the happiest- the natives, who love children, showered her with colorful stones.

All throughout our stay- we were entertained by music and national dances during our lunches and dinners. The colorful costumes of the dancers, their long nails and graceful dance movements mesmerized us. Sonia and I tried to imitate their movements. But, alas! We were not as graceful.

It was hard to leave Ceylon, we had fallen in love with it. We were sad that it ended so soon.

We parted with feelings of amazement of how such a small island offered such a wide variety of natural resources and taught us so much.

Our visit to Srinagar and Gulmarg, India

Srinagar, the capital of Kashmir, was one of our unforgettable trips. This was the base of many treks, such as the *Shankaracharya* hill, where-at its highest point-is the *Shankaracharya* Temple. Kashmir is the disputed and divided territory at the northernmost corner of Pakistan.

Though, Srinagar belongs to India, we had to get special permission to visit. After traveling to Delhi, we took a small plane to Jaipur, where we stayed in a lovely hotel for a few days.

Going to Srinagar in a small plane is an experience of a lifetime. We were going on this trip with our friends, the Hendricksons and their two children. As we entered the plane, we saw cages and cages of small chicks. We sat in the front of the plane but, still, we heard the cacophony of the chicks. At first, we were uncomfortable, but, later, it became like music to our ears, we thought it was very funny. We were frightened by the small plane flying between two huge mountains. The mountains were getting closer and closer. I started seeing the trees in detail, side by side, I was getting nervous and tense

"Ben, if I extend my arm out of the plane's window, I will touch that mountain." I said nervously.

"Yes, I was thinking the same thing." Ben replied thoughtfully.

After that harrowing experience, we landed; we thanked God that we arrived safe. We started thinking about the return. The people at the airport told us; "The pilots fly those routes daily, they are very experienced, and we should not worry."

Srinagar is built on a high plateau, surrounded by snow-peaked Mountains. A multitude of rivers and lakes in the region create a spectacular landscape. Nestled in all this grandeur was our very own houseboat on Dal Lake. An amazing amount of tomatoes and watermelons grew on top of straw beddings on the water. We agreed that Srinagar is one of the most beautiful places we have ever been.

Our houseboat had two bedrooms, a living room, and a dining room. Next to it was the kitchen boat. The cook prepared wonderful meals, and the helper served us. During the day, small boats came filled with a variety of fruits and vegetables; others brought souvenirs and toys. The owner of one of the vendor boats told us that he could get us anything we wanted. Ben and our friend Henry Hendrickson decided to ask for something that was out of the ordinary. Hendrickson said. "I bet he doesn't have Cuban Cigars."

So they decided to ask the man.

"Yes *Saab,* I've the best," was his enthusiastic answer.

He dove into the loaded boat, and-to our amazement-he produced a cigar with a band that said, "Cuban Cigar. Made in India."

A boat came everyday and put fresh flowers in each room. In order to go to the village, we took a small taxi boat, *Shekara*. These taxi boats were very ornate, with hand carved woodwork and an awning to shade the passenger seats. The seats were covered either in red or shiny material and the awnings had velvet ribbons streaming in the breeze. The driver of the boat stood on the edge of the *shekara* and paddled with a long heart-shaped paddle. It felt like a time capsule from the exotic past when Shah Jehan had his palace on top of the hill.

Levon and Carol Hendrickson enjoyed horseback riding twice a week together in Lahore. Since the area was well known for its horses, they wanted to ride and found some horses. While they were galloping through the woods, the horse that she was riding suddenly came to a dead stop in front of a tree. Carol flew over the horse's head and hit her head on the tree. She fell to the ground, and with Levon's help she eventually got back on the horse and slowly walked it back to the stables. We were all worried about a concussion, Levon was visibly shaken. That was the last time they rode horses in Kashmir.

Shopping was the best. Their Kashmir shawls were excellent quality, hand embroidered with striking exotic designs. The brass work covered with papier-mâché had intricate and colorful designs. "This is a funny looking bowl, it reminds me of a boat." Sonia pointed.

"*Memsab*, this is a beggars bowl."

"What do you mean?"

"This bowl is used because it is easy to carry; the inside being brass and the outside papier-mâché."

There were so many beautiful items to buy as souvenirs. We did not know which ones to pick.

Visiting the hilltop garden of *Cheshmashahi* was another highlight of our trip. The place was well designed with cozy corners, stone seats and statues. It was covered with unusual plants and trees of various sizes. Water cascading in the middle of the long garden gave a peaceful feeling. It all helped capture the romance, and previous splendor, of a royal era. In my minds eye I could see Shah Jihan romancing with his wife in one of the hidden corners of this unique garden.

Our guide took us fishing in the northern area of Srinagar, two hours drive from the city, on rough roads. We were near snow-peaked mountains, where a river flowed with a tremendous force. *What a spectacular country*! The air was crisp and invigorating, the closer we came to the mountains, the cooler it became. We stopped at the foothills and saw dark rocky surfaces jutting out of the snow-covered mountains, as though peeking through a white veil.

"What a view! We are so close to the mountains!" Levon said.

"I feel like I am closer to God!" I exclaimed in a solemn excitement.

Fishing was excellent. Within half an hour, Ben, Levon and Henry, had caught their limit of nine trout each. The warden kept a keen eye on them to make sure they didn't catch too many.

Our guide brought cooking equipment and fried the fish. It was the most delicious fish ever! We packed some in an ice chest to take back to the houseboat.

As our vacation time was nearing an end,we were concerned about the dangerous flight back. Again, local people reassured us that these pilots are experienced, they fly this route everyday.

Flying back to Jaipur was not as bad. I guess we were used to it, and we were expecting the flight to be frightening. Vacationing in Srinagar, Kashmir in the summer of 1969 was one of our unforgettable trips, the beginning of many.

Gulmarg

We decided to go to the highest golf course in the world. This was in the Hindu Cush Mountains over 8,000 feet above sea level. The only way to go in 1969 was to walk or go on mules. The climb was treacherous, but those mules were steady on their hoofs. I was petrified and did not dare look down. On one side, a steep precipice yawned in front of us like the mouth of a huge monster. On the other side a towering cliff looked down on us like ants in this majestic setting.

The mules were familiar with this narrow footpath and traveled single file. Because the climbing was slow, we adapted to the elevation and the thin air. It took us a long time to get to the golf course.

Gulmarg, a town founded in the sixteenth Century by Sultan Yusuf Shah. Inspired by the beautiful grassy slopes- emblazoned, with wildflowers of different varieties, the Sultan named it *Gul-marg* (meadow of flowers). The town stands in the imposing Himalayan peaks, like an eagle's nest.

This mountain resort of such exceptional beauty has the highest golf course in the world at an altitude of 2,650 meters. (8694 feet). The resort has become the country's premier ski resort in winter. The golf course was built by the British. Colonial influence is seen both in design, and in the rules and regulations of the golf course.

The weather was cool and crisp. There was snow on the surrounding areas. One minute, it rained, and the next minute, the sun shone. The weather was so odd that within minutes of getting wet from the rain, we were dry. It was exhilarating! We played a few holes, but the course was very difficult-too many hills and rivers! We each hired a ball-boy to make sure that he watched the balls and directed us to them.

"Did you find my ball?"

"No *memsab,* (madam)I can't find it"

"Be sure you watch the ball!"

"Yes *memsab,*"

"I'll use another ball. Be sure you follow it to see where it falls!"

"Yes, *memsab.*"

"A-y-y! It fell in the creek!"

"Can't you locate it?"

"No."

"You're supposed to watch-and find them!"

"I can't find it."

"This is my last one!" I played it and then asked, "Did you follow the ball?"

"Yes, *memsab.*"

The ball-boy's pretended diligence made me angry. He finally did admit to me, "I can't find it."

Having lost all of my golf balls, I regrettably stopped playing. Ben, Levon and our friend continued playing. My ball-boy was clever. Every time the ball landed in a brook, he pretended to not see the ball. Later, we found out that the ball-boys collect them to sell back to the club.

The ball boy's behavior spoiled my pleasure in playing golf in that golf course.

Descending the golf course was more frightening than climbing up to it. I was worried about the children; Levon was good on the mules, but Sonia was not accustomed to this type of dangerous terrain!

Finally, we made it safely to the bottom of the mountain. Vacations like this revived in us our adventurous behavior. We were always looking for places to go and see.

Our Trip to Armenia

The Union of Soviet Socialist Republics (USSR) started to allow tourists to visit their country in the summer of 1970.

Ben had not seen his sister, Arpineh, since her migration to Armenia in 1943.

"We should go and see her and her family before leaving Pakistan." I said to Ben.

It took a few months to get our visas. The American Embassy advised us, "Be very careful. Do **not** associate with anyone except relatives. Be suspicious of strangers."

We had heard so many stories! We told the children not to talk to strangers. The authorities might be nice, but may trouble the relatives after our departure.

After lengthy consultations with American Embassy personnel and people who had visited the Soviet Union, we decided to go ahead. We booked the tour with *Intourist* of USSR (the tourist office of the Soviet Union).

Ben wrote to his sister in Yerevan, Armenia, to tell her we were coming.

Armenia is a borderland nation between the East and the West. The cultural division has washed back-and-forth since the days of ancient Rome and Persia. Armenia is also the first nation to adopt Christianity as its national religion. With the oldest Christian church – Etchmiadzin- which has witnessed the Christian tradition, both ancient and unique.The church is built on top of a pagan temple. In 1970 I descended under the altar and viewed the worship area where the ancient Armenians sacrificed animals to different gods. I felt the eerie sacredness of the area.

When Armenians think of their Caucasus neighbors, they say: "God allotted neighboring Georgia the fertile valleys and the forests. God left the wealth of oil to the Azeris who laugh all the way to the banks of Europe and Asia. And finally God blessed Armenia with lava and rocks!"

Our route was via Kabul, Afghanistan and Tashkent, Uzbekistan. The reason to stay in Kabul was to buy presents for relatives. Kabul had changed since we visited it years ago. Russian-made cars filled the streets using a type of gasoline that polluted the air with a horrible smell.

We found new shops, with ready-made dresses, jeans, nylons, make-up and many other items not found in Lahore, Pakistan. It had become a shopper's paradise. For two days we raided every shop and department store in the city. Our suitcases were bulging and we had to buy an extra suitcase!

As we packed, we removed all the tags from the new items- for fear of customs confiscating them.

On our way to Tashkent, the capital of Uzbekistan in the USSR, the plane was filled with Uzbeks returning from their vacations. We saw that many of them carried coats made of sheepskin; Afghanistan is famous for these types of coats. The skin side of the coat is embroidered with intricate geometric and flowery designs. The wool is on the inside of the coat. An odor of sheep permeated the plane.

There were also a few tourists, some American government officials, and teachers.

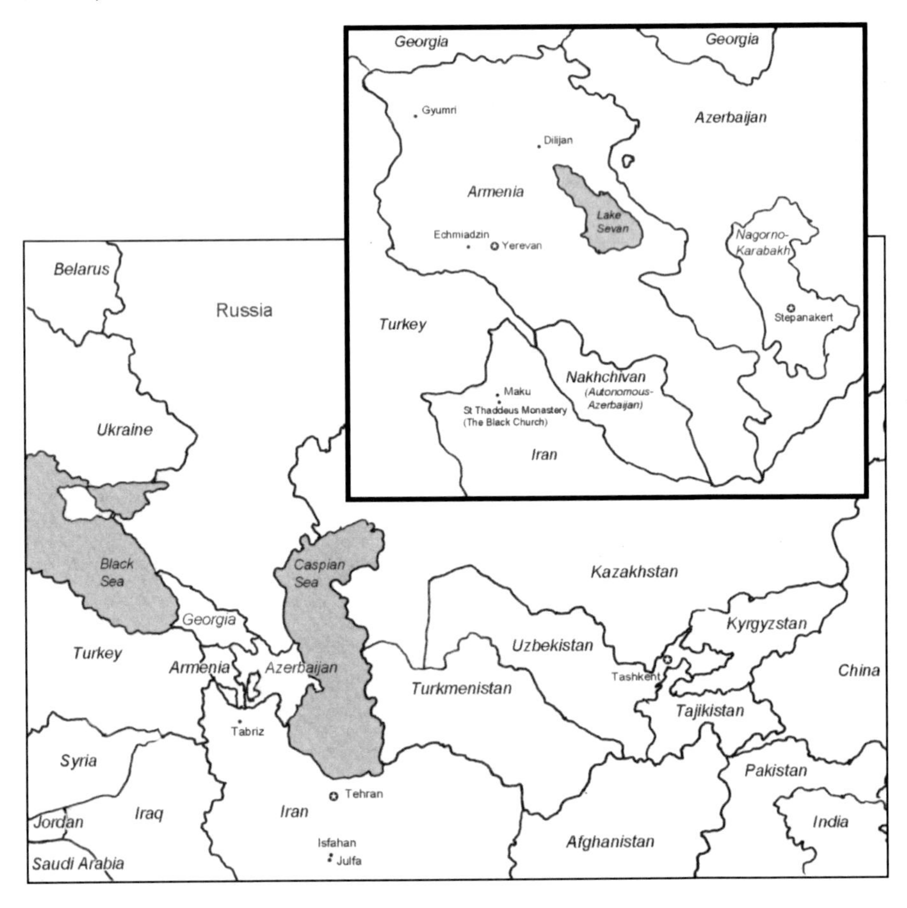

Uzbekistan, one of the six Turkic Central Asian republics, is land-locked, north of Afghanistan. Tashkent is the capital. Bukhara and Samarkand are the main cities. They are the largest cotton exporters in the world. Uzbeks are a mixture of Mongol and Iranian people. Eighty-eight percent are Muslim. We wanted to stay a day in Tashkent to see the sights, but we were nervous about entering the Soviet Union.

When we arrived, the customs people announced, "All foreigners stay in the room. All Soviet citizens proceed through customs."

Customs officers took each of these people to a room, examined them from head-to-toe, checking all the clothing, including the seams of each dress, each pair of pants and each coat. They counted the money each person had and turned every pocket inside-out. We felt sorry for the natives- but, we trembled, not knowing what awaited us.

Most of the Uzbek women had ankle-length skirts with pockets. They wore long-sleeve shirts, jackets, and kerchiefs on their heads. Under their skirts they also wore colorful pants with a wide upper waist, tapered from the knees down. Their shoes were old fashioned boots with thick soles.

Some of the men wore European clothing. Others wore traditional loose fitting shirts made of cotton that reached almost to the knees. The trousers were wide at the waist and narrowed below the knee before reaching the ankles. Men also wore embroidered skull caps.

Five hours later the foreigners turn came. First, the individual travelers went through and then the families. When our turn came, we declared everything- including the amount of money we had. The inspector was so tired that she glanced at our suitcase and at the money we had in hand. Without counting it, she motioned for us to go through.

Surprise! We were so relieved!

They drove all the foreigners to the best hotel in town, which was not what we had anticipated. The lobbies, and the stairs, were dark. When we reached our room, we were disappointed; it reminded us of a sleazy motel, not a first class hotel.

We had nothing to eat or drink. The children were hungry.

"Here's the dining room." Said Ben.

"Mom, I'm thirsty." Said Sonia.

"What about you, Levon?"

"Hungry and thirsty." Growing more impatient by the minute.

"We'll use our dinner vouchers to buy some sandwiches."suggested Ben.

Other Americans had the same idea; we chatted with one of them. He was passing through too. He was a university professor, and he was going to a conference.

We asked the waiters, who were conversing with each other, if they could bring us something to eat. Half an hour later, the food had not come. Ben said, "Do you think the cook went shopping for meat at this time of the night?" We all laughed, which released some of the tension.

The waiters were extremely rude. Ben approached one of them and said, "The children need water."

A waiter brought a bottle of water and took a dinner voucher in exchange.

"Ben! Did you see that! He grabbed the dinner voucher instead of the beverage voucher!"

As it turned out, the waiter brought mineral water, which smelled like sulfur. The local people are used to it, but the children had a hard time; it tasted like medicine to them.

Then the waiter went to another visitor who was sitting at a nearby table.

"Sir! It's late. We're closed."

"Can I have something to drink?"

The waiter banged on the table and said, "**Do you understand English! "**

The American was stunned!

In a surprised tone, he responded, "I ... think I... do"

"WE ARE CLOSED!"

The American gave an angry look; he turned and with a shrug he left the dining room. He looked tired.

We went to our room still hungry. As I walked in, I realized that there were other occupants- a multitude of cockroaches were having a party on the floor in our room. I cringed. I gave the children their nightgowns and locked the suitcases to prevent any unwelcome visitors from crawling inside.

All this time, water dripped from the ceiling, in the bathroom.

"Here! Use your toothbrushes;" I told everyone, "I'm going to pack them back into the suitcases."

We informed the hotel manager about the dripping water. The

Soviet Union had sent their sputnik into space, so we joked "They may use their advanced technology to stop the leak." Two men came from the maintenance department with buckets. They left a single bucket in the bathroom underneath the drip, so much for Soviet technology.

I was furious! We were tired so we all went to bed.

In the middle of the night, we jumped up when we heard a rumbling. The windows rattled! At first, we thought it was an earthquake. But, then, we heard bells. I looked from the balcony; and I saw that a tram was right in front of the hotel. The noise of the tram reverberated at night when everything was quiet. We went back to bed. After two hours, the same happened which made us jump from our deep sleep. This went on untill morning. We were all tired, hungry and irritated.

Using the bathroom became a problem: by morning the water had overflowed. And there was an inch of water, everywhere, on the bathroom floor and, some had even reached the bedroom.

I packed in a hurry, in order to be on time for breakfast, hoping that—this time, at least—we would succeed in making it to breakfast **on time.**

"Give me everything!" I told the children. "I'll pack it all and I'll lock the suitcases. I don't want cockroaches in them!"

As we approached the dining room the matron shooed us away in the same rude manner as the waiter had the night before.

"Breakfast will be served at eight o'clock." she said.

My watch read ten minutes **after** eight. I pointed to the wall clock, but it didn't matter—she threw us out, **again** anyway!

I was angry and we walked away from the dining room.

Here I suggested we take this opportunity to look around. After so many bad experiences inside the hotel, the gardens delighted us. Gorgeous marble statues of mermaids stood surrounded by colorful beds of bright flowers. Beds of ivy surrounded the statues of mythological figures.

Just breathing in the fresh air helped to clear my head.

I felt wide awake, in this tranquil, isolated garden. I felt much more ready for the day's adventure. (*I am glad I suggested looking around).*

Half an hour later we returned to the dining room. But, on our way, the sight of two waiters carrying our entire luggage shocked us.

We said, “Where are you going with our suitcases? These are ours!”

“We‘ve been looking all over for you! Where have you been? The bus is waiting.” they said,

“But our plane is scheduled for the late afternoon!”

“You are going to the airport **now**! The bus is **waiting** for you.”

His curt words shocked and angered us.

“The children haven’t had anything to eat!” I said.

I felt glad that I locked everything and the suitcases were ready for our departure.

“Let’s go! Hurry!” Said the waiter.

We had no choice but to go to the airport immediately. We thought, maybe we can buy something to eat there.

Of course, the prospect of sightseeing in Tashkent went “down the drain”.

On the way to the airport, men in long traditional Muslim garbs, lounged in the sun- enjoying the beautiful weather. Cows grazed in the green lush meadows, and a mule led donkeys, with jute bags on their backs filled with vegetables.

We checked in at the airport. Sure enough, we **were** scheduled for the late afternoon. This meant we had to spend a whole day at the airport, instead of sightseeing as we had planned.

We found a sandwich counter at the airport- none-too-soon!

“We’d like sandwiches for the children, please. “ Ben told the sales lady.

“Give us your vouchers.” she said.

So he did.

“No. These are for the hotel … Not for the airport.”

“Well, then we’ll pay cash.” Ben told her.

“We can’t accept money. We only take airport-vouchers.”

Ben and I argued with her- it made no difference. Eventually, we both gave up, and we all took seats in the reception area--hoping for something to eat, later, on the plane.

More than 24 hours had passed since we had last eaten anything! By now, we no longer felt hunger.

The airport, an old building with high ceilings and concrete walls, reminded me of a huge factory. We were ushered into a large hall where a few travelers were already seated. The chairs we found were metal seats and most uncomfortable!

“Mom. I’m tired. These chairs are so-o-o hard.” Said Sonia.

"Go!" I told the children. "See if you two can find any shop with comfortable chairs."

They came back in a few minutes, each with an unhappy face.

"Mom! Dad! This place is boring!" Levon spoke up. "It looks like the airport is filled with old torture-room chairs!"

We were all exhausted. By afternoon I felt angry and frustrated.

Finally, our plane arrived and we checked in. As we started our journey, the captain began speaking in Armenian. Wow! The captain and stewardesses were Armenian. We were thrilled!

During our stay in Lahore, Pakistan we had not heard or met a single Armenian. This was a welcome surprise. Our emotions overwhelmed us and once again, I could hardly withhold tears of joy.

This plane was an experience. Seats were not assigned. So, when we boarded, transit passengers had occupied most of them. Sonia and I sat together. Ben sat one row in front, and Levon sat two rows behind us. Suddenly, Levon jumped up, "Water is dripping on my head, and guess what, Mom! I have the seat belt in my hand. Look!"

We found him another seat and double checked our own seat belts. Sure enough, only one was secured. All the others were torn-off. We were unable to buckle-up. Next, Sonia's seat cushion fell off! "Mom what shall I do?"

Ben and I straightened the seat and made Sonia comfortable. I prayed that we arrive safely in Yerevan.

We met an American couple and we told them our experience. They were sympathetic, a lady offered a small piece of salami sausage to the children. But the children felt embarrassed, to accept it. However with a little encouragement, Sonia finally took the sausage.

We met Armenians from Yerevan in the plane. One of them worked in a hospital, and we asked her if she knew Ben's sister.

She said, "Yes! I know her daughter, she is a doctor in one of the hospitals."

"Please inform her that we'll be in Yerevan at Armenia Hotel."

"I definitely will inform her. She'll be thrilled!"

By now we had nothing to eat. But, as we approached our destination, (Yerevan, Armenia), we forgot our hunger.

At the Yerevan airport, a van met us from the *Intourist* office. When the guides realized we were Armenian they were elated, but also upset when we told them that we had nothing to eat for forty-eight hours. They held the van and brought a box for the children with sandwiches, boiled eggs and other food.

Although Levon and Sonia were too embarrassed to eat, I noticed how they were eyeing the box. The moment we reached our hotel room, they attacked the food like wolves and within minutes all was gone!

We expected to see Ben's sister Arpineh at the airport or at the Hotel Armenia. But, Alas! No one came to greet us.

We thought, *maybe tomorrow.*

Hotel Armenia was in the center of the city, by Lenin Square (presently Independence Circle). Lenin's huge statue was prominently set on the south side of the square with his hand pointing to the north. Right across the hotel stood the imposing Natural History Museum with its beautiful ornate columns.

The lobby of the hotel dazzled us with oriental carpets with vibrant colors, surrounded with comfortable sofas. Crystal chandeliers hung at each end- it reminded us of a sultan's reception room.

At one corner, near the entrance, we noticed the check-in counter. The slow elevator stood in the opposite corner as though it was there as an after thought. Most people used the wide red carpeted stairs. Ben and I went toward the elevator, Levon and Sonia climbed the stairs pretending to be royalty.

At each level of the hotel, a full-bodied lady sat with an apron around her waist and a kerchief on her head. She watched our every movement. *A Soviet kind of hotel security?* We were told, "Give her a bottle of cognac – she will give you the best service."

We heard drums that afternoon, on our way to our room. We looked from the balcony and we saw hundreds of what we thought of girl scouts, and boy scouts. We were told "They're Pioneers and Octoberians." All kinds of military men, and veterans, marched proudly around the Square. They were celebrating the anniversary of the Soviet Union's victory of WW II.

I asked someone nearby "Are they Russian or Armenian?"

She was offended, "Of course! Armenian!"

We had never seen so many Armenians in uniform, marching with such dignity. I had goose bumps. We all had tears in our eyes.

The next day, we took one of the scheduled tours. We came back to the hotel in the late afternoon. Still, no one greeted us. Nor were any messages left for us.

"Ben. Do you think your sister and family are afraid to see us?"

In front of the Genocide Monument in Etchmiazin, Armenia

"Maybe. The American Embassy said that they are likely to be harassed after our departure."

So we were cautious. The hotel people were trying to help us, and we were surprised that no one came to meet us. A quiet man, in a hotel uniform-behind the reception counter-with a round red face-short hair and an indifferent look- speaking from one side of his mouth- suggested, "Why don't you take a taxi and go to their house?"

"Can we? Isn't it dangerous?" I questioned.

They laughed, "On the contrary. They'll be very upset if they found out that you came and left, without seeing them."

In the afternoon, after coming back from another of our scheduled tours, we took a taxi. "Driver! We're scared from going to our relative's house; we don't want anything to happen to them."

"*Tzavet danim*! How can you think that way? Hop-in I'll take you there."

He was sympathetic, when we arrived, he refused any money. We knocked on the gate of Ben's sister's house. As we were knocking, the postman came and delivered a letter.

"Ben! Look! It's the letter you mailed a month ago from Pakistan!"

His sister almost fainted the moment she saw us. She thought she was seeing ghosts. There was much jubilation- hugging, kissing, crying- we were all crying and laughing at the same time.

We found out later that the lady traveling with us on the plane had forgotten to inform Ben's niece about our arrival. Sure enough, the letter that just came was our letter that Ben had sent a month before our departure from Lahore, informing his sister that we are coming to Yerevan.

A high wall surrounded the stone house, the iron-gate was the only entry way. Inside, fruit trees surrounded us; the aroma of the flowers transported us into a different world. Later, a tour of the garden revealed a special pit for barbecue. There were chicken coops in the back of the house. They had two bedrooms, a living room and a dining room.

I went shopping with Arpineh. She explained that in the Soviet Union you waited in line for everything. When they sell-out, they close the door and tell everyone, "Come back tomorrow."

At the meat market, the butcher recognized her. He put a large amount on the side for her. She had to stay in line and when her turn came she paid extra –under the table- This was the same for bread, vegetables, or any other item, such as shoes.

She made one of the Armenian dishes that we all liked- *Dolma*- (Lamb/beef- stuffed vegetables)

DOLMA

3 green peppers
3 firm tomatoes
3 med. Zucchini squash
3 Tbsp. chopped parsley
2 cloves garlic
1 8-oz. can tomato sauce
2 Tbsp. lemon juice
2 med. Onions, chopped fine
½ cup rice
1 ½ lb. ground lamb/beef
3 Tbsp. chopped mint leaves(option)
Salt & pepper to taste

Scoop out centers of green peppers and squash. Do the same to the tomatoes but add the pulp to the meat mixture. Mix all ingredients and fill hollows of vegetables, but not too full. Arrange side-by- side, in a pan, add one cup water, cover and bake in medium oven for 1½ hours.

ALMOND GOUREBIEH COOKIES

1 cup flour
½ cup Crisco and butter
1 pkg. blanched whole almonds
½ cup sugar

Mix butter in mixer until it is a paste. Gradually add sugar. Add enough flour to make dough. Taking a little at a time, form a long roll and cut in pieces, or "S" shaped pieces. Press one almond on each piece. Bake in a 350 degree oven for 15 minutes. They should not be brown.

Ben's sister, Arpineh, was a radio announcer in the Arabic language. It was the Soviet answer to the voice of America, broadcasting to Arab countries.

Her husband, Gaidzag, was an interesting personality. He was a poet and a writer, he knew seven languages. He loved Armenia. He and his family, migrated to Armenia in 1948, with many other Armenians from around the world when Stalin opened travel to the USSR to repatriates. Gaidzag was disappointed in the Soviet System. He was working in the children's library.

One of his workers was once disgruntled and jealous from Gaidzag's position, went to the communist leaders of the area and pointed a finger at him, in court, he falsified against him. Gaidzag was surprised, knowing that he had helped this man many times; this was during the time when Stalin was ruling with an iron fist. Gaidzag was put in jail and eventually sent to Siberia.

It was very upsetting to hear him tell the way he was treated in jail. He was forced to hard labor in sub zero weather. His family was furious. They sold what they had and raised money and did every

Visiting the Lepedjian family in Yerevan 1970

thing to prove his innocence. Finally, after two years, he was released- sick and emaciated.

Gaidzag and Arpineh had four children. The eldest daughter, Maro had a doctorate in chemistry, the second daughter Anahid, was an engineer and the third daughter, Tamara, was a Pediatrician. Their son, Aram, was twelve years old, attending a special music school and playing the piano. We had heard that American blue jeans were the rage in the Soviet Union and brought him a pair. He went to bed hugging the jeans!

"We were worried when we did not see you at the airport." Ben said and explained what they told us through the embassy.

"Things are much better now. During Stalin's time it was bad, we watched what we said." Gaidzag said.

"Brother, sometimes we felt the walls were listening to us." Arpineh continued. "The young communist members stooped under the window and listened to your conversation, you did not dare say anything anti-government."

Ben wanted to meet electric power engineers of Yerevan. Gaidzag was a friend of the Minister of Water and Power, and he arranged such a meeting. Once at the ministry, we were invited to sit at a huge table. Ben being an electric power planning engineer started asking many technical questions. We watched in amazement as a highly specialized engineer was called into the room to answer each specific question. By the end of the meeting there were twelve engineers. They each expressed respect for someone with so much diversified knowledge. They were highly specialized and eager to talk with Ben.

After the meeting, the Minister of Water and Power invited Ben to the main hydro electric power station at Lake Sevan, something that Ben really wanted to see.

Lake Sevan was about one hour's drive from Yerevan. As we entered the city limits of Sevan, there was a black limousine parked on the side of the road. They signaled us and we stopped.

Gaidzag said, "The mayor of Lake Sevan is here."

The mayor, a short man with a jovial personality, dressed in a black suit, approached with two of his men.

What Now? I thought. We were surprised to see him come towards us with a bottle of champagne and glasses.

"Welcome to our town!" he said His helper opened the champagne and poured it into the glasses.

"*Genatzet*! (Here's to your health) Welcome, and let's drink to your visit."

We never expected such a reception.

After about ten minutes of welcoming talks and drinking to each other's health, we continued on our way toward the electric power plant, with two limousines. As we arrived, we were ushered into an elevator, I was skeptical and worried. The elevator kept descending on and on. It was only a few minutes, *but for me it felt like a never ending downward plunge.*

"How far down do we have to go?" I asked.

"Not much left," someone said.

We finally reached the bottom. As the doors opened, the scene was massive. This was the generator room of the dam. There were huge turbines about two to three stories high. I had never seen anything like it. Ben, tried to explain to me and the children what was happening, and the function of each instrument. The children were terribly excited, especially Levon who was mesmerized by all the giant electrical equipment.

On one side of the room, there were huge windows and we could see the concrete dam and the water flowing down it. How fascinating! After realizing why we had to come so far down it was not as intimidating going up.

Once out of the dam, the mayor and the minister invited us to take a boat ride on Lake Sevan. At the pier we climbed into a motor boat and sped off. The Minister wanted to show us how clear the water was, so he dipped the cup into the lake. O-O-P-S- He lost the cup. The boat was going too fast; but the second attempt was successful. We all admired the beautiful clear water of Lake Sevan.

The Mayor was explaining that Lake Sevan is one of the largest high altitude lakes in the world. It is situated in the central part of the Republic of Armenia, at the altitude of 1900 meters above sea level. The name Sevan literally means Black Van. It is said that long ago Armenians came from the areas around Lake Van and saw that the lake was almost black and reminded them of Van. (730-714BC).

. The Mayor continued, "The lake was well known for it's *Ishkhan* (prince) fish, which they exported to Moscow, specially for the Premier and the Politburo of the Kremlin."

We visited the island where there is a church- *Sevanavank*. A monk greated us and explained, "With the order of the first King of the Bagradit Kingdom- Ashod I, three churches and a group of cells

Vicky at Sevanavank - Lake Sevan, Armenia 1970

were built by monks in 874."

"The island was used for worship, pilgrimage, and a place of exile for Armenian nobleman who had fallen into disgrace. In 859 Ashot I, led a battle from the island against invading Arabs and the Ottomans. During the battle, monks and clergy fought alongside the army. Five hundred years later the Persians and the Ottomans divided the Armenian Kingdom."

After the tour, we were the luncheon guests of the Mayor and the Minister of Water and Power. They insisted that we eat the famous *Ishkan* fish. They made us realize that in their communist country, everyone is equal. The workers, the drivers, us, the Mayor and the Minister all sat at the same long table.

The fish was delicious. They loved their vodka. They took turns in standing up and toasting. After a few words of welcome, they drank bottoms up. "*Genatzet*! Brother Ben, for having you as our guest!"

"*Genatzet*! Fellow Armenian for being amongst us!"

"*Genatzet*, Ben for your health and happiness, and long life!"

Everyone was wishing something, and every time, at the end of the wish, we were supposed to empty our glass of vodka and then they immediately refilled it up.

"I am sorry, but I can only drink one glass." I said.
"Fine, we understand."
Being a woman they accepted.
Ben took a sip but was unable to empty the glass every time.
"It's an insult if you don't drink all of it." said the Mayor.
"My health does not allow me." said Ben. This, they accepted.
That same evening we had tickets to go to the opera to see *Anoush*. A popular Armenian opera.
"We need to go early so we can make it to the opera." Gaidzag said. As he began searching frantically through his pockets. Then in an unhappy voice he declared. "Unfortunately the tickets are at the house and I need to go there to pick them up."
We were running late, the minister volunteered, "Driver, take Gaidzag to his house so he can pick up the tickets and hurry back to the opera."
"Yes I'll take him, hurry Gaidzag!"
They dropped Ben myself and the children at the opera house. Ben's sister was waiting there, she was worried. When she saw us she took a long breath.
"Where is Gaidzag?"
"He went to pick-up the tickets from the house."
"We have only ten minutes for the opera to start, I thought that he had the tickets with him. He will never make it!" She was livid.
The time of the opera came and we still were outside waiting anxiously for Gaidzag. We were on pins and needles, we were sure we'll miss the opera, when finally we saw the minister's limousine arrive with Gaidzag, we started breathing.
We finally entered and it was already ten minutes passed the time of the opening scene; they held the performance until we were seated! According to Ben's sister, "I just can't believe this! Something like that has never happened before and it can never happen again in the Soviet Union."
We enjoyed the *Anoush* Opera greatly. The actress was a famous Armenian star with a beautiful voice. The opera starts with happy scenes, with popular songs, but the ending of the opera is tragic, almost everyone left the opera with tears in their eyes.
During sightseeing we noticed that the hills were scattered with black stones, after a closer examination we recognized the semi-precious stone, obsidian, Armenia is rich with minerals.
The fresh fruit and produce of Armenia was not only large in

size, but also had a hyper taste like nothing that we have every experienced. A tomato tasted more tomato like. The same with all the fruit especially the tennis ball size apricots.

"Apricots were known in Armenia during ancient times. Apricot seeds were found in an archeological site in Armenia in an Eneolithic era site. Its scientific name is *Prunus Armeniaca* (Armenian plum) Alexander the Great exported apricot trees and white heart cherry trees from Armenia to Europe." Gaidzag explained. He was proud of the vodka he had made from the apricots of their tree and served it almost every night with dinner.

Every morning Ben's sister Arpineh collected eggs from the chicken coop and we had fresh egg omelets.

It was fun to collect and eat fresh fruit from their tree.

Collecting mulberries in the backyard, Yerevan

"Aram, climb the berry tree, let's collect some mulberries." said Arpineh.

"Fine mother, I'll first bring the white sheet and make it ready."

We each held a part of the sheet under the branches and gave direction to Aram to where the ripe looking berries were.

"Aram go to the branch on the right, shake harder!"

"Ha! Ha! Look at those beautiful berries come down." Ben said with a glint in his eye.

"Ben, stop tasting them you won't leave any for us!" I screamed.

It was time for us to leave Yerevan and the family, this was the hardest part- to say goodbye. I enjoyed the magnificent pastoral surroundings, loved the Armenian architecture and elated at the archeological sights. In a short time we became closely attached to Armenia and its people. We had to say goodbye to all.

Moscow

Our next stop in the Soviet Union was Moscow. our hotel was in the outskirts of the city.

We were disappointed, since we had to travel half an hour by bus before starting any tour.

We went to the *Intourist* office in the hotel and complained.

"We reserved a first class hotel... It was supposed to be in the center of the city." Ben stressed.

"This is a first class hotel."

"Please transfer us to another hotel closer to the center of Moscow then."

"You want first class hotel?"

"Yes."

"OK, give one hundred dollar more and we will upgrade you,"

We were tired and agreed and paid the hundred dollars. After taking the money they ushered us back to our room and gave us two extra blankets and said.

"Here now, this is your first class hotel room."

We argued, but no use. They would not listen; they were very rude and uncooperative.

We went and saw the fabulous *Bolshoi* Ballet in the outstanding and ornate opera house. All the chairs in the orchestra had red seats. Surrounding the orchestra were the second and third level booths with dazzling gold-color wood and red drapes. There was a central booth which was larger and more elaborate than the others; we assumed that must have been the one for the tsar and the tsarina when they visited the opera house.

We were lucky to find tickets for one of the booths close to the stage. It was thrilling to watch the fairylike ballerinas dancing. We rented binoculars but we did not need them. We were close enough (two booths away) to see the expressions of the dancers, the sweat forming on their forehead, the wrinkles as they smiled.

During intermission with lights on, the opera house looked stunning. The hallway was filled with people talking and drinking. Most women wore long dresses and men were in suits. It was elegant.

We were the odd ones amongst them with our ordinary American pant suits.

We visited *Gome*, the largest department store in Moscow. Most of the other stores were almost empty. We were surprised when we saw a long line of people standing outside a shoe store to buy shoes.

There were no lines in the souvenir store, so we bought a few souvenirs. When we stepped outside the souvenir store, we saw the store employee of the shoe store close the door gesturing, she said a few words in Russian. Some of the people standing in line showed anger and left murmuring. Others, like sheep, just turned around and with a resigned expression, left. We felt sorry for those people.

I thought I was in a fairyland when I saw the spectacular St. Basil church.

Our guide explained, "It is a Russian Orthodox Cathedral, erected on the Red Square in Moscow, in 1555-1561, on the order of Ivan IV of Russia to commemorate the capture of Kazan and Astrakhan. It marks the geometric center of the city. It was the tallest building in Moscow until the completion of Ivan the Great Bell Tower. In 1928, it became a State Historical Museum."

It is part of Moscow's Kremlin and Red Square UNESCO World

In Red Square, Moscow, 1970

Sonia and Levon in front of the Kremlin, 1970.

Heritage site since 1990.

The Cathedral design shaped as a flame of a bonfire is very unique. From every angle the building was shimmering.

According to legend: the tsar, Ivan the Terrible, blinded the architect so that he would not be able to build another one like it.

There was a long line by Lenin's tomb, but it was moving fast, as you entered the tomb you felt the cold air. It was quiet and eerie, I had goose bumps! In single file we followed each other. His body was in a glass coffin we were surprised to see that his skin looked very real. It gave the impression as though he had just died.

At the Kremlin museum, we were dazzled with the unbelievable beauty of the carriages of the Tsarina. Most carriages were covered with precious and semi–precious stones- masterpieces of art. There were sixteenth century carriages and closed sleighs. The guide explained that many originated in European artistic centers such as London, Paris, Vienna and Berlin.

Lenin square was buzzing with tourists from all over the world, each with their own guides, speaking in different languages. People were friendly and helpful. We took buses, went sightseeing on our own and we never felt pressured or restricted.

We decided to take a walking tour of the suburb we were in. It felt like any other city with people walking to or from work. As we approached a grocery store we went in and found that they sell only cuts of fresh meat. Right at that moment we saw a robust woman arguing in Russian with the butcher. We did not understand what they said. But we assumed that the butcher was charging her more than he should.

Suddenly we saw her pick-up the meat and throw it on the counter with a huge **BANG**! She started screaming at the butcher and we were sure a fist fight would follow, fortunately there was the counter between them. We immediately got out of that store. From outside we could see and hear the furious argument. It was time for us to leave, and continue our walk.

A few feet away, a young boy approached us with some Russian military souvenir pins.

"Chewing gum?" he requested.

We had already given all our chewing gum out to other people. Levon liked one of his pins.

"I will give you one ruble for the pin." Ben said.

"Thank you," The young boy was happy.

"Ben, why don't we go and take the subway?" I suggested.

"Good idea."

"Wow! Look at those paintings, the whole underground looks like a museum."

We were very much impressed: each station was designed on a different theme and each more beautiful than the previous one, very attractive, clean, and colorful with outstanding architecture. We decided to take a ride. We were enjoying our ride, when, we realized we had passed our exit.

"Oh! No! We passed our station." I said disappointedly.

"How do we come back?" chimed in Sonia.

"Let's get out at the next station." I suggested.

When we exited, there were three tunnels, one more colorful than the other.

"NO! We are lost! Which tunnel do we take to go back?"

After turning in circles, we found someone who knew a little English and helped us out.

Our stay in Moscow was short but very enjoyable; it was time for us to say our goodbyes to this exceptionally beautiful city.

At the airport, after a long wait, we boarded our plane. We had first class tickets. We learned the hard way: there were no first class seats in Soviet planes.

"Why did you charge us for first class tickets if there wasn't a first class compartment?"

"Oh! You want first class! HERE! Come!" *Hmmm!*

The stewardess briskly led us to the front of the plane where there was a table and two seats on each side. She said, "Here is your first class." *O-h-h here again another first class experience!* We not only attracted attention but we had a very uncomfortable ride all the way to London.

Our Visit to Singapore

Ben had eight weeks of vacation coming and was entitled to go home to Chicago. We decided to go via the far east and return from the west. Thus making a round the world tour.

Our first stop was Singapore. Attractive buildings, lovely promenades and beautiful gardens, along with the hospitality of the people made us feel welcome.

On our second day, a young man approached us. “I’d like to show you my city.” He said.

At first, not knowing what he really wanted from us, we felt uncomfortable with the offer, but after walking with him a while, we became friends.

“You have a beautiful and a very clean city,” We told him

“Yes, we do. We’re very proud of our city.” said the young man.

He took us to many lovely shops. Full of fine china, fine pottery and other household items.

We offered to pay him.

“No. Thank you. Helping tourists experience our culture first hand is my pleasure.”

. We visited the Bukit Timah Nature preserve and were captivated by the exotic birds in the forest. We spent time strolling among pagodas in the Chinese and Japanese gardens.

Our cable car climbed high to Mount Faber, Sonia had never ridden a cable car. She was nervous. I too was uneasy. But tried not to show it. Especially, when we were above a wide river, with ships sailing below. We began to take pictures of each other making faces, clowning. Eventually we were all laughing at our foolishness. The panoramic view of the harbor and islands were spectacular.

The oddity of seeing St. Gregory an Armenian church in Singapore brought tears to my eyes. Built in 1835, on Armenia Street its architecture includes well proportioned Roman Doric Columns. A guard opened the door for us when we arrived.

The small sanctuary, with its semi-circular alter had a wooden cross on the wall, and Armenian writing above it. The wooden pews had rattan backing reflecting Singapore’s tropical climate. As we entered, we felt the peace and sacredness of the place. There were very few pictures. The sun’s rays entering from one of the windows, left me with a feeling of deep mystical reflection. This was one of the highlights of our visit to Singapore.

The Memorial Garden was tucked within the tranquility of the tropical landscape that surrounded the church. *Khatchkars* (ornate tombstone crosses made of tufa stone) were scattered in the garden as a remembrance for the Armenian people who lived their lives in Singapore. From the writing on these tombstones, we pieced together the kind of life they led- hard, demanding and challenging. Some tombstones told the story of their escape from the Armenian Genocide by the Ottoman Turks. Other tombstones were of prominent Armenians, such as those of the two brothers, Archak and Digran Sarkies, builders of the Raffle Hotel in Singapore. Many of the writings described the generosity and help the government and the people of Singapore demonstrated during the eighteen hundreds. I was moved!

"Are there any Armenians living here?" I asked the guard.

"No." he replied.

"A priest?"

"No. Once a year an Armenian priest comes to Singapore to celebrate mass. Armenians from around the world attend the celebration. All the Armenians left Singapore. Many migrated to Australia."

We felt happy that the church was designated as a National Monument by the local National Preservation Board.

As we left the church, we found ourselves in a bazaar by the river. An endless variety of stores with extraordinary treasures and trinkets beckoned me to shop. My first purchase was batik material for a dress.

Our hotel was in the center of the city, on a quiet street. The most imposing hotel was the Raffles Hotel built in 1886. A majestic building, they called it the "Grand Old Lady Of The East," the hotel was the favorite retreat of writers and movie stars. As we had discovered from the church, it was built and managed by the two famous Armenian Sarkies brothers.

We loved Singapore, it is a fascinating city, but our time was up and we had to leave.

Manila

Manila, a city of wonders! An exciting city- full of surprises and so cosmopolitan! The strong American influence is still evident.

The day we arrived, the Philippine president's wife, Mrs. Imelda Marcos, was giving a reception in the hotel we were staying. Hundreds of people were crowding the halls, music everywhere, the television media had taken over.

Pakistan did not have television at the time. We did not realize how much we missed watching TV. So we were glued to the TV in our hotel room. As we watched we saw that the gala parties, on TV were happening in our hotel.

"Why don't we watch what's going on in the lobby?" I suggested.

We all agreed. We rushed downstairs, the place was flooded with gorgeous girls, actors and actresses, dressed in Philippine style clothing.

We were in awe as we watched the stunning gowns of the beautiful women and the dashing men walking through the large lobby. The hallways were filled with young people, laughing, conversing loudly and music permeated the air. The joyous atmosphere was contagious and we all felt a thrill at being a part of it.

The next day more sightseeing and shopping! The shops were filled with monkey-pod wood. (We bought a gorgeous salad bowl with carvings on it. We still use it.) Ben bought a shirt made of papyrus-type material popular among the men. I ordered a dress with a hand embroidered design.

I was surprised, the finished dress was brought to our hotel room the next day. How could they finish it in one day? It fit me well and I looked stunning in it.

I loved the plates and lamps made from sea-shells, but hesitated in buying them since we had to carry them onto the plane.

We took rides to various parts of the Philippines. One sight we viewed from a distance was the island where a volcano had erupted a week before our arrival.

We were introduced to a drink made with coconut juice that we drank with a straw inserted in a green coconut. M-M-M Delicious! I wish I could remember the ingredients of the concoction.

The market was filled with an unbelievable variety of bananas-tiny ones, red ones, long and thin ones, some just for cooking.

We visited the cemetery where World War II American soldiers are buried in a serene and peaceful surrounding. Crosses lined up with military precision reminding us of the sacrifices made for freedom.

The most inexpensive public transportation in the Philippines

Visiting a Jeepney wookshop in Manila, 1970

is the Jeepney. These are the original US military jeeps that were left over from World War II, and are known for their flamboyant decorations with vibrant colors, tin roofs, and crowded seating.

We met friendly Italians, who were going to an "Italian night" celebration. They insisted that we join them. We were surprised to see so many Italians in Manila.

There was singing, dancing, Italian food, presentations and jokes- and of course, all in Italian. We hardly understood half of it. The friendly atmosphere reminded us of home. We had one of the most enjoyable experiences.

The best part of these trips was that both Levon and Sonia were being exposed to multiple languages and customs as they tasted unique foods and experienced different cultures.

Visiting Home

At Hawaii Airport, a stretch limousine stopped in front of us and the driver said; "I'll take you for the price of a taxi."

"Fine. We're going to Hilton Mandarin Hotel." Said Ben.

The driver took us to a hotel, and as soon as we stopped, he unloaded the luggage and disappeared.

"Ben! Look at the sign. It says; 'The Reef Hotel.' Where is the driver? This isn't our hotel!"

"Aloha! How can I help you" said the hotel's uniformed person as he approached us.

"We are looking for the driver that brought us to this hotel. This isn't where we have a reservation."

"Let me see... No, you're not registered. But we can accommodate you though, be seated please. We'll easily arrange it."

We looked around for the driver of the limousine. We saw our luggage sitting in the middle of the lobby. The children were fast asleep on the couches beside the registration desk. The driver and his limousine had vanished. We did not have energy enough to look for the Hilton Mandarin Hotel.

We realized that he had tricked us. The driver would get a kick back from this hotel. We were furious. Our spirits were dampened. I felt like a clap of thunder hit me and I was ready to jump on the driver, but alas! He was nowhere to be found.

We were so tired and it was getting late. Reluctantly we accepted to stay in this hotel. To this day I feel cheated and we missed staying in a luxurious hotel.

For a week we did some sightseeing and resting. It was at this time that we bought matching Hawaiian moo-moos for the women and shirts for the men. We noticed that as we were sightseeing Levon always stayed behind.

"Levon why don't you join us?" I asked

"Forget it! We look silly dressed like this, everyone is looking at us," he answered with disgust.

"They all realize we are a family," replied Sonia.

In Pakistan driving is on the left side of the road like the British. While Ben was driving in an area where there was no traffic, without realizing he was on the left side of the street. Suddenly a car started coming from the opposite direction, Ben said look at that guy he is

At the USS Arizona Memorial in Honolulu, 1970

playing chicken with me. As he came closer, we suddenly realized that we were the ones on the wrong side of the road. We all screamed in unison and Ben jumped and brought the car to the right. I could imagine how the opposite driver was angry and probably cursing.

After a one week of rest in Hawaii, we left for Chicago.

In Chicago, most of the time, Ben was busy at the main office. My sister had organized a week of parties for us to renew our friendship with our old friends.

On our way back, in New York, we were united with my brother Garabed and family from Detroit, my sister Artemis and family from North Carolina. We visited museums, art galleries, theaters and restaurants. In one of the restaurants my brother befriended a piano player. All throughout dinner they alternated playing at the piano. My sister played Chopin, Beethoven, my brother played tango and other popular pieces. Music took wings and transported my emotions to another place.

Via London and Beirut we reached Lahore, Pakistan. Thus we ended our round the world home leave.

Having Pets

In an apartment, it was not easy to have pets. Levon wished he did have one. His friends lived in houses with large gardens, They had more room for pets. We bought Levon a beautiful parrot with rainbow-colored feathers and a red beak.

Under Levon's tutelage, the parrot soon acquired an enviable vocabulary--as well as a sensational wolf whistle, we all enjoyed listening to its chatter. But the wolf whistle was its favorite.

The parrot was confined in it's small cage. So occasionally, we allowed it to fly around the screened balcony. Like humans it loved the freedom. Besides, people passing by enjoyed listening to its chatter and laughed.

One day, I heard the door bell ringing, followed by fierce banging on the door. Startled, I jumped! "*What's happening*?" Someone was cursing and shouting. I wondered as I opened the door to find one of our neighbors, who also was the wife of Ben's work colleague standing there shaking with anger.

"**What's the matter?**" I asked puzzled

With bulging eyes, she glared at me and shrilled:

"**What kind of son are you raising? What vulgar example are you giving him and what kind of mother are you anywa**y?" I'll teach him a lesson for being so rude and disrespectful to me." She rushed in and headed to the balcony.

I could not believe that Levon could be disrespectful to her.

"**What did he do**?" I asked confounded. (He was not at home at the time.)

"He gave me a lewd whistle as I was passing!" she exclaimed, almost foaming at the mouth.

Well, I immediately realized what had happened, and beckoned to her to follow me to the balcony. And I'm sure you can guess what the parrot did at that very moment: looking directly at the woman, he gave a masterful rendition of his wolf whistle. "Where is he? Where is he?" she kept saying.

After a few moments of embarrassed silence, the parrot repeated its wolf whistle. When it finally dawned on my choleric neighbor that her ill-conceived anger was unwarranted, she apologized profusely. But I was angry and disgusted at her behavior, as well as the ugly words she used.

I accepted her repeated apologies, of course, but decided right then that I never wanted to associate with someone who behaved with such reckless foolishness and who couldn't control her temper.

Levon kept asking, "Can I have a cat?"

We kept saying, "No, you have the parrot and one pet was enough."

One day the door bell rang and I was waiting for Levon to open the door. He did not. Someone kept on ringing the bell. I went to the door, as I opened it, Levon's friend was standing there, I told him

"Levon is inside. Why don't you come in?"

"Please open your hands,"

I wondered why, but I did it, anyway. The next thing I knew, he had put a beautiful tan colored, fiery blue eyed Siamese kitten in my hands. Before I could say a word, he had disappeared. Our son did not say a word. The sneaky pair had planned well. They knew that once I had seen the kitten I would melt and accept it. This was the most gorgeous kitten I had ever seen. I turned. Confronting Levon, I saw his "funny" smile.

"How can you trick your own mother, you know we said, 'no'!" I scolded.

But I could not let the beautiful kitten go.

We all loved her. But, as she grew, she started to be active and destructive. She climbed up the drapery on one side of the room, ran across the railing and slid down the opposite side of the drapery; she was ruining them and the furniture as well.

While we were at school we had to confine her in Levon's room. We realized she enjoyed the companionship of the Parrot. After school we always found the cat cuddled next to the parrot's cage. They seemed to take pleasure in each other's company.

After a while, the cat started to tease the parrot. She would go next to the cage and move her tail back and forth; the bird would follow the cat's movement like a hypnotic dance. One day we saw the parrot peck the cat's tail. The cat jumped three feet in the air with a big MEOW! She never learned her lesson. She kept on teasing the parrot, and the parrot kept on pecking the cat's tail. It seemed they both enjoyed this game.

We had the parrot in the balcony, it was flying around, and it used to enjoy pecking on the wooden frame of the screen netting. We did not realize it had pecked it so much that the netting had separated from its frame. The parrot made a hole and escaped. We looked all over for him. Our *chowkidar* (guard) found him in the evening and brought him back. We repaired the netting. But after a few months he had done the same thing, and this time we never found him.

John- a colleague of Ben, and his wife, Mary, lived in our apartment complex, both enjoyed Levon's company. Levon was in ninth grade at the time. John taught Levon how to create a chemical recation by using an iodine compound. He called it "contact-explosives," because it would explode with a loud pop when you touched or stepped on it.

On April 1, 1969 while I taught my sixth grade class, I noticed Levon, who was supposed to be in his class, come to my section of the building, he was surprised to see me. Seeing his quick movement, I knew he was into some mischief.

"Levon! What are you doing here?'

"Nothing, Mom. My friend and I are only going to the bathroom."

"You should go to your classroom."

"Don't worry, Mom. I will. I've got study hall."

Twenty minutes later, the bell rang and the students started to change classes. As they stepped into the hall, we heard "POP! POP!" I heard crackling noises from all over the school. Hilarious! Students were jumping, looking under their shoes, touching the ground, but they could not see anything. Pandemonium permeated the air.

"WHAT'S HAPPENING?" Everyone screamed.

There was nothing in the hallway. The iodine compound stuck to their shoes and carried into each of their classrooms. As it dried, their foot contact to the floor created a reaction with a big "BANG!".

I wanted to crawl into a hole!

I knew Levon organized this and I also knew that he was sitting in his classroom with an 'angelic face'. No one suspected him of doing anything wrong. The school was in turmoil all day long.

Levon also used this compound on the stairs at our apartment. No one realized they were stepping on wet iodine compound, but as it dried the "POP! BANG!" began.

Levon was so upset with the neighbor lady who called him names, that he used it mostly around her apartment. He got his revenge. She never thought Levon had anything to do with it; she blamed the other neighbor boys, who had been caught earlier playing with firecrackers. In reality, they had been in cahoots with Levon all along.

Ben and I scolded Levon, “Don’t use it again around here... or anywhere else!”

Conversely, Sonia was a little angel. She was taking ballet lessons, she loved dancing; and she participated in every activity at school. (Every Christmas she helped me make a papier-mâché *piñata*).

A *piñata* was a novelty in Pakistan and no one had made one before. Our base was chicken wire: we twisted it to the shape we wanted it to be; we covered the formed shape with strips of newspaper dipped in a solution of flour and water; (it took a long time for it to dry). After it dried, Levon and Sonia painted the piñata with watercolors. We had filled it with candy and small toys. Two days before Christmas, we joined with other ladies from the apartments and invited all the servant’s children of the complex to join us for an exciting Christmas party.

Each child received a little bag with candy and presents. I sewed each bag with shiny red material I found. (Sonia prepared ribbons to tie them). There were about fifty children, all dressed in colorful clothing, well groomed hair, and well behaved. All enjoyed every minute of it. It was a joy to hear their laughter and see their smiling faces.

During this time many young travelers passed through Lahore on their way to India. We saw young addicts arriving from Europe in unhealthy condition and in tattered cloths. Some could hardly breathe. Marijuana and poppy plants grew wild all over this region; as we were playing golf, Levon pointed to a patch of weeds on the side of the golf course.

“Mom. Look! These are Marijuana plants, see! They grow wild.”

“Levon. Make sure you stay away from those plants!

“Don’t worry mom, I’m not that crazy.”

On her way to India, following a guru, a twenty year old American girl stopped in Lahore. The school invited her to come and talk to the high school students. She had stopped taking drugs but the damage was obvious. We all were shocked to see her appearance: she looked like a 60 year old woman with half her teeth missing and whatever left was black, her face was wrinkled, and she was extremely thin, reminded me of a skeleton. (obviously malnourished).

She considered the guru a great teacher of life and followed him. He had helped her reform herself and that saved her life. She encouraged our students to stay away from drugs:

"I ruined my health. Many times, they rushed me to the hospital near-death." She said.

It was a good education for all the students.

Christmas party at the apartments for the workers' children

Vacationing in Europe

Two years after our last vacation, we were thankful to leave the hot July weather of Lahore (so hot the asphalt stuck to your shoes!) and depart for Europe. Local people in Denmark wore summer clothes and many were sunning themselves in swimsuits. For us it was cold. We wore jackets and coats.

In Copenhagen, we visited the famous mermaid statue; we were surprised to see how small it was. It represents the fairy tale by Danish author Hans Christian Anderson- the story of a young mermaid who fell in love with a prince who lived on land and often came up to the edge of the water to look for her lover.

At the world famous amusement park, Tivoli Gardens, another surprise awaited us near the Pantomime Theatre. We came face to face with one of Sonia's girlfriends and her family, from Lahore. Both girls enjoyed riding the merry-go-rounds, the famous wooden roller coaster, the world's tallest carousel.

Tivoli Gardens reminded us of Disneyland. No wonder: Walt Disney, after visiting the gardens emulated its happy atmosphere.

Hans Friis, friend and colleague of Ben from the American University of Beirut, met us at the hotel. We followed his car to Forum (a suburb of Copenhagen where they lived by a lake). His wife Helga and son Peter greeted us. Peter is a few months older than our son Levon.

Hans and Helga took us to a fjord where not many tourists visit. The view was spectacular! The pounding of the waves against the steep hills emanated the power of nature and I watched with awe the rise of the rocky terrain from the seashore, imagining *Vikings climbing those steep heights to shore.*

Next to the fjord we saw an open air theater.

In Copenhagen

Our friends invited us to sit down in this natural setting and watch the enactment of the Danes welcoming the Vikings from the sea. The actors wore original costumes and spoke in Danish. Our friends translated it for us. We enjoyed beyond words, the acting and the pastoral surroundings.

What a memorable day!

The next day we visited a museum where marine explorers recovered an original Viking ship in 1962. The museum was built around the ship since it was so fragile to move. Our guide described the scientific method used to restore the wood that had been sub merged in the sea for many years. The ship was kept in sea water for a while and gradually exposed to air. Otherwise the wood would dry quickly and come apart. This process took them over a year.

Our visit to the Viking village was fascinating! As part of a class, university students lived the life of the Vikings for one year in this village. They lived in mud huts with thatched roofs that had an opening in the center for the smoke to go out. They used horses for transportation. The students were not provided with modern facilities so that they could learn how their ancestors lived.

Viking village in Copenhagen.

We saw them till the land with ancient Viking tools. All the students' food came from the land they lived on. They made their own cloths with home-spun material.

We admired the way they lived and the students' perseverance of the harsh life proved invaluable in rediscovering their roots.

Dubrovnik

Our next stop was Dubrovnik- which was in Yugoslavia at the time. We fell in love with its walled city, which goes back to the middle ages. We marveled at its winding cobblestone streets, its small quaint shops, and narrow stairways leading to picturesque houses built along inclines.

In Yugoslavia, a communist country, we did not have difficulties in traveling wherever we wanted.

I still hear the bells of the church of the old city. We happened to be in the center of the city when a group of young people sitting on the steps of the church began to play their guitars and sing, the ringing of the church bells accompanied them.

We took a ferry boat from the city harbor to the nearby garden island. The island was covered with attractive plants. We visited various parks. Sat around- enjoyed the sunshine and the calm atmosphere.

As we went further into the island, we suddenly found ourselves in a nudist camp area. The "skinny dippers" dove from high rocks into the sea- you won't believe how fast we pulled our kids out of the area and retraced our steps to the harbor.

The second day, an American group arrived at the hotel where we were staying. Peace and quiet went out the window! We found it disturbing to hear loud American voices in the hallways, complaining and de-

Dubrovnik Church in the old city.

manding. One voice still rings in my ears. An American lady who, with a shrill voice, screamed in the hallway; "I want toilet paper in my bathroom!... **Where is the manager! I want to speak to the manager!"**

"Oh! Mom. How rude!" said Levon in a disgusted way.

"Remember how you should never behave." I told him.

We hiked along the rocky seashore of Dubrovnik, we visited small villages and enjoyed the hospitality of the gracious people.

On our return we stopped at Lake Geneva, and gazed in wonder at its beauty. From the center of the lake, a spectacular fountain of water shot up into the sky! What a thrill!!

Alas out vacation was too short. We arrived home to Lahore, Pakistan, exhilarated and ready to face life.

At Lake Geneva

Another political Conflict

About the end of 1970 the political situation between India and Pakistan began to deteriorate again. We could **feel** the tension! The American community and especially Ben's company-decided to have meetings and discuss what to do in case of a flare up.

Sure enough, war between the two nations broke out.

Bengal, which was on the eastern side of India, was partitioned by the British in 1947, because of religious differences of the population. The western part went to India, and the eastern part joined Pakistan. This section was named East Pakistan. The population was 88% Moslem. But the language was Bengali. The language created a barrier between East and West Pakistan. Politically the West dominated East Pakistan, thus creating resentment among the East Pakistanis.

East Pakistan leaders fled and set up a government-in-exile in West Bengal, India, in 1971. Eventually, the Bengali irregulars received support from the Indian Armed forces, resulting in the Indo-Pakistan war of 1971. With the help of India, East Pakistan won the war and became independent, calling themselves Bangladesh. About 210 million people live in Bengal, and 60 percent of them live in Bangladesh.

Second Evacuation from Pakistan

When the war broke, we were ordered to close all the curtains and keep the house in darkness. Electricity was cut off most of the time so we used candles. During the day we saw the Indian planes drop bombs on the military bases, make a U turn above our apartment complex and leave. We were terrified!

The company decided that all the women and children should go to Islamabad, the capital of Pakistan, where the American Embassy would provide refuge.

Islamabad was safer because it was further away from the Indian border and the Indians had agreed not to bomb that area for the safety of the international community.

The kids and I were to leave for Islamabad and from there travel out of the country. The men had to stay in Lahore.

"Ben, I wish you were coming with us."

"The government won't allow any of the company men to leave."

"Can't we stay here and celebrate Thanksgiving with you? It's only two days away?"

"Look! We even received a letter that women and children must leave tonight for Islamabad, where it is safer."

We did not want to go. But when the orders came, we had no choice. It was not safe. The next day we each packed a suitcase. The two kids and I left with our driver and drove to Islamabad to the American Embassy.

One of the directors at the Embassy said, "We have a very nice residence, the lady of the house is in the United States, you and the children will be comfortable there."

The house was huge! The downstairs had a living room, a den, a dining room and a kitchen. The servant's quarters was on the side and the bedrooms were upstairs. Each bedroom opened onto a large veranda with a beautiful view. But, alas! We were indoor-bound and afraid to go out to enjoy the view. Every so often, we heard the bombing and the exchange of aerial fire between the Pakistani and the Indian fighter planes. The fear of stray bullets kept us inside even though Levon was curious to watch.

At night, we made sure that the drapes were tightly drawn before lighting the candles. We kept our spirits up by playing a card game called "war," which sometimes lasted three days. Our driver bought the vegetables and meat from the market during the day. The host's servant cooked the meals. He was not used to having children in the house, so there was a little conflict. We made him happy by paying him a little more.

In Islamabad, the American Embassy asked all the evacuated children to attend school and the teachers from Lahore to resume teaching. I was happy about it, but it was not easy: we had to be on alert all the time. I was teaching math and science to the handful of students from my junior high class that had come from Lahore. Many times the air raid siren sounded during class, and all of us ran for shelter. Our days were often filled with frightening and traumatic moments while waiting in the dark hallways for the "all clear" siren. After a while it became a part of everyday life.

"The siren is blowing again! Everyone into the hallway.... get away from the windows!"

"I'm scared! It's dark in here," said one of my shy students.

"It's OK! Come kneel by me. Don't be afraid! I'm next to you. Hold my hand." I held her shivering hand, eventually I could feel her relax and I was happy to see her calm down.

"The siren is blowing again... all's clear. The planes are gone. Now, back to our classroom."

Worried parents started to keep their children home and many others left the country. The school decided to close early for the Christmas holidays.

One night, our host took us to the American club, there was a movie. He thought we would enjoy it. In order to go there, we had to drive without the car lights. It was pitch dark, eerie. There were pot-holes: we had to be careful not to go off the road. Everyone watched the road and gave instructions to the driver.

"Go to the left! There's a big hole on the right."

"What happened to the moon?"

"There is no moon tonight."

"We should be close. Look for the parking lot entrance on the left. It should be open."

"Here it is. Turn in."

Once we were there, we enjoyed ourselves. It was a relief to see other Americans who were going through the same experience. It was refreshing to do something other than play the game "war" by candlelight.

Every Wednesday, we waited by the phone to hear from Ben,

from Lahore. The phones were inconsistent and hard to hear through so we had to yell into the handset.

"Hello? Hello? Vicky? Are you there?"

"Yes, Ben. I can hear you. We've been waiting for your call."

"On Thanksgiving Day, I invited all our single friends, who had let their families go. The turkey which we'd ordered from Denmark was delicious. The cook prepared all the trimmings, I wished you were here," said Ben.

"I'm so glad you invited them...We miss you!"

"I can't wait to see you...and my cat," said Levon.

"That cat is so active! It's driving me and the cook crazy."

Sonia took the phone. "Hi Dad"

"Sonia! I saw your teacher yesterday. She sends you her love." said Ben

Sonia giggled and was happy.

"Here! Mom wants to speak to you."

"The driver is restless. He misses his family." I said.

"Tell him to wait a little longer. There's talk that a few of us with families might leave Lahore and finish the project in Chicago."

"Should we come back?"

"No. It's dangerous. Also, after dark, there's a curfew. No one can go out. I'll call you next week. By then, I'll know more about the decision of the company."

We were happy that he invited others for Thanksgiving Dinner, but sad that we were not there to enjoy the turkey.

Because of the political situation, many of the Harza company consultants were called back to the United States. Ben was asked to leave Lahore. He started to sell everything that we had. Unfortunately, before leaving, we had received our Thanksgiving and Christmas orders from Denmark. This included three months supplies of food and Christmas presents for everyone. We were hiding the presents with the food away from the children.

Ben without realizing had asked a shopkeeper to buy the food in bulk and never removed the Christmas presents that were for the family.

He gave away many items from the house, and he had to abandon many more. I felt sad. Many memory items: baby pictures of the children; letters from our parents; Lahore was under curfew after six o'clock. Ben had little time to pack and organize everything. My not being there, created hardship and loss.

Our driver had to go to Lahore to bring Ben to Islamabad. It made him happy; he had missed his family and he was eager to go.

During this time the American Embassy sent our host to Washington DC. We had this huge house all to ourselves. Loneliness and fear especially at night, became our companion. All three of us slept in one room.

Finally Ben arrived tired and drained, he had a grueling drive. Before he rested he explained to us what had happened.

"Train tracks run parallel to the road to Islamabad and as we were driving, Indian planes attacked any train they saw on them. Many times both the driver and I had to jump and hide in the trenches by the roadside. The bombing was fierce! We had to pull over three or four times. The Indian planes broke away as we came closer to Islamabad. We thanked God that we weren't injured or killed."

Ben had brought Rupees with him since the banks were closed. I had the idea that we could buy gold jewelry with that money. Wherever we went, they refused to sell gold, it was considered contraband during the war. Our friend told us to go to a specific jewelry shop. The moment we entered the shop, with a nervous and concerned look, the jeweler immediately locked the door! Closed the drapes! And drew the shades!

"I have these 24 karat gold bracelets and these rings," said the shopkeeper.

I bought three bangles, a gold necklace with turquoise stones and three mother of pearl gold rings.

"Please, please! Don't tell anyone that I sold these to you."

"Don't worry. We won't."

"Do you have other items we can buy?"

"I'm sorry. This is all I have. You know it's illegal to sell gold." After buying jewelry, we still had Rupees left.

The Embassy told us that a caravan of Americans would soon leave Pakistan via the Khyber Pass to Afghanistan. They advised us to be ready at five in the morning, and be at the Embassy with our suitcases. Only two suitcases were allowed per family. We registered, and went through passport-control right-away. The next day we arrived at the Embassy bright and early with our suitcases.

We boarded one of the two school buses filled with families. A truck carried our luggage, a few embassy cars, and escorts were in the front and in the back of the caravan, with walkie-talkies and telephone communications. The Embassy sent news to both the Indian government and the Pakistan military that a convoy of Americans were heading toward Afghanistan. They, in turn promised to stop hostilities and not to resume until after the caravan had crossed the border.

We were happy to leave the war zone but sad, we had to leave Pakistan under these conditions. Pakistan-the land of contradictions, like an old lover-you can't get out of your system...seductive, annoying, magical, familiar, and inspiring.

Our bus in which we traveled did not have heating. We were freezing! December snow covered the Khyber Pass. Our buses lumbered along the steep, curvy road.

There was jubilation in the bus as we neared the Afghan border. When we crossed the border, Americans were waiting for us. Under huge tents, they had peanut butter and cookies for the children-they welcomed us with "open arms"; nurses and doctors inquired to see if anyone was sick.

"Levon! Look! There's peanut butter on the table." Sonia said.

"Oh! Boy! Let's go get some; I've not seen peanut butter for a whole year." Said Levon.

"Ben! Did you see those portable toilets?" I pointed.

"Yes. I'd never seen one like that before."

These portable toilets were made of hard blue plastic with white roofs. Inside they looked like any regular toilet with a seat and a place to wash your hands. It seemed strange to us since we had never seen anything like it.

The mud- camouflaged bus we traveled on to the Pakistan -Afghanistan border.

"Sonia is scared. She doesn't want to use this toilet. I think I'll have to persuade her by going with her." I said.

After a little rest and passport control by the border police, we continued our journey without escorts. Everyone was singing, thanking God that we got out without an incident. The route ahead was harsh. We had to go through the Hindukush Mountains with snow all around and thanks to the experienced drivers with steady nerves and good vision we continued on those sharp- curvy roads.

"Sonia. Come sit next to me." I said.

"Mom, I don't feel good."

"Come close. I'll wrap this coat around you." I felt her forehead.

"Sonia! You feel very hot!"

"Yes...mom, I've a headache."

By evening she started feeling worse. She was burning-hot! I was worried. We still had an hour's drive. We tried to make her as comfortable as possible. It was past midnight when we reached Kabul, Afghanistan. At the hotel, we wanted to see a doctor, but none were available.

"Here Sonia, drink this hot soup, you'll feel better." I sat beside her and made sure she ate something and gave her an aspirin.

I kept on checking her temperature, I was concerned.

By morning after a good rest she was feeling much better.

Our first priority was to secure air fare to get out of Kabul to go home to Chicago. We were only able to buy tickets up to Tehran. Ben's company had a large center in Tehran, Iran and a contract with USAID. We thought this will give us a chance to visit Tehran, see some of our friends, do some sightseeing, and then head for Chicago.

We thought it will be easier buying tickets from Tehran for the rest of our trip. So we relaxed and having been in Kabul before, we knew the markets and the places to visit.

We had the shock of our lives. No one would exchange the dollar. We met some merchants, who produced bundles of dollar bills.

"Here, you want play money?"

"What do you mean? These are American dollars!" I said.

"Madam! They're worth nothing!"

"Why?"

"The dollar has no value now."

We listened to the news and found out that the dollar was floating, its value became like play money in Afghanistan. No one would accept it. (*The floating dollar is when the dollar is under a flexible exchange rate regime. In 1971 President Nixon removed the dollar from the gold standard, thus devaluating it.*)

Well! This was where our rupees, which we thought was the play money, became very handy and precious. Their value was much better than the dollar. We were able to buy many things with the leftover Rupees including our airfare to Tehran.

Tehran, Iran

Tehran had a sweet and sour feeling for me; this was where we were evacuated the first time in 1965 during the India and Pakistan war. This was the city where I lost our third baby. Here we were again, another war between the same countries, another evacuation. We decided to stay only a few days.

Alas! Little did we know that we would spend nine years in Tehran and be present at a very historical revolution, again turning our lives topsy-turvy.

When we evacuated from Pakistan in 1965 and returned to Chicago, the Iranian Electric Power Planning Department head, with the department workers, came to Chicago for training in "power planning" from Ben. When we returned to Pakistan in 1968, the Iranians once more requested training from Ben's office. They followed him to Lahore and after three weeks of training by Ben, they returned to Iran. As they were returning, they expressed their wish, that after Pakistan, Ben would come to Tehran, Iran and be their consultant.

Ben had his heart set to stay in Tehran with the company. So went to the Harza company administrator to see about an opening. There were none. He was disappointed. We decided to sight-see.

Before leaving Ben went to see the Iranian workers that he had taught electric power planning. We waited for him to come back and after two hours, he came to the hotel in an Iranian Government limousine, like a big shot.

"Is that dad getting out of that limousine?" I asked Levon.

"Yes mom, dad; the VIP!"

Ben approached with a lively gait, smiling.

"Am I dreaming?" I said, "What happened?"

"The ministry wants me to stay here."

"I thought there weren't any positions available?"

"Mr. Puya... I didn't realize that he was the minister of the electric power planning department. All he did was call the Harza Company representative in Tehran and in five minutes he created a new position for me!"

"Well! Does that mean we are staying here?" I asked, eager to know about the change.

Ben nodded as he began to explain.

"I went to the office and asked to see Mr. Puya. Since I did not have an appointment, the secretary curtly turned down my request.I gave him my card and asked that he give it to Mr. Puya. I hardly reached the front door when he came running after me, we hugged, and both of us started talking at the same time.

"'Why didn't you tell me you were in Tehran?' he asked me."

"'I'm only here for a few days, on my way to Chicago,' I told him."

"People in the office were surprised at the warm reception. It never occurred to me that Mr Puya was a high level minister in the government."

"'You can't leave; I was waiting and hoping that you'll be free from Pakistan to come and work in Tehran.' he told me."

"I explained that there weren't any positions and that I had already asked. We will be leaving in a few days."

"That can't be. You can't leave, I won't let you!"

"He then picked up the phone and asked the chairman of Harza Engineering Company to open a position in Tehran. I could not believe my ears when Mr. Puya said 'done, now you're staying.'"

We were delighted with this news.

First, we had to find housing that was centrally located. We found a nice apartment and within a short time we moved in. Since

Arrival of some of our furniture from Lahore to Tehran, 1971.

we had left Lahore with only the clothes on our backs, we had to buy everything else not knowing whether our remaining belongings still in Pakistan would find their way to us.

The apartment was well located, adjacent to the American Embassy and close to the local shopping areas as well as the American commissary. We had a view of the well manicured Embassy gardens. We would have enjoyed our stay more but, after a while, our sloppy neighbors made our life miserable. He was a co-pilot, and the wife a stewardess for Air New Zealand. They loved having fun and drinking beer. They fed their huge dog in the kitchen, and after every meal the roaches had a picnic with the spilled-over food. The dog enjoyed chasing the roaches; the owners thought it was funny!

Soon, the roaches invaded our apartment and the apartment above. We had to move.

We found a comfortable and a pleasant house with a swimming pool, in the Darous area on Mesbahe Karimi Street. On the lower level, a large living room and a dining room divided by a column. Adjoining the dining room and living room, there was an atrium with a small pond and a waterfall. We kept fish in this pond and surrounded it with colorful potted plants and flowers.

Parians at home in Tehran, 1972

We used a room on the first floor as a music room and library. The room next to the kitchen became our commissary goods room with shelves and a huge deep freezer for our frozen supplies. The main entrance door was made of beveled-glass and beautiful wood. Off the entryway was a foyer that led to the living room. Another door led to a Middle Eastern style bathroom—with no toilet seat.

Like a giant corkscrew, the circular stairs led to the bedrooms on the second floor. The spacious landing, led to two other bedrooms, and a master bedroom with a balcony which overlooked the swimming pool and the neighborhood gardens. The landing was large enough for me to do most of my sewing. I enjoyed the view from the large balcony that was next to it. The hallway led to two bathrooms. One of the bathrooms was also the Middle Eastern type without a seat.

All the second floor balconies had beautiful views of the trees. The facade and the balconies were made of pink marble.

The living room had two large glass doors that opened to a marble terrace overlooking the pool.

The heating system was in the large basement next to the storage area, where we could enter from the kitchen and from the courtyard.

Following the Iranian custom of privacy, the property had high walls all around and an iron gate.

At the end of the second floor hallway, a door led us to another balcony. Here- with one more step up: we could reach the roof of our next door neighbor.

The rent was high, but we fell in love with the house, so we decided to stay and signed a lease. We registered Levon and Sonia into the The Tehran American School. This was December mid-year. After a few days Levon said "You know mom, the junior class is working on subjects that I completed as a sophomore in Lahore."

"My! I didn't realize how advanced the Lahore American School was."

Both children went to summer school at TAS while I volunteered to teach. This school was only for American citizens. The system was based on American public schools. The curriculum was the same and all teachers had to be qualified and certified. I did not expect to teach full time for I knew that the classrooms were full and all teachers were already assigned.

At the end of summer, the principal came to my class and surprised me. "Vicky, we're very happy with you. We want you to teach full time."

"I thought all the classrooms were taken." I said.

"This year the enrollment was higher than we expected, so we need a teacher for the fifth grade. Will you accept?"

I was available; I had the qualifications and already working- I felt elated! I had two days before school opened. I was given a small room and 34 students. With desks one on top of the other and not enough books to go around. It was a challenging year.

The one convenience about the school was that we had buses to take us back and forth. Both Levon and Sonia were on the same campus but different levels, there always was a late bus for students who participated in the after school activities.

New classrooms were needed because the student enrollment mushroomed. The school board decided to build a larger school and bought property for this project. This was an enormous undertaking and would take a few years for each phase.

In the meantime, they leased a fenced property in a beautiful valley. We later found out that the buildings were used as housing and a hospital for the psychologically disturbed.

All the elementary grades moved to this property.

The first day of orientation, I went to pull paper and pencils for my class, from the supply room. While I was inside I accidentally closed the door and found myself a prisoner in a padded room with no way to get out; there was only a small window on the door and no door knob. How could this be? Then I remembered that this was a building for the mentally disturbed.

I panicked! **Banged** on the door! No one heard me, my heart was racing. I screamed, **"Help! Help! Open the door!"**

After ten minutes, which felt like ten hours, another teacher who needed supplies opened the door from the outside. Oh! What a relief! "What happened?" she asked.

"I came in for supplies, and didn't realize that this door doesn't open from inside! "

I jumped out. And I made very sure that a proper knob was installed and the room was off limits to the students.

I was invited to help work on the next year's curriculum that summer, from Kindergarten to twelfth grades. I worked on the math, reading and creative science curriculum. The school promoted creativity with a special program of advanced science classes. I was

Vicky with her 5th grade classes, Tehran American School 1973-4.

Tehran American Elementary School- Lavisan Campus

in seventh heaven; it was a challenge to research, to learn, and to make recommendations.

The administration was very receptive to the ideas and opinions the teachers gave while building the new school.

The campus consisted of many buildings; each with eight to twelve classrooms with a teacher's lounge, bathrooms and a storage room. Some classrooms were built in such a way that walls opened to become one large room. These were designed especially for open classrooms; there were small cubicles, with glass doors, for one-on-one instruction, and a space for lab work. Each building

Christmas at Tehran American School.

was named for an Iranian city, for example; Isfahan, Shiraz, Tabriz, etc.

The elementary buildings were ready within two years. Three other teachers and I, started with an open classroom for the fifth grade. It was an exciting time for all. Students improved greatly and enjoyed being in an open classroom environment. We had no discipline problems.

With the winding down of US involvement in the Vietnam war, we suddenly had many American military families move to Tehran. American pilots were brought in to help the Shah train the Iranian air force. The student population grew by two thousand at the elementary and junior high school levels.

There were twelve fifth grade classes with twenty three to twenty five students each. We moved to a larger building, even then we had two of the fifth grade classes in another building.

Each building had to have a coordinator to organize and help with the curriculum for each teacher. The administration asked me to be the coordinator of the building my classroom was in. I needed to meet after school with the other coordinators and the assistant principal at least once a week. Many times I met with teary-eyed teachers to settle arguments, help solve problems and organized special programs, just like a principal.

Transferring two thousand students a day became a tremen-

Vicky with Masters of Education diploma.

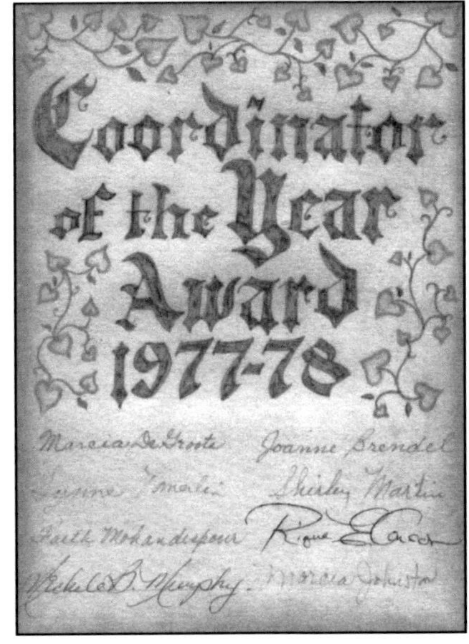

dous undertaking. The school hired a special person and a staff for this job. Everyday nearly hundred school buses lined up on campus like giant orange caterpillars and two thousand students ran like ants in every direction. It was a breathtaking sight! – a regulated chaos. The beautiful campus thrived and buzzed with activity under the majestic snow covered mountains.

The school followed the rules of the American public education and all teachers were certified with the necessary degrees. They believed in continued education of their teachers. For that reason, they contracted with the University of Alabama and brought professors from Berkley, Duke, and Alabama to teach graduate courses. They offered these courses after school hours and I registered for education and counseling courses.

During the day, the professors visited the classrooms, evaluated the teachers and suggested ideas. After a tiring day of teaching, I found it difficult to attend classes. I devoted my weekends to writing papers and studying. Finally, after two and a half years of grueling studies I graduated with a Masters Degree in Education.

I would have earned a double Masters Degree if I had taken one more course in counseling, but the political conflict prevented me from doing so.

Living in Tehran

"Whether at Naishapur or Babylon,
Whether the cup with sweet or bitter run,
The wine of life keeps oozing drop by drop,
The leaves of life keep falling one by one.
ge of the field!"

From the Rubaiyat of Omar Khayyam
Translated by Edward Fitzgerald

Our house became a center of activity. Both Ben and I encouraged Levon and Sonia to bring their friends home. We enjoyed seeing the young get together, swim, play games and listen to music.

Ali, our servant loved the children. He made sure that they were ready for the bus. He helped in buying the groceries, kept the house clean, and prepared the meals. We had a pleasant life.

American families always stayed together. We enjoyed many parties and social events. Tehran, at the time, was a cosmopolitan city with beautiful shops, galleries, and restaurants. Its many night clubs created an exciting atmosphere. Its restaurants gave several dishes to choose from, and there was music everywhere.

Not all night clubs served alcoholic beverages. For example: At a Chinese restaurant, the waiter approached and asked, "Do you want 'special' tea?" We said "Yes". He brought two teapots. One of the teapots had tea, the other had beer. They had to be careful since drinking alcohol is looked down upon in Moslem countries.

One of my favorite Iranian dishes is *Fesenjan:*

FESENJAN

1/3 kilo walnuts
1 chicken, or duck or ½ kilo lamb or stew meat
2 cups pomegranate juice
1 cup dried plums (aloo)
3 tbsp shortening
2 onions

Clean duck, chicken or meat. Cover with water in a saucepan and cook on slow heat until done. Chicken cooks very quickly, so it needs only a few minutes cooking time. Grind nuts and one onion in a meat grinder or blender until very finely ground. Cut and fry one onion in a pan with shortening. Add nuts, fry and stir constantly to prevent burning– about 10 minutes or before nuts turn dark. Add this to cooked meat with its water. Simmer ½ hour.

Add pomegranate juice (or alternate sauce) and plums. Simmer another ½ hour. If sauce turns dry, add a little boiling water. Serve with plain rice.

Note: If you are unable to get pomegranate juice, use this alternate sauce: 3 tbsp. Tomato paste, ½ cup sour grape juice or 1/3 cup vinegar, ½ cup sugar. Half this sauce recipe if you are using dried plums.

MAST VA KHIAR

2 medium-sized cucumbers
1 teaspoon salt
1 cup mast (Yoghurt)
½ teaspoon pepper

Peel cucumbers, cut in small pieces, add mast and seasoning. May be served as an appetizer or as a meal accompaniment.

One of the easiest things for me to make is funny cake for the young people:

FUNNY CAKE

1 ½ cups flour
1 tspn vanilla
1 cup sugar
1 tspn vinegar
½ tspn salt
1/3 cup oil
1 tspn Baking soda
1 cup cold water
¼ cup cocoa

Sift dry ingredients into ungreased 8x8 pan; make three holes in mixture. Into first hole put vanilla; into second hole, vinegar; and into third hole, oil. Pour 1 cup cold water over all this and stir until well mixed. Bake at 350 degree. About 30 minutes.

Besides eating the food of Iran, we enjoyed going shopping. The shops where full of exciting antiquities as well as modern items. Ben and I enjoyed looking for Persian carpets, they really captivated us. Each city in Iran had its own unique carpet designs.

The beautiful Kerman carpets brought high prices. The Herat carpets consisted of mostly silk. The Kashan Carpets depicted mythology and displayed a variety of birds and animals. Kashan is famous for their *kilims. Kilim* rugs are flat, tapestry-woven carpets made with kemp, cotton, wool thread, cloth or cotton thread. *Kilims* can be purely decorative when hung on walls. They function as rugs, saddle bags, and small floor coverings. Many have geometric designs. A famous *kilim* is the *Ardabil kilim* rugs. *Kilims* cost less than carpets. Wool carpets were the most popular, but silk ones were striking and the most expensive.

We visited souvenir shops filled with jewelery made of mother of pearl. We valued the delicate drawings depicting stories from Omar Khayyam, or hunting scenes of the shahs.

Brass shop in old city (top left). Artisan working on copper (top right). Visiting the Freedom Monument of Iran with the Borges (bottom left). Christmas in Tehran (bottom right).

The picture frames of inlay with brass, copper and mother of pearl are exquisite! We went to a factory to observe the craftsmen working. Their creations were detailed and meticulous, with the end results; beautiful. After observing how they were made, we appreciated the inlayed designs more.

Vicky and Sonia visiting a mosque

The artisan took long thin pieces of brass, copper and mother of pearl; he applied glue and bound them tightly together, forming a design. When dry, he cut this combination horizontally into thin slices and glued them next to each other on a wooden surface. They made picture frames and boxes with attractive designs decorated with these patterns.

Another interesting handicraft is their enamel ware.

When we asked about a vase, the artisan explained that the base is brass and it is decorated with enamel paint.

A visit to the crown jewels turned out to be the highlight of our first year's stay. We were captivated with the exquisitely designed tiaras, with diamonds and rubies.

"Mom look." Sonia said. "The queen in this picture is wearing the emerald and diamond necklace that's in this display case."

"You're right."

We saw many brooches with rubies and emeralds and many gifts from other nations given to the Shah throughout the years. A globe with precious stones depicting the capital of each country truly amazed us. An unbelievable number of fine quality jewels helped create a dazzling sight. The royal family housed them in a vault museum of the Central Bank of Iran, which was heavily guarded. The public could visit only for a few hours on certain days of the week.

Ben traveled to all parts of Iran as part of his job. Whenever

Levon graduating from Tehran American School (TAS) 1973

possible, we accompanied him. One of our visits took us to Karaj Dam, where he designed all the lighting. We were excited, especially our son, Levon. Later, we overheard him telling his friends about our visit; "We went to my Dad's dam. It was huge with lights all over the place!"

Another of our trips took us to an area near the Caspian Sea, the location with the most beautiful hotels. The ministry gave us the red carpet treatment at the government rest-house that we stayed in.

As we explored the towns around us, we heard people speaking Armenian.

"*Parev* (hello) we are visiting." I said to one of the residents.

"Hasming! Come here! Meet these Armenian people!" He called to someone with excitement, a group of smiling people rushed to our side. They made us feel as though we were heaven sent.

"Where are you from? Very few Armenians visit this faraway place." Said one of them.

"We're from America... living in Tehran." I said.

"*Pari yegak hasar pari*, (Welcome. A thousand times, Welcome) Apparently, many survivors of the 1915 Ottoman genocide of Armenians escaped south and settled here.

One of the men wanted to show us the community hall: "My father brought the wood of this building from Russia."

"The wood is so ornate! Who carved it?" I asked.

"Members of my family." Said one of them.

"Come and see inside. We have had many parties and family gatherings in this hall. The floor has special wood that lasts forever."

Indeed it was huge, a beautiful hall with a shiny wooden floor and a high ceiling with beams.

You **must** come to our house and have a meal with us."

"We don't have time."

"We insist!"

"We can come and have coffee with you." I replied.

When we did go to their house, they gave us a feast! And before you knew it, all the Armenians of the neighborhood came to welcome us. Each carrying an Armenian delicacy. We ended up with more than fifteen people. It was heart warming.

What we experienced on that occasion was traditional Armenian culture. Hospitality to strangers! Kindness! Good fellowship!

Speaking of kindness to strangers, back in Tehran, one day, it was close to dinnertime, when Sonia had not come in from cheerleading practice. Ben and I were about to call the school when we heard the bus arrive. Sonia rushed in!

Sonia in flag girl uniform - TAS football game, 1977.

"Mom! Dad! A friend is having problems and I'd like to help her."

"What kind of problems." I asked.

"She and her husband lived in an apartment, but their lease expired. The landlord rented it to another couple. They don't have a place to stay. They're leaving Tehran in two weeks; they're waiting for their papers and airline tickets."

"Why didn't they tell this to their landlord so he could have extended their stay?"

"They said the landlord is heartless. He wants them out."

"Sonia...**who** are these people?" I asked in a somber tone.

"The husband was hired by the University of Tehran. He is a mathematician. She... I think,... is a psychologist. The University closed for summer vacation. So they're getting ready to go home. They asked me if they could stay with us. I told them that 'We had a room. You can stay for two weeks. But first, I have to ask my parents."

Sonia, a soft hearted person, always felt sorry for other people who needed help.

"Sonia, how long have you known these people? Where are they from?"

"About a month ago I met her at one of the meetings at school. She seems very nice; they're from the United States."

"You actually told her they can stay here?"

"Well... Yes. They don't have any money; they'll live in their car if we don't take them in!"

"We'd like to meet them and see what we can do." I said.

Sonia rushed out of the room and out the gate. Suddenly, we saw, a young couple come in with suitcases. Sonia's eyes and expression reflected the words **PLEASE**!

We were surprised. *I smelled something fishy*!

For a few days, life was pleasant. We went to work early every morning. *I wondered why they slept-in half the morning.* About two days later, a truck came filled with boxes. Unknown to us, they had checked our basement and decided to bring all their household belongings. We asked Sonia if she knew about this, she did not.

About the fourth night we heard shouting coming from the bedroom. Her voice overpowered his. Sonia did not know what was going on. This started to happen every night. On the weekend, we saw her scream at her husband. I suspected he was too weak to confront her. His self esteem was very low. He just bent his head down, he looked emaciated and ill.

Ali, our servant, said, "Madam. These are bad people. I wish they'd leave."

Two weeks went by. They stayed and enjoyed our cooking and our hospitality. They always had an excuse for delaying their departure. At the end of two months our nerves were shattered from their fighting. When we asked them to leave, I couldn't believe my ears when I heard what she said.

"You have so much here; you must share this comfort with us."

"Are you saying that we must! The audacity. We both work hard for what we have. Nothing is free." said Ben.

"You should share it with us! We have nothing!"

Immediately after that confrontation, we looked for their sponsors. Since she met our daughter at school, I asked the principle if she knew these people. The principal said, "We hired the wife at first, but fired her because she was not stable and was creating conflict between teachers and students."

The principal was surprised; she thought they had already left for home.

The tension began to create conflict in our own family. To my amazement she confessed that she was jealous of our peaceful life, jealous of our relationship and wondered why we never fought.

Personalities like that, are contagious; Ben and I started arguing, as well, over non-important issues. That is when Ben offered money to buy tickets for them to leave for the United States. We also found their sponsors and asked their help. Previously the sponsors had offered tickets, but they had refused to leave.

Finally after three months of misery, and with the help of their sponsors, we bought their airline tickets, took them to the airport, and forced them to leave.

Ben and I made peace and returned to our happy life. Sonia learned the hard way not to trust everyone and we all learned something about "kindness to strangers."

Our Vacation to Spain and Portugal

We had to postpone our trip to Spain and Portugal until Sonia recovered from whooping cough. Both Ben and I isolated her taking turns to keep her comfortable. Once Sonia recovered we could leave Tehran for Spain and begin our vacation.

Madrid enchanted us. The old city illustrates Moorish culture and architecture. We had to walk through a maze of narrow streets in the old city in single file. We admired the ornate tiles covering the façade of old Moorish buildings. At the Museo Nacional del Prado, we were mesmerized by El Greco's paintings.

We visited the famous Flea Market. We eyed the trinkets and leather goods. We lost our way among a sea of people. Many evenings we enjoyed the Flamenco dancers. What a fiery performance! The strumming guitars. The stomping of feet. The women wore bright dresses. The male dancers- wore tight fitting outfits. What passion!

The Museo El Greco in Toledo, south of Madrid, was one of the highlights of our visit. El Greco (the Greek) a painter, and architect was born in Crete. He signed his paintings Domenikos **Thetocopoulos** in Greek characters, followed by Kres (Cretan). El Greco settled in Spain in 1577. His paintings express intense religious feelings. He captures the mystery of the spiritual World. And many of his paintings are exhibited in the Prado Museum.

The Burial of the Count of Orgaz (1586-88) is one of El Greco's most famous paintings: oil on canvas, 480 x 860 cm. The light colored heaven with angels above, gives a mystical feeling dividing the earth below with icon-like faces, including his own. The Burial of the Count of Orgaz's funeral is a masterpiece of spatial composition.

During our train ride to Lisbon, Portugal, it saddened us to see the squalor in which people had to live.

Lisbon greeted us with a huge statue of Christ. It overlooked a long bridge. We visited the 'Shrine of Our Lady of Fatima'.

On our way, while sightseeing, we realized how narrow the rural streets were. Many times, Ben stopped the rented car on the side of the road to allow cars from the opposite direction to pass. We had many near-misses. They made us nervous! Picturesque small towns spotted the area near Fatima. Cobblestone walkways and quaint shops dotted the area. We noticed that every second-story building displayed pots, over-flowing with flowers hung from windows and balconies. Friendly people greeted us and invited us into their shops.

One highlight of our stay were the bullfights. We saw one in Spain and one in Portugal. They were both similar and different in their own way, we preferred the Portuguese version. Before the bullfight, there was a parade with *matadors* and *bandarilheiros,* their attendants in colorful costumes. Then came the *Cavaleiros*, their horses protected by thick leather aprons. When the bull appeared, people clapped and cheered.The *forcados* a group of eight men wrestle the bull to the ground. In Portugal, the matadores fight the bull but its life is spared. Unlike the bullfight in Spain, where the matador kills the bull in front of a frenzied audience shouting "*Olé! Olé!*"

In Portugal, while sightseeing we came upon a hilly road lined with trees on both sides creating an archway over the road. On closer examination we realized that we were in a forest of cork trees. This was a novelty for us. Five people with axes were shaving the bark. One of them said that new bark will grow shortly. Later from the market, we bought beautiful hot plates made of cork and tile.

We continued our drive. A few miles later we heard something like a bomb. PANIC! We saw a plane flying overhead apparently it had passed the sound barrier. At the market a shop owner told us that a military base is close-by and it happened regularly.

We continued on our way and settled in Estoril where we had reserved a pension. A five minute walk brought us to the most beautiful beach where we spent most of our remaining vacation days. After two days in Estoril, Ben developed an intense cough and gasping for air, that increased while he ate, which frightened us. We all were terribly worried.

Aside from keeping us awake at night, we felt bad because we knew that this was disturbing the other residents in the pension. At the clinic, he was diagnosed with whooping cough.

What a nightmare!

We rented a cabana on the beach where Ben spent his days resting. Levon and Sonia enjoyed the beach, and joined in the other daytime activities. Soon, we returned to our home in Tehran. But it took a long time for Ben to completely recover.

A Visit to an Armenian Village

The wife of a missionary, who is a colleague of mine, invited me to go to Isfahan with her and her husband to visit an Armenian Village. I was thrilled to join them. It became one of the most exciting times of my stay in Iran.

Shah Abbas occupied the Armenian territories in 1589. He was impressed with the hard work of the Armenian people of Julfa. Their carpets, their brass work, their gold artifacts, and their fine artisanship, especially their work with silk. He wanted his people to learn from them.

Shah Abbas forcefully transferred all the families to Iran and he named the village Julfa, Isfahan. He essentially enslaved the craftsmen, the carpet weavers and the masons. The Armenian carpets, woven in Julfa during that time, have hidden words and signs of the cross. The enslaved weavers hoped that their relatives will recognize the names, the signs, and learn about their whereabouts. He allowed them to build a beautiful church, but, with a circular dome to evade the attention of Moslem fanatics.

I had not seen such a beautiful church before. Frescos covered the walls, described the life of Jesus, and many depicted scenes from the stories of the Bible. Many years later a bell tower with the Armenian design of a sharp steeple, added beauty to the structure.

Armenian church with mosque like dome, Isfahan

The main wooden gate of the old city became the exotic entry way to the city of Isfahan, reminding me of a sight from *One Thousand and One Nights*. We saw Armenian symbols and designs on the huge gate, the craftsmen had carved their names on the corner of the wooden gate in Armenian lettering.

Inside the gate, shops lined the street with utensils of copper and brass. It reminded me of the old city of Jerusalem. Further inside, I heard an unusual banging on metal, as though a group of performers were making music using percussion instruments. We rushed to see where that cadence originated. It surprised me to see rows and rows of men in their *shalwars*, (baggy pants) sitting cross-legged in front of their shops, banging hot copper into pots and pans. The workmen seemed unaware of the syncopated music they were making.

I was looking forward to seeing the Armenian village. On our way to the chief's house, we met a group of young ladies and children, dressed in long traditional Armenian dresses with coins sewn on them. I admired their silver belts (*Sevada Kamar*) with ancient Armenian designs. It reminded me of my grandfather's handmade silver jewelry which was handed down for generations.

We walked along unpaved roads with stone houses on both sides. I remembered the old stories that my grandmother used to tell me. History books that I had read haunted my memory and I started experiencing what life was like at the beginning of the last century.

I became like a large doll from outer space to the women and children. They had never seen an Armenian woman dressed in pants with short hair. They bombarded me with questions.

"What's your name?"

"Where do you come from?"

"What do you do?"

They followed me everywhere. Children touched me. They wanted to hear me speak. They spoke the eastern dialect, unlike myself who spoke the western dialect.

This became a dream for me. My American friends watched, fascinated by the way the people acted towards me.

As we entered the chief's house, the lady of the house greeted us. "*Pari yegadzek*" (welcome).

The rooms of the house built next to each other, surrounded a courtyard. Wall to wall Armenian carpets covered the floor. Carpets

Vicky with Armenian women and children of the village, Julfa, near Isfaha

also covered the seats. Only a few pictures hung on the walls. The chief was happy to see me; he showed me through the compound.

"This is the room where we dry the grapes that turn into raisins." He explained. The drying grapes hung on trellises they looked like giant garnets in the sunshine, which beamed into the room from the small window.

"Those are beautiful grapes!" I exclaimed.

"Yes! We are very proud of our vineyards. They are just a few miles away. They are the best quality red grapes."

The chief led me to another room, completely empty, but for a half-woven carpet.

"In this room we weave our carpets. My daughter is weaving one which will bear her name on one corner. When she gets married, the carpet will be part of her dowry."

I could see some of her friends, and family, sitting, socializing and helping.

"Each daughter weaves her own carpet with their mother and friends' help."

. "What an attractive carpet! Did you design it?" I asked.

"Yes," Said the young lady proudly.

The unfinished rectangular carpet had multiple geometric designs in the center. In each corner, she wove vibrant colored flowers inside a small circle- triangular shapes stuck out of the circle like the rays of the Sun.

"What inspired you to make this design?" I asked.

"I like geometric designs. The corners show my hopes for the future; a happy, healthy, and prosperous life."

As we continued our tour of the village, I noticed many houses in ruins.

"Why are there so many houses reduced to rubble?" I asked.

"The owners of these houses migrated to Armenia. The last thing they did was pull the house down. They did not want to sell it to a Muslim family. If an Armenian family wanted it, they gave the house to them."

We recognized the fear, and the animosity, between the Christians and the Muslims.

"The Armenian farmers work hard, produce vegetables for the market. Many times, the Iranian Moslems find opportunities to attack, and steal the produce. We have to be careful." He explained.

As we continued our walk, we saw a group of people coming toward us with a young man dressed in a suit, on a white horse. Colorful material covered the horse and people were rejoicing as musicians playing Armenian instruments accompanied the rider. They had a *dunbag*, (a drum-like instrument); a *zurna*, (a high pitched flute like instrument); and a *duduk*, (a reed instrument).

"What's happening?" We all wanted to know.

"Come; join us." They motioned, "We're going to the wedding."

A wedding party was taking the groom to the bride's house. We joined the extraordinary gathering. The musicians started to play louder when we entered the courtyard of the bride's house. Everyone started dancing an Armenian group dance.

"You must join us." Someone pulled my hand to bring me into the center of the group. **There I was!** Dancing and enjoying myself.

The men were in suits, and the women were in elaborate Armenian dresses, they were long and colorful with all kinds of coins sewn on them. The tradition was for the married women to use kerchiefs to cover their heads, but the unmarried eligible girls did not.

Eventually the bride came out of the house surrounded by her family. She wore a long red flowery dress with a vail of stripped design. The groom walked up and greeted her and they both walked the short distance to the church in a somewhat solemn pace, while the rest of the crowd escorted by musicians created a joyous racket of singing and high spirits.

We all walked to a quaint church. It was not as ornate as the one in Isfahan. But it was large enough to accommodate the people of the village. The priest greeted us.

Unfortunately, we did not have enough time to stay for the duration of the ceremony. The family wanted us to stay to enjoy the meal, but we had to leave. Leaving this town was like leaving my family behind. Before I knew it tears rolled down my cheeks. This was a very emotional experience for me. With a heavy heart I parted from the people and the city.

Bride and groom on their way to church, Julfa.

Qara Kelisa (Black Church)

St. Thaddeus Church, also known as Qara Kelisa, is revered by the Armenian Orthodox community and is one of the oldest surviving Christian Churches of Iran.

Armenians believe this to be the first church constructed in the year 68, by one of the apostles of Jesus- Saint Thaddeus, who traveled to Armenia to preach the teachings of Christ. Armenia was part of the Persian Empire at that time.

On the anniversary of St. Thaddeus Day, We joined one of the church groups and went on a pilgrimage.

It took two days by bus from Tehran, to reach our destination. Our children made friends traveling with the group.

We became emotional, because we knew that Armenia was so close, just on the other side of the Arax River.

As we approached we saw the two conical domes of the church. Everyone was speaking at the same time some pointing, some crying, while others prayed and sang. I was astounded. Surrounding the church we saw rows and rows of tents for new pilgrims arriving from all areas.

St. Thaddeus Church was called the Black Church because it had two pyramid shaped cupolas; originally built with black stones. The white structure, which was the main church, was added to the original building in 1810. Part of the monument was destroyed during the Mongol invasion in the 13th century. Throughout history the church was renovated.

We had hardly settled in our tent, when we heard music and singing. We rushed out and what do we see? An Armenian folk music group playing the *tambour* and *duduk*. The people were dancing the circle dance. Someone pulled our fourteen year old Sonia into the circle. I was overcome with emotion seeing people dance to the rhythmic music.

We were amazed at the number of people and tents, especially non-Christians. We approached a Moslem family.

One of them said, "Our parents and grandparents were Armenian. During the genocide they were forced to become Moslem."

"Mom! Dad! Come and see! They have a whole lamb hanging down here."

"People make a wish and sacrifice a lamb. They donate the

meat to the church to give to the people, it's called *madagh*," I explained.

Neither Levon nor Sonia had ever known this religious custom. They were upset. They approached the carver and asked, "Why did you slaughter this lamb?"

He responded, "I prayed to God that, if my son recovered, I'd donate a lamb to the church, which they'll cook and distribute to the people." Our children stepped away with mixed feelings. Levon and Sonia went horseback riding. Later we hiked, and found all kinds of carved *khatchkars* (stone crosses) scattered around the mountain, which made us realize that this area was part of old Armenia.

The Qara Kelisa Church and the tents of the pilgrams around it.

One of the Armenian ladies asked, "Would you like to go to see Mount Ararat?" I was thrilled and said, "Yes!" She said, "Hop-in. The bus is waiting."

On our way we passed by a village up in the mountains surrounded by high walls. The houses were made of stone, and the roads were unpaved. It surprised me to see the local people wearing Armenian clothing but Muslim headgear.

The group leader explained, "This whole Armenian village was forced to change their religion and become Muslim. Thus the Turks did not massacre them." I could not believe my eyes. I never imagined that a village like this existed.

After leaving the village we drove toward Armenia. At the border we stopped.

"Oh look! Mt. Ararat!" someone exclaimed.

"How majestic!" I announced.

It was covered with snow, stunning; we were all crying and singing Armenian folk songs. Mount Ararat is the symbol of Armenia. According to history the original Armenians came from the foothills of Mount Ararat. They became the first Christian nation in the fourth Century.

The second morning, about five o'clock, I woke up to a haunting melody. I dressed and went out into the chilly air. Someone was playing the clarinet on a hilltop. Unexpectedly, I saw others coming out of their tents and, like me, going toward the sound. So inviting, I could not resist climbing the hill. I saw Ben, Levon and Sonia were also climbing towards the music. Before I knew it, hundreds of people were climbing that hill. I was mesmerized by the sight of the musician when he came into view, silhouetted against the rising sun. No one talked and all climbed toward him. It was captivating; to this day I get goosebumps when I remember the moment.

After a while he finished playing and told us the fascinating story of this music. He was a music professor in one of the Universities in Tehran.

He began, "*A shepherd fell in love with the daughter of the richest man in the village; they both were secretly seeing each other. When the shepherd asked the hand of the daughter for marriage, the father refused, and would not allow his daughter to see the shepherd.*

The shepherd had the ability of playing the duduk, (traditional Armenian reed instrument), while playing; all the lambs followed

Sonia in front of our tent (top left). Local Armenian musicians playing the *duduk* and *dhol* (drum) top right. Vicky helping at the kitchen at the camp (bottom).

him wherever he went. The father saw that the daughter was very much in love with the shepherd. He also heard about his amazing ability. The father asked the young man to show what he could do. He asked him to collect the lambs from another hill. Once he proves his ability, then he will allow his daughter to marry him. They agreed on a day. That night the shepherd went to the opposite hill and prepared himself. Meanwhile the rich father collected thugs and dug a deep trench between the lambs and where the shepherd was staying.

In the morning, everyone was there when the shepherd started his music to call the lambs. The lambs on hearing the music, started walking towards it. On the way, one by one, they fell into the deep trench and died. Of course, none of the lambs reached the shepherd. When the shepherd realized this he threw himself in the trench and killed himself. The rich man's daughter seeing this also threw herself in the trench and killed herself."

When he finished the story we were all in tears. This story reminded me of Romeo and Juliet.

The professor said, "This was the music the shepherd played." He pointed to the people saying, "All of you, when you heard me playing, you left everything and climbed the steep hill to come and listen."

I enjoyed the magnificent natural vistas, enjoyed the pastoral surroundings filled with ancient ghosts of the Armenians. Knowledge of the present is the sum-total of ones past.

We returned back to Tehran filled with happy thoughts; thankful that we had the opportunity to witness and be part the comradery of this unusual festival at this historic monument.

The shepard's captivating song.

Persepolis

So while the vassals one by one were speaking,
One spied the little crescent all were seeking,
And then they jogg'd each other, "Brother! Brother!
Hark to the porter's shoulder-knot a-creaking!"

Dreaming when dawn's left hand was in the sky
I heard a voice within the tavern cry,
"Awake, my little ones, and fill the cup
Before life's liquor in its cup be dry,"

From Rubaiyat of Omar Khayyam
Translated by Edward Fitzgerald

One of our friends, a colleague of Ben's from the American University of Beirut, surprised us with a visit. Professor Yervant Kalayan, an archeologist, came to study the archeological sites in Iran. He and his wife stayed with us for a few days. We decided to join them on their trip to Isfahan.

After enjoying the sites, the churches and the beautiful mosques, we went to see the ruins of Persepolis, situated 70 Km northeast of the modern City of Shiraz.

Mosque in Isfahan with Professor Yervant Kalayan

The ruins are an imposing complex of palaces built by the "Achaemenian King, Darius the Great. He reigned around 518 BC. This was the seat of Persian monarchs until Alexander the Great destroyed it in 330 BC. These were the remains of the Achaemenian dynasty, when Persia's empire stretched from the Nile to the Danube.

The Persians called Persepolis *Takht-e Jamshid* (Throne of-*Jamshid* and his wife *Peseh*) Persepolis comes from the Greek word, for Persian City (*Peres polis*). In 1979 , UNESCO declared the citadel of Persepolis a **"World Heritage Site",** one of the 80 treasures featured in the art and travel documentary series on 'Around the World in 80 Treasures' presented by Dan Cruickshank.

"Dad! It says we're entering the ruins from the Gate of All Nations," said Levon.

"Yes, it's also known as the gate of *Xerxes.*"

"There's an inscription on the door with three different Languages." Levon continued.

"The translation in English says 'be kind to travelers, respect other people and cultures'."

"Mom! Look at that symbol. It looks like a big bird." Said Sonia.

I laughed and gave Sonia an approving nod. "This is a symbol of the Zoroastrian religion for the Great God *Ahura Mazda*. I see other symbols like the four elements; lion for fire, bull for earth, lotus flower for water and eagle for air." I said.

"Oh Mom! How do you know all these things!"

"I read about it in a book."

In 1971 the Shah of Iran, Shah Mohammed Reza Pahlavi; built a luxurious tent city next to the ancient city of Persepolis. The city planners designed it in the shape of a star on 160 acres. The city was to pay homage to 2,500 years of the monarchy. Guests included innumerable VIPs, such as the Duke of Edinburg, Princess Anne of England, King Haile Selassie of Ethiopia and others.

"It was a lavish celebration," the guide continued. "Guests drank 5,000 bottles of champagne. The central tent was the Shah's reception hall, twenty giant crystal chandeliers hung throughout the tent. Each dignitary had his own tent."

"This must be the tent where Princess Ann stayed." I said.

"How do you know?" asked Sonia.

"There is a sign with her name on it. It looks like a luxurious hotel room." I said with admiration "All units have bedrooms, showers, bathrooms and sitting rooms. It would be fun to spend a few days in one of these tents."

"Could we stay here?" said Sonia.

"Oh no. This is not a camping tent." I said.

"These chandeliers were made especially for this occasion." Said the guide.

In front of the entrance to the tent city at Persepolis (top).
Levon and Sonia in the Persepolis ruins.

Stunning red Persian carpets ornamented the floor of the huge red tent. *I could imagine what it looked like with all those kings and dignitaries sitting on red chairs, in sparkling, colorful costumes.* We were dazzled. Sonia and I pretended to be dignitaries attending a meeting; we walked in a majestic stride, sat on the red chairs, and laughed, as everybody followed our example.

The ruins of the Apadana Palace- where King Darius had his receptions- was located at a higher level. I admired the intricately carved reliefs along the staircases, which depicted representatives of 23 different countries in the Achaemenian Empire. These showed how they dressed, what kind of weapons they carried and what treasures the subjects brought from their homeland to please the king. I felt the greatness of the empire.

"This is exciting! Look! The Armenian delegation relief presenting their gifts. They're in traditional Armenian clothes." Said professor Kalayan.

The Palace was equally impressive. We needed more than a day to admire the carvings. Each pillar told a story about the life of Darius and his people. It depicted the story of the wars, the prisoners, the slaves and the wealth of the country.

During the war with Alexander the Great, this city was destroyed by the invading warriors. Work was being done to restore it. Professor Kalayan took hundreds of pictures of almost every pillar, every carving, he could lay his eyes on. All admired the ruins, Professor Kalayan being an archeologist, was explaining the history of the place. It was an educational and a fun trip!

We visited the tomb of king Darius the Great, which was simple but striking. Again, it reflected the Zoroastrian design and beauty.

Tomb of Darius the Great in Persepolis.

Caravanserais

In Iran, the Caravanserais are spread about 40 Km apart from each other, along the old caravan routes. These were inns built around the sixteenth and seventeenth centuries where travelers rested during their journey.

Caravanserais were the motels of the desert. Today, many are in ruins. With a group of teachers, and their families from Tehran American School, we stayed in one of the restored-caravanserai in the middle of the desert.

The minibuses were our camels. After traveling on an isolated road in the middle of the hot desert, the caravanserai, with its castle like walls, was a welcome sight. Once inside the gate, we were greeted with the strong, odor of camels. The inner wall, separated the rest area of the camels from the complex set of rooms- as well as a restaurant.

A water fountain, in the center of a huge square courtyard, in the middle of the desert seemed surreal. The rooms surrounding the courtyard each had circular entrances, and a dome with a very small window. It reminded me of the ancient Biblical caves. Once we entered, it was cool and comfortable.

In front of our room in a caravanserai, 1973.

"Mom. Where's the bathroom?"

"Sonia, come with me. Let's find out." I said.

"I see a sign on the other side of the courtyard." said Sonia.

"Yeah, you're right; these are common bathrooms for the whole compound."

"To wash" I continued, "We have to go outside to the fountain, which I see is in the middle of the courtyard."

We were given kerosene lamps for room lighting, fortunately, we had brought flash lights with us.

After dinner, a group of us, thrilled- and eager to investigate, decided to venture outside the caravanserai's walls to examine the stars. We were in complete darkness. I was afraid of getting lost. I held my hand out. The darkness engulfed my hands; we did not dare walk far for fear of getting lost. We held hands, and stayed together. This experience reminded me of the three Wise Men who followed the star to Bethlehem.

"This is fascinating. The sky is so clear! I can see every constellation!" Levon said.

"Incredible" I exclaimed. Now we understood how desert people were able to find their way.

Our biggest fears were the desert scorpions. Fortunately, they stayed away from us.

On our return we all sat around the courtyard and told stories. After a while, there was nothing else to do but go to bed.

The next day the sun greeted us. After breakfast, we said goodbye to our host and left to visit another caravanserai. One of them

Visiting the caravanserai where Shah Abas stayed.

was the caravanserai where Shah Abbas stayed while traveling, it was in ruins, but the rooms looked larger, more ornate, and was once an attractive building. Again imagination took its wings taking me to the era where Shah Abbas and companions often travelled in the hot desert, welcoming the cool rooms, and gathering in the restaurant for a sumptuous dinner and entertainment.

We learned that, thousands of years ago, the area was submerged in water. We were able to gather fossils of fish and plankton.

"Dad, look at how the stones are shining from the sun." Said Levon.

"Yes! The whole place is covered with shale." Answered Ben

We were amazed at the terrain

"Watch where you step!"

"Why?"

"You see these funny looking mud trees, they are termite nests." said one of the teachers.

I cringed. "Here I was about to step on one...." I said.

"Termites munch the woody part of a plant and as they eat they secrete a mud like solution and surround themselves with it. This takes the shape of the wood they are consuming." Explained a teacher.

Our drive home was long, but pleasant.

After returning home we were truly amazed- and surprised- at what we had seen and experienced. We could not sleep; we sat around talking and reliving our experiences. It was the best education for us, as well as for our children.

Our Visit to Isle Of Man

The Isle of Man is located in the Irish Sea between Great Britain and Ireland. Internally self-governing but a British Crown dependency- Tynwald, the island's parliament– is the oldest in the world. The island is influenced by Celtic and Norse cultures. It is 221 square miles - 32 miles long and 14 miles wide.

According to legend, two giants Finn McCool, an Irish giant and a Scottish giant, had a fight. The Scott fled to Scotland. Finn McCool was angry, so he took a big chunk of land from Lough Neagh and threw it at the Scott. But it did not reach him; it fell instead, between the two islands of Ireland and Scotland and became the Isle Of Man.

Ben's work associate and friend Tom McCreedy and his wife Ethel met us at the airport and drove us to Douglas, the capital.

"Our house is too small we'll steal your daughter Sonia who will stay with my seventeen year old daughter. And we'll take you to the hotel" Tom said

Sonia started giggling- she was happy. She liked Susan who was a few years older than her, blue-eyed, long blond hair and soft complexion– an attractive girl. I also liked this arrangement.

The next day we dropped the girls at the multi-story recreation building which was the pride and joy of the city. Ben and Tom went to play golf at the highlands next to the hotel – one of the most picturesque locations, with the sea surrounding its three sides. As they were playing the wind was blowing fiercely and the golf balls were flying further than they normally would go.

The sea breeze, the sun and the surrounding greenery put me in a happy and invigorated mood. As I walked down the beach it surprised me to see that the water had receded to low tide. People were collecting the exposed crabs. I remembered there had been a full moon the previous night.

After the men returned from golfing we went to pick up the girls. As we drove up, we noticed people rushing to get out of the multi-story recreation building.

"Susan! Sonia! Why is everybody rushing?" I asked alarmed.

"On our way out, we heard the fire alarm, since we were near the door, we left, we could hear people running down the stairs." Susan said.

When the girls told us this, we did not think it was anything serious. Since it was tea time, we went to the hotel to drink tea and enjoy small sandwiches.

As we were enjoying our tea, the phone rang, Susan answered it then **screamed**. On the phone, her friend had told her to rush to the hospital and give blood. The special glass of the building they had just come out of had melted down, burning hundreds of young people. Many others running down the stairs were injured by the stampede.

We were stunned! How horrible!

Susan rushed to the hospital.

We drove to a high spot close to the recreation center, where we saw the ambulances arriving and leaving; it made me shiver.

"Oh! What a terrible sight! I can't believe this!" I said with tears in my eyes.

"I wonder what caused this!" Tom inquired.

"God saved our girls!" I replied with a shiver in my voice.

"OH-m-y! What would have happened if they'd decided to stay a little longer!" said Tom as his voice cracked with emotion.

"Thank God they came out when they did!" said Ben, as though he was praying.

We were terribly concerned. We felt sorry for all those young people who did not have a chance to get out.

Later, when Susan came, she lamented that many died from their burns, from smoke inhalation and being trampled!

We felt sad and it made us realize how life was so fragile.

We didn't have much time left, so we decided to continued our sightseeing, but the experience left us with a heavy heart.

Tom took us around on the island. I had heard of heather but I had never seen it. It grew all over the island; we came to an elevation from which I saw a sea of pink heather.

"Each Heather flower has thirty seeds, so a plant produces thousands of seeds per season." Tom explained "Flowers bloom in late summer."

The rocky northern part of the island had spectacular views.

I sat atop a high rock and listened to the music of the waves as they rolled back and forth- hitting the rocks below with a tremendous force (BANG).-foam splattered everywhere.

The fort, we visited, was built during the time of the Vikings. We learned about the influence the Celts and the Norse had upon the

The McCreedys with Sonia and Ben at the fort. Susan and Vicky (insert)

origin of the island's culture, history, music and language.

Every time we passed a bridge, Tom said: "Good morning, 'little people'."

I was curious. I asked, "Why do you say that?"

"This is the home of fairies, 'little folks', or 'themselves'. If you don't greet them, you'll have bad luck."

Touring Isle Of Man with the McCreedys.

I thought he was joking! But the next time we crossed a bridge, he said, "Hello, 'little people'," and he made me say hello as well.

Tom continued: "One day, I crossed the bridge without greeting, and on the other side I had a flat tire! Since then, I always greet them."

Tom insisted we go and have lunch in a pub. I thought to myself that *pubs offer lunch*? But, as I entered, I smelled the delicious aroma of food. It was very inviting. This was the first time I ate minced pie, in my mind *minced pie was always too sweet* – I was wrong, it was scrumptious; savory meat, made with special herbs and spices.

While admiring the carved wood paneling surrounding the bar, I noticed a division between the bar area and a small room. This was odd. I asked Tom, "Why is the bar divided?"

"This is one of the oldest pubs. In early times they separated the men from the women. The women stayed in that room and ordered their food and drink from that window."

Susan wanted to show Sonia her great grandmother's house. As we drove, I saw high walls surrounding it. Tom said "This is the haunted house!"

Indeed no one wanted to go in. The grass around it was over five feet high. The house was built in the seventeen hundreds, the windows were boarded. *We could almost see the ghosts peeking at us through the cracks of the broken windows.* I wanted to go in but Tom told us not to go. He said, "The floors and walls are creaking; the house is old and neglected. Since great grandmother died a long time ago, no one has lived in it. It's dangerous."

To say Good-by to the McCreedys and their beautiful Island home, was the hardest thing to do. Even though we stayed a short time, I felt a special warmth towards this unusual island.

Guam

Guam, the largest island in Micronesia, is the only possession of the United States in the western Pacific Ocean. It is near the Philippines. In 1521, Ferdinand Magellan had declared it a Spanish territory.

During the Spanish American war of 1898, the United States, took Guam over, as part of the Treaty of Paris. In 1941, Japan captured the island and mistreated its people, the Chamorro. US troops recaptured it in 1944 and established a military base.

The young man sitting beside me on the plane looked nervous.

"I'm going to Guam for military training." He said "And I already miss my family."

I tried to cheer him up by pointing out the sandy beaches, and the lush green vegetation from the plane window.

We fell in love with this thirty-mile long, four-to-twelve mile wide Island, surrounded by coral reef.

"Come Sonia. Let's go for a walk on the beach." I said.

"Mom! Look!... Coral!"

Our hotel was by the beach. The tide brought in coral from the sea and scattered it over the sand.

On our walk to the beach in the mid afternoon, we saw the waiter, running toward us "Take cover!" He yelled at us. We looked up. The sky was blue. Not a single cloud. So I wondered; *why does he want us to take cover?* Within seconds, a downpour, drenched us. We had never experienced such a phenomenon!

"I can't believe this! Where'd this come from?" I asked.

This was an everyday occurrence. This hot, humid island is located in "typhoon alley."

We saw beautiful Catholic churches scattered over the island as evidence of Catholicism, introduced by the Spaniards. We drank in the beauty of its green and blossoming landscape. We felt the Chamorro's kindness and their love of family as we walked among them and found a tour guide that invited us into his home. The contented spirit, of those who had little, and lived in shacks, refreshed our spirits.

We left this beautiful island with heavy hearts. We had enjoyed the Chamorro's hospitality and their love of people.

The Iranian Revolution

With them the Seed of Wisdom did I sow,
And with my own hand labour'd it to grow:
And this was all the Harvest that I reap'd-
"I came like Water, and like Wind I go,

Yesterday this Day's Madness did prepare
To-morrow's silence, Triumph, or Despair:
Drink! For you not know whence you came, nor why;
Drink! For you know not why you go, nor where.

From the Rubaiyat of Omar Khayyam
Translated by Edward Fitzgerald

The Harza engineering contract with the Iranian government expired in 1978. The Chief of Water and Power asked Ben to stay, to work, as a system planning consultant, at double his salary. Ben accepted and was given a car with a driver at his disposal.

It was at this time that President Carter visited the Shah, and criticized him for his human-rights policies, Carter insisted he give more voice to the masses.

In order to please President Carter, the Shah allowed his people to demonstrate. (Before, this time demonstrations were never allowed.) Little did the Shah know that the small group would soon increase to a huge throng of people.

The Shah allowed Khomeini to come to Tehran from exile. Khomeini's wife and grandchild became our neighbor. Khomeini's people were happy that we lived next-door because they believed that an Iranian would be more dangerous than a foreigner.

A wall separated us. On one corner, attached to our common wall, was a little structure for garden equipment. The men piled-up sandbags and propped-up guns on its roof to protect Khomeini's family. We were terrified. We lost our privacy; they were watching us, as well. But inside our compound we felt safe.

Americans received threatening notes. Homes and cars were vandalized. Tomato, egg and rock throwing at school buses forced the school's administrators to close early for Christmas vacation. A Christmas letter was circulating in Tehran among the Americans:

Christmas in Iran

When the wise men went to Bethlehem stable,
They started from here or so goes the fable.
Upon seeing a star, they left Sepah Square
'Couse that was before the cannons got there.
The anniversary is close but all we can hear
Is the rumble of tanks, not eight tiny reindeer.
But Tehran is all calm, there's "barf on the coo"
"Snow on the mountain" (translation for you).
With oil workers on strike we don't drive too far,
But we are in luck; we do have a car.
There's no gas for cooking, but warm is the town
From burning buildings all the way to the ground.
When the crowds with their matches started fooling around.
And the soldiers just watched, we really were down.
Iran customs is closed and no mail gets through,
Sure hope this greeting makes it home and to you.
The lines to the U.S. aren't ringing a bell.
Strike bound workers cut off phones when they leave
Demanding their price and want all to believe.
Our work is just great though it isn't much fun
To hold meeting and talk o're sounds of a gun.
The people are friendly, well most of them are
We're telling ourselves cleaning words off our car
Of "Yonkes go home," (can't they learn how to spell?)
We really aren't scared; but to some it is hell.
We've been kicked from our buildings by workers-all Persian
But we're told by their leaders it was just for diversion.
"Keep a low profile" we are now being told,
"If you go out at all it really is bold".
But Americans aren't built to hide and to shiver.
So we go where we want, but sometimes aquiver
All this sounds so bad and we know you must fear.
But it's really been fun and we're in good cheer.
We surely are thankful that we have each other
With only good wishes for friends foe and brother.
Merry Christmas to all, and to all a good night
Remember we're here, and for goodness sake write!

The "Go Home Yankee" painted on our gate frightened us.

Some friends lived in areas where they felt threatened. We invited them to come and live with us until it quieted down. Our three upstairs bedrooms became home to three different families.

Everyday became an uneasy party. Because of Christmas we had accumulated enough food in our freezer to feed an army. We invited other Americans over for meals, mostly those who had no way to buy necessary groceries for the Christmas season, especially women married to Iranian men. In a way, it was very good for us. All our activities were during daytime. Sunset brought curfew. Everyone closed all their doors and windows. Many times, electricity was cut off, so we bought kerosene lamps and flashlights. We had to be careful with flashlights for it was hard to find batteries.

We missed the children. But, we were glad they attended Universities in the United States.

A friend asked me, "Would you teach in a Montessori school? Many of the teachers left the country, and we need teachers."

I told her, "I'd be glad to teach, as long as transportation was provided."

One of the teachers who taught in the same school lived close-by so I started teaching. She picked me up and dropped me at the house, so it was very convenient.

The Montessori school was located in a beautiful area near a main road. We drove to the school on a wide, spacious thoroughfare with lovely trees dividing the four lane boulevard. We continued driving around a huge circle with the Shah's enormous bronze statue in the centre.

The day the Shah departed Iran, we heard gun shots close by. We were terrified! We guided the children to a centrally located room with few windows.

News came that as soon as the Shah and his family left the palace, the military cadets started fighting with each other. Those who did not want the Shah to leave, versus those who did. Guns were readily available. Many were getting wounded. We wondered: "Will everyone join in?"

Parents picked up their children from our school.

Chaos!

People ran in different directions. We left once the children were picked up.

We saw a mob closer to the circular road.

"Everyone is heading toward the circle," my friend said.

"This person is signaling… He wants us to stop. He's pointing to the back of the car." I said.

I started shivering. I said to myself "Good luck! *Don't say anything. I don't want them to know that we are American."*

"Vicky, look back and see what he's pointing at." My friend said.

"He wants the box of Kleenex."

"Let's give it to him."

We stopped and gave him the Kleenex box.

"*Khanoum* (Madam) do you have any towels in your car? We need them for the wounded."

"Sorry. We don't." My friend answered in Farsi.

"Thank you for the Kleenex."

The mob with fingers showing the victory sign left the sidewalk and came onto the road.

We were petrified!

"Vicky! Make the victory sign in return and smile!"

Our car approached the circle. The mob was getting closer and closer to the center. It was a terrifying situation; my friend and I were giving them the victory sign and smiling. At the same time **shivering!** We were afraid that they would recognize us as Americans and attack us. Like twigs dropped into a fast-flowing stream, our car was swept into the throng.

My friend concentrated on driving the car, avoiding the people. Fortunately, they left us alone. Their aim was to get closer to the statue. The circle was now a sea of people, like a crowd leaving a sports stadium. Slowly, we eased our way out. The crowd was shouting!

"Down with the Shah!"

Some were by the Shah's statue. Pushing! Trying to shake it out of its base. There was a kind of hysterical elation in the air.

We finally reached home. As we arrived, we heard on the radio, that they had toppled the Shah's statue.

Weapons from the armory had found their way into the hands of teenage boys, who had probably never handled firearms before. The boys, some about ten years old, were running up-and-down the streets, yelling, waving their guns, and jumping into cars to tear off along the highway, shooting in the air- *Success has a thousand fathers but failure is an orphan.*

I was terrified! That was the last time I ventured to go beyond a few feet away from home. Our friends, one-by-one started leaving Iran. Our neighbor, Khomeini's wife and grandchild were receiving visitors nonstop. Long lines of veiled women were standing outside, waiting for their turn to welcome her and kiss her hand.

A few days later Ben drove to a close-by market for a newspaper. On the way, he saw that people were coming out of the American compound with all kinds of goods- especially guns and ammunition.

Ben said, "I tried to pass as fast as I could. A young man with a gun stopped me and asked for a ride. I couldn't say no. I stopped and let him into the car. I only nodded my head for if I said one word the young man would know that I'm not Iranian and who knows what he would have done? After half a block, the young man asked to "be dropped"- what a relief! I took a deep breath! After that experience I decided not to take the car out alone, again."

The driver of the Government car was picking Ben from home every morning and bringing him back after work. There were times they had to avoid certain routes, because there were mobs rioting, or fighting between the Shah's people, and Khomeini's people. They had to avoid areas where the mob burned tires and attacked liquor stores dumping the drinks on the road and burning them.

Night time was eerie, we could see the red of the bullets flying accompanied by the shouting, it reminded us of laser shows. Many who stood on their roof, screamed and shot in the air, not realizing that bullets would come back down and hit them or others who are next to them. We decided to close the doors and windows and draw the drapes so we will not attract attention.

Our servant, Ali, had a hard time coming to our house. His relatives and friends scolded him for helping the American family. He kept telling them that we were Armenian and Palestinian not American. Some people started following him to see if he was coming to our house. So he found all kinds of ways to avoid or lose them. As time went by things started getting worse.

This was history-being-made in front of our eyes. Very few people get to observe firsthand a revolution in progress.

They started to ration gasoline. "Madam. You stay home. I will go and stand in line for gasoline," said Ali.

"Be careful, Ali."

"Don't worry, madam. We also need some meat and vegetables. I'll go and buy them."

After two hours, he came back. We were concerned.

"There were so many people that I had to stand in line. There are very few vegetables. The farmers are afraid to come to the city and many are busy fighting. I brought some *barbari* bread." (long flat loaves with delicate crust that were baked fresh everyday).

He was our great protector.

There was a mosque about a block away from our house. According to history, the Shiite Moslem sect regrets that they did not help Ali's sons, Hassan and Hussain, in the battle of Karbala where they were killed. On the anniversary of the battle, on their way to the mosque, at night we watched the processions of devotees, march past with green flags. As they walk, they flogged themselves with chains or hit their chests, chanting; all to the rhythm of the banging of cymbals. Most of Iran's Muslims, and part of Iraq's, are Shiites.

This year's procession was much larger, the chanting and the cymbals were louder, and flogging was more fervent, they sounded more fanatic. It was eerie. We closed all the drapes and stayed indoors. "Oh! How I wished I could take a picture of this procession!"

But I knew if I did they would kill us.

The First Hostages

John, an American soldier, needed some money. He was looking for someone to fill the shipping container to pay part of the expense of taking it to the States. We gave him our carpets, brass tables and souvenirs, to pack in the shipping container. Since we never imagined Iranian mobs would attack the American compound, we thought our goods were on their way to the United States.

We waited for John to respond to our messages, but he didn't reply. So we went to his house, but it was locked. We assumed he had already departed.

After two weeks, John phoned.

"Hi, John... You sound awful!" said Ben.

"I'm sick. I'll be leaving next week. I've been held hostage by the *Mujahidin* (Khomeini's young rebels). I was one of the hostages that they took from the American compound. They bused us from one courthouse to another... everywhere people spat on us! They threw eggs and tomatoes at our bus! They screamed at us! I became ill." He continued "Fortunately- but I don't know why- they

The American Embassy after it's take-over -1979

released us after two weeks. Our container was in the compound when I was taken hostage. I don't know where it is now."

"Before you leave the country, is there a way you can find out what happened to it?" Ben asked.

"No. It's in the hands of the *Mujahidin*."

"Noooo!... (Pause) I hope you feel better."

We were both stunned!

On his way to work, Ben, heard that a mob had overrun the prison. Crowds of people on the street reminded Ben of a New York City parade- cheering and applauding only with cars full of revolutionaries, who raced by with guns pointing out of each window.

We were terribly upset! We thought: "Maybe we can salvage some of our goods." Our servant, Ali helped us find two young *Mujahidin*, who had guns, who took us to the American compound.

The streets were packed.

There was a carnival-like atmosphere. People, leaning out of their vehicle windows, were yelling "*Allah-ou-Akbar*" (God is great). We maneuvered three roadblocks. One of the walled-in compounds was locked, and the guards did not allow us in; but we were able to get into another American walled-in compound closer to the city.

"Oh! What a mess!"

Everything was in shambles: inside the building were broken children's toys, furniture, debris, broken glass, and household items piled a foot high. The looters took everything they could carry, and destroyed whatever was left. We could not contain our feelings. I started to cry. We were shocked. We were angry!

"How could they do this?"

Mere words could not express our feelings except.

"Oh my God! We lost everything!"

With a heavy heart, we went home wondering what to do. We thought—like in other places, things will quiet down and our life will return to normal.

But we soon realized that this situation was different. In Lahore, the Pakistani government protected the Americans. Here the Iranians were against the Americans.

Getting out of Tehran, Iran

What, without asking, hither hurried, whence?
And without asking, whither hurried hence!
Another and another Cup to drown
The Memory of this Impertinence!

From Rubaiyat of Omar Khayyam
Translated by Edward Fitzgerald

While Ben was at work, in mid-February, he was told that the Iranian workers won't allow any Americans to enter the office building. His Iranian colleagues sympathized with him. They liked him. They advised him: "Stay home until the political situation stabilizes. Until life turns back to normal."

We needed to get out of Iran! We gave our car and all of our clothes to our servant, Ali, and his son. With deep sadness, we gave our piano and music books to Mr Abbas Bahrami, who helped Ben at his company. We packed a suitcase, and we asked Mr. Bahrami, to "Mail it to us when things calmed down."

We called the Embassy for instructions to get out of the country. We told them, "We will be ready in about a week."

The person on the other end of the line, at the Embassy, said, "Buddy, you better be at the Hilton Hotel by six p.m. **today,** with one suitcase each. We'll process you and put you on the last American plane."

"One suitcase?! What do we do? What does one pack in one suitcase? What about our important papers? Our picture albums? Our jewelry? We have only five hours!"

We gave our library and two sets of encyclopedias to our Iranian friends.

We called a taxi to take us to the hotel; but no taxi driver was willing to risk his life **driving any American, anywhere**.

We were about to go crazy when Rique Carson- one of my colleagues from the American School- came to see if he could help. What a relief! We hugged him!

"Rique! God sent you to us. We need to be at the Hilton Hotel by six o'clock. Can you drive us there?"

"Of course I will."

We informed the landlord that we were leaving.

We loaded the car.

While loading the car, the landlord came and started to argue with our servant. He told him "Get out!"

That confrontation made us very angry. What right did he have to treat our servant like that!

"Please stop treating Ali that way. He was a good servant and helped us." I said.

"I'm sure the servant will take over my house. Many other servants have!" he said in an angry tone.

Many rumors circulated. As the expatriates were leaving, the servants had locked the landlord out, saying, "Everything is ours!" They also extorted money from the landlords.

In many areas thugs entered the houses and forced the occupants to give them their money, jewelry and their possessions. Anarchy reined in the city.

"We told you! Ali is a good servant. He's not that kind. He'll not take over the house." I kept saying.

Of course all this fell on the deaf ears of the greedy landlord. In spite of being rich already; he was ready to grab everything we left behind. We were angry, frustrated and disappointed. We asked the landlord, "Let Ali have the things we've given him."

It was upsetting, but we ran out of time; we had no choice but to leave. As we were leaving, Ali was thrown out. The landlord took over our house with all our belongings and the things that we gave to Ali earlier stayed in the house. We never found out if Ali got the things we had given him, but at least his son did have the car.

The Hilton Hotel was vandalized. That once elegant hotel was in shambles. We could not find a room where we felt safe. Everything was bullet ridden.

We were grateful to our friend for getting us to the hotel and helping us find a room.

"Rique! Why don't you come with us?"

"I need to stay, I have a nice landlord. He's taken good care of me."

"Oh! I just remembered! The champagne and caviar are still in the freezer. We were going to celebrate our departure!"

I was not sad about all that we left behind, the food in the freezer and many more items, but I was furious that we did not enjoy the champagne and the caviar before we left.

"It made me angry that the rude, conceited! Insatiable! Greedy! Landlord was now enjoying our champagne and caviar!"

Ben and I huddled in the hotel lobby with other Americans. For the fourth time in our lives, we felt the terror that war refugees experience when fleeing the violent upheaval of a conflict.

None of us could conceal our fatigue, our fright, and our bewilderment. Even the men, who tried to console the women, and the women, who tried to comfort the children, could not disguise their anxiety.

An embassy employee instructed us to: "... be ready, with our suitcases, at 5:00 a.m. ready to leave for the airport."

"The *Mujahidin*," he said, "want you to leave early for your own safety, while it's still dark, and the rioters are sleeping."

Later, we saw the Ayatollah making a speech on Television. He said, "Americans should be allowed to leave Iran, unharmed, and should not be deprived of their personal possessions."

Well, obviously, the Iranian mobs didn't follow the wishes of the Ayatollah.

Wild stories circulated. Everyone, waiting in the lobby, turned somber. As the minutes crept by, the atmosphere became so oppressive that we could hardly breathe.

American women, married to Iranians, had to leave with their children. Many of those unfortunate women- who waited with us in the lobby- wept in despair. Their wails of anguish could have shattered a heart of granite. Others just sat silently, in a corner, wondering- I'm sure- "How will this chaos end?"

That night, not even fragments of sleep could release our exhausted bodies and tormented minds from that terrible reality.

The lock had been smashed from the door of the room where we spent that dreadful night. So we piled chairs against it, in a feeble attempt to protect ourselves. Of course, intruders, wearing heavy boots, could have demolished the door and the chairs.

All night long, we laid awake and listened to blasts of gunfire and the shrieking mobs- sounds that Dante forgot to mention in his description of Hell.

At 5:00 a.m. we stood in-line with the rest of the Americans in the hotel's lobby. Before allowing any of us to board the bus, the *Mujahidin* inspected each suitcase for weapons or any items bearing the Shah's image. They confiscated all jewelry that had coins minted with the Shah's picture, or members of his family. Each of us had to go through five separate stations, to be searched at each one. With malicious glee, the revolutionaries made a mess of our suitcases. No question about it– those lads enjoyed their work!

Luckily, and in a moment of foresight, I had sewn valuable coins in the lining of our suitcase, and- to this day- it gives me great satisfaction to know that those soldiers-of-Allah never found them!

After a detailed search, we were herded onto several buses. Three armed revolutionaries boarded each bus. One stationed himself in the front, another in the middle, and the third in the rear. The manner in which they positioned themselves gave us good reason to worry. They anticipated the possibility of an attack on the bus by a frenzied mob.

As our bus bumped its way to the airport, a guard, who looked to be fifteen years old, strutted along the aisle, swaying with the motion of the bus. He kept his finger on the trigger of his rifle, with the safety catch off.

What if that fool stumbles ? I thought, terrified. I'm sure, the thought went through the mind of every passenger. None of us dared to disobey the guards' orders to remain silent. It's amazing how obedient one becomes when thugs-with-assault rifles- bark loud orders. Only after the power-drunk "*Mujahidin*" had frightened us to their satisfaction, did they allow our convoy to continue.

I'm sure these *Mujahidin* will impress their grandchildren in the future with stories of their bravery during the Revolution of 1979.

As we rode on quietly, suddenly, someone started crying. Others covered their heads from fear. As we drew nearer to the airport, a truck pulled alongside. And then, leaning out the window, the driver spat on our bus.

None in that bus, ever harmed that truck driver- or even held the slightest ill-will towards him. In fact, none of us knew him! Yet, he hated us! He hated us with every cell in his body, and with every drop of blood flowing through his veins! I saw hatred in his bulging eyes and contorted face! If his well-aimed expectoration had been a bomb, we'd be dead. He hated those he didn't even know!

How strange... how terrifying ... are the ways of mankind!

Our convoy was forced to stop several times. Each area of the city seemed to be under the control of a separate revolutionary group and each group had to demonstrate its authority by boarding our buses to interrogate and search us as they pleased.

Although the airport was a mere six miles from the hotel, it took two hours to reach our destination.

Two words can describe the scene at the airport: **Utter chaos!**

All this happened on February 22, 1979.

"How can I ever forget the exact date?" I ask.

We were met by a multitude of foreign reporters with dozens of television cameras. It seemed like legions of armed men, swarming, everywhere. Even though we were told by the embassy people, "Do not talk with anyone!" Sure enough! Some couldn't resist their few minutes of fame, so they began to blabber into microphones. Someone, eventually reminded them to "Stop talking!"

After waiting about five hours, the *Mujahidin* herded us through customs. Again, I worried that my jewelry would be discovered, and confiscated, during the customs inspection. But, to my great relief, that didn't happen.

Suddenly, as I began to board the plane that promised a trip to safety, one of the *Mujahidin* fighters gave me a royal fright as a farewell gift. He strutted towards me and snatched my purse from my hand. He opened it and rifled through its contents, and occasionally stared at me with fierce piercing eyes. After what seemed like an eternity, he allowed me to continue. I froze! I could not move, at first my bones turned to concrete, and my blood became ice water! I felt as if my feet were chained to cement blocks!

Frightful rumors circulated all around us. We heard that many American citizens, suspected of espionage, were taken at random and whisked away to unknown destinations.

There were three stations where revolutionaries checked our luggage. As I walked towards the plane, I carried my jewelry in a small purse that hung from my shoulder under a light coat. Layered atop that coat, I wore a heavy fur coat, and I carried a larger purse in my hand which held my cosmetics and travel papers.

It is a good thing the *Mujahidin* were inept at baggage inspections, because they never found either my jewelry, or the coins I had sewn into the lining of my suitcase.

On the plane, no one dared say a word. It was quiet. Eerie! If we had to communicate with one another, we spoke in whispers. We knew we were not yet out of danger.

Before takeoff, the ever-present revolutionaries entered the plane, came down the aisle and ordered us to give them our passports. They scrutinized each of us as if looking for a specific person.

We heard that a week before the Iranians ordered a Pan American plane to turn back.

The *Mujahidin* entered that plane and confiscated any jewelry with the Shah's likeness. An American couple was whisked away. We were told: "No one knows what happened to them."

Our plane took off without any further incident.

After an hour of flight, the captain's voice suddenly came over the loudspeaker:

"This is the captain speaking. **Congratulations!** We just left the Iranian air-space. We'll celebrate with champagne and ham sandwiches."

Both treats were forbidden in Iran by Khomeini.

The captain continued, "The American-guard from, the American embassy, is safely on board."

"Ben. Remember? That's the guard who shot a revolutionary, while the embassy was being attacked during the first hostage-taking. The Embassy must have smuggled him on-board."

All of a sudden, we heard patriotic songs over the loudspeakers. Everyone cheered!

I glanced around and I saw tears running down the passengers' cheeks and I felt warm tears running down my own.

Ours was the last Pan Am Flight to leave Tehran.

We landed in Frankfurt, Germany.

FREEDOM!

Passport control: **"Ben! I can't find the passports!** I had them in my hand!"

PANIC! In the excitement, I left our passports on the plane.

What a mess! A worker went to search the plane and sure enough, he found them.

We were lucky!

The Americans in Frankfurt welcomed us with open arms and assigned us to different hotels.

We arrived in Germany in February during the cold weather. The snow covered streets reminded us of Christmas. Since we were not used to harsh winter weather, we froze.

Unfortunately our hotel didn't have proper heating. We asked the manager for extra blankets, but with a cold stare and an equally cold "NO." She refused our request.

The hotel employees were so rude that the next day, we decided, to leave Germany never to return.

We left for the Far East, and visited Thailand for the second time.

The **WELCOME HOME** sign, at the airport in Hawaii, brought tears to our eyes. We vacationed in Hawaii and we ended up in California.

Epilogue

We settled in California, in 1979. It was a turning-point in our lives. We faced an uncertain future; this was our third evacuation... and the worst! Aside from that, we lost our household furniture and most of our souvenirs and mementos. But, worst of all, we were emotionally shattered.

We did not know what the future held. Ben's company, Harza Engineering wanted him in Chicago, but we did not want to go there. We hoped his company had a branch in California, or somewhere else in the West. Our aim was to settle in California away from the snow and the ragweed that afflicted me with hay fever. Ragweed, we were told, did not grow in the West.

We rented an apartment.

My cousin, Luther Derian, introduced us to a mutual acquaintance, Sebouh Tashjian, who had a high position in the Commonwealth Edison Company. Through Sebouh's recommendation, Ben found work at the Southern California Edison company as an Electrical Power Planning Engineer. We now, looked forward to a normal life, a calmer existence- in a free country!

My Masters degree in Education along with the many years of experience, placed me in an overqualified situation for a public school teaching position. Unfortunately, Proposition 13 required the School Administrators to economize by hiring less qualified teachers. This denied me the opportunity to teach in a public school.

It was during this time that we met a lawyer who was advising a travel franchise (Golden Globe). Fascinated by our stories about our round-the-world travels, he encouraged me to become a Travel Agent.

"I have no idea what a travel agent does!" I told him.

"We promise to teach you. We'll even help you to find a place. And, we'll help you to acquire the necessary licenses." He told us.

We formed The Golden Globe Parian Travel Agency in three months.

Once again, on November four, 1979, the Iranian militants stormed the United States Embassy in Tehran and took 70 American hostages.

I wondered. *If I knew any of them?* It grieved me to learn that our friend, the school superintendent Dr William Keough, was among them! He and I had worked together.

The news depressed me!

For safe keeping the Tehran American School had placed all their records at the American Embassy. The school physically transferred to Islamabad, the capital of Pakistan, where it was safer for the students. Dr. Keough returned to Tehran in order to retrieve the school's records from the U.S. Embassy, when he was taken hostage!

Our family listened to the news every day, we prayed for the release of all the hostages. Finally Dr Keough was released. He was ill, and died soon after.

* * *

Levon and Sonia wanted to continue their education in Illinois where we lived for a number of years.

Sonia, our daughter joined us in Alhambra, California, in June. She had been attending Elmhurst College, (my alma mater) in Illinois.

She began attending California State University of Los Angeles. (CSULA).

A few weeks later, Levon, came from Carbondale, Illinois. He was attending school there. He transferred to the Art Center College of Design in Pasadena in September.

We moved into a house in the City of Duarte.

Ben retired from Edison and opened a small electronic shop.

We were happy. But our happiness did not last.

1982 was the saddest year of our lives! We lost Sonia! We were inconsolable! A reckless driver crushed all the hopes and dreams of our vivacious 22 year-old daughter! Our grief was overwhelming! We remember the pleasure of hearing her sing, while she played the piano and the guitar.

She still lives in our hearts.

Ben closed the electronic shop to join me in the Travel Agency business.

We felt better when my sister, Artemis, and her family came from North Carolina to live near us. Their love and warmth, gave us the incentive to look to the future in a positive way.

I took the required courses and received my Certified Travel Consultant degree (CTC) in 1988, from Wellesley, Massachusetts. I also studied and became a notary public.

Levon married Maro, in 1990- a lovely girl from Yerevan, Armenia. Arthur and Sona their two children, bring us much joy.

On September 11, 2001, the terrorist attack on the twin towers in New York stopped us from taking a group of tourists to Armenia.

Many people thought this to be the best time to travel, because of the improved security. Therefore, after a week, Levon and I accompanied a smaller group to Armenia for the consecration of the new Cathedral in Yerevan.

Later, we saw Pope John during his first visit to Yerevan, we continued taking groups of tourists to Armenia.

Ben became a real estate broker, a real estate appraiser, and a notary public. He continued playing golf three times a week.

I semi-retired by August of 2003, moved my office to the new addition of our house, continued to take groups to Armenia, and I formed new groups as well, for cruises.

I Joined the Armenian Allied Arts Association (AAAA) - and became the president for four years. In that capacity I had the opportunity to encourage young talent.

I enjoy the musical programs of Tuesday Musicale of Pasadena, of which I was the treasurer and (at the time of publication) I am the president.

My role as President of San Gabriel Valley Ararat Guild is also satisfying to me, because I am helping the Mission Hill Ararat Home-for the aged.

Looking back, we liken our lives to ships sailing from port- to-port. We sustained furious storms and enjoyed calm seas.

We had finally found a welcoming-port in Los Angeles, California, where we settled for quieter lives, albeit busy ones.

We celebrated our 58th wedding anniversary in September of 2011 and were getting ready for our 59th and 60th. We looked forward to a happy life.

Ben's wish was to print the memoir his father had dictated to his mother in Armenian. It was about his father's enlistment in the Ottoman military and his escape and later rescue of thousands of Armenian survivors of the 1915 Genocide. There were many documents and affidavits from prominent leaders of the time both in Armenian and in Arabic. Ben translated the Arabic documents, I translated the Armenian to English and Levon edited it to become a book entitled: Crows of the Desert. Unfortunately after three weeks of publishing, on April 28, 2012 I lost my loving Husband to a stroke.

I was glad that he at least got to see his wish come true with his father's book. Now a feature documentary film has been made of it and the story of his father will become part of the history of the Armenian people.

ACKNOWLEDGEMENTS

The help and encouragement I received in writing this book is greatly appreciated.

My brother Garabed, who after a terrible car accident listened to my manuscript as it was read to him and reminded me of the chronological happenings in our lives. Also the encouragement of his family.

My thanks go to my sister Artemis, who stood by me and provided me with many photos of the family. Also the suggestions given by my nieces Sylva Etian and Arda Derian and my cousin Luther Derian

Many thanks to my niece, Nina Turpanjian, who proof read the original manuscript.

Also I greatly appreciate the support I received from my writing groups, especially from David Quintero, Gordon Dyer, and Rosa Lara.

My son Levon and his wife Maro were very helpful in finalizing and editing.

Of course, my deepest appreciation goes to my husband Ben, who was always there to help, proofread, and stand by me and encourage me to continue at all times. Without his help I could not have been able to accomplish any of this.

Parians 1961

Leaving Chicago 1973- Levon to stay behind to attend the University

Sonia, Levon, Ben and Vicky in their new home in Duarte, California, 1981